ARCHITECTURE AND SPECTACLE:

Architecture and Spectacle: A Critique

Gevork Hartoonian
University of Canberra, Australia

Routledge
Taylor & Francis Group

LONDON AND NEW YORK

First published 2012 by Ashgate Publishing

2 Park Square, Milton Park, Abingdon, Oxon OX14 4RN
711 Third Avenue, New York, NY 10017, USA

Routledge is an imprint of the taylor & francis Group, an informa business

First issued in paperback 2016

British Library Cataloguing in Publication Data
Hartoonian, Gevork.
    Architecture and spectacle : a critique.
    1. Architecture, Modern--20th century--Case studies.
    2. Architecture, Modern--21st century--Case studies.
    3. Architecture--Aesthetics. 4. Historicism in
    architecture. 5. Communication in architecture.
    I. Title
    724.6-dc23

Library of Congress Cataloging-in-Publication Data
Hartoonian, Gevork.
    Architecture and spectacle : a critique / by Gevork Hartoonian.
        p. cm.
    Includes bibliographical references and index.
    ISBN 978-1-4094-2293-8 (hardback)
    1. Architecture, Modern--21st century--Themes, motives. 2. Architecture--
Aesthetics. I. Title.

    NA687.H37 2012
    724'.7--dc23

                                                            2011045502

ISBN 978-1-4094-2293-8 (hbk)
ISBN 978-1-138-27406-8 (pbk)

Contents

List of Figures

Acknowledgments

I am grateful to the editorial board of the Ashgate Publishing Group, and to Valerie Rose in particular. Thanks especially to Sarah Wardill for her careful desk copy editorial work. I would not have been able to produce this volume without the OSP grant (outside study program) I received from the University of Canberra, where among my colleagues I would like to thank Jen Webb, Stephen Parker, Peter De Deckker, and Rodney Moss. A generous grant from Cox Architecture (Canberra) sponsored the copyright expenses. Special thanks are owed to Mark Wigley for facilitating my access to the Avery Library, Columbia University. I am also grateful to Kenneth Frampton for our memorable lunchtime conversation, which routinely took place after attendance at his "Doctoral Research Colloquium" course, spring 2011. Most enjoyable was Shaowen Wang's company, during which time we visited and photographed buildings in England and Germany. I want to take this opportunity to express my appreciation of Nayere Zaeri for her kind hospitality on the many occasions that I visited Philadelphia. Special thanks to Routledge Taylor & Francis Group for granting the copyright of *Crisis of the Object* (2006). The present volume is a revised and expanded version of the earlier manuscript.

Introduction

This book presents a criticism of contemporary architecture, the thematic of which is centered on the disciplinary history of architecture. Through a discussion of architecture's problematic rapport with technology and aesthetics, the aim is to present a critical understanding of how architecture thrives through the production and consumption systems of capitalism. Whereas at one point in time in contemporary history, architects were able to use available techniques and materials and charge architecture with aesthetic sensibilities (image) associable with the *machine* and/or *place*, in the present age of digital reproduction the image is valorized beyond what was experienced through the spectacle of old carnivals and stage-sets, one main task of which was to dramatize the event and/ or the play respectively. During late capitalism, the image has become a spectacle with wide connotations, which surpass the frescoes whose operative domain remained confined to the interior space of religious buildings. These developments concerning the function of image in culture are discussed by a number of critical thinkers as they explore its consequences for architecture.

What makes this book's approach to the spectacle permeating contemporary culture unique is the following. First, and as far as the question of technology is concerned, architecture's periodic crisis should not be considered a style issue, but rather one that echoes the developmental process of capitalism. Second, the overwhelming presence of image in contemporary culture, which has been intensified by the recent turn to digital technique, is useful because it highlights the presence of image in Gottfried Semper's discussion of the tectonic of theatricality. This is clear from the distinction the German architect made between the core-form and the art-form. Nevertheless, he saw their relationship and its aesthetic connotation as being based either on an ill-defined notion of poetics, or on the potentialities of surface articulation of the element of wall which has been at work since Renaissance architecture.

Laying aside the notion of poetics, which in romanticist discourse is delegated to the capacity of an artist/architect, this book pursues a reading of the aforementioned

Semperian rift that is imbued with the idea of "nihilism" advanced by contemporary thinkers, and above all with Walter Benjamin's notion of "wish-images." Thus we have the claim that image is as much a by-product of technique as it is a part of the architect's conscious and, at times, unconscious attempt to embellish the constructed form. What this means is of twofold significance: on the one hand, it recognizes the presence of *image* in Semper's discussion of the tectonic of theatricality. On the other, it demonstrates the ways in which the image could waft architecture into the aesthetic world of commodity fetishism. Thus arises the need to highlight the difference between the architecture of theatricality and that of theatricalization. Apart from the nineteenth century's struggle to address the crisis of the object caused by the availability of new material, techniques, and building types, Semper's significance today lies in the formulation of an architectural theory which suspends the smooth transition of architectural traditions, foreshadowing the idea of the crisis of architecture as a recurrent theme in modernity. Obviously, this reading of Semper is motivated by contemporary literature and the work of architects who constantly try to deconstruct the received traditions of architecture, even those with tectonic connotation. It is my conviction that, paradoxically, such "radicalism" in design enables the historian and the critic to discover the ways in which the disciplinary history of architecture survives in capitalism. No matter how critical we might be about the return of the surface and the organic in parametric design today, these returns have raised essential questions for both architects and historians concerning a discussion of the tectonics that is centered on critical historiography.

The present book addresses what is particular to architecture, and its capacity to breach the schism between art and science. Securing a tight relationship with technique and technological transformations, architecture is in trouble when it comes to re-presenting ideas extraneous to the art of building, even when the suggested externality is untenable. And yet, if *autonomy* is internal to modernism, then an argument should be advanced to suggest that, since the inception of modernity, architecture has to abandon the symbolic and iconographic realms, and enter into a network of relationships that is central to the periodic formations of capitalism. Therefore, the proposition presents itself that only in modernity does architecture arrive at a paradoxical awareness of what is architectural, that is the culture of building.

In my previous writings, I have taken advantage of the issue of autonomy and underlined the significance of the tectonic for contemporary architecture. Central to this position is research that concerns both the technical and the aesthetic and the way they inform the tectonics of the column and the wall, or the roof and the enclosure, for example. History witnesses architects' endeavors to rethink tectonic culture along with transformations that take place in the realm of technique and aesthetics. In modernity, however, architecture's autonomy, the desire to uphold its disciplinarity, is constantly challenged by a logic that wants to see all cultural artifacts in a temporal state. If architecture's durability is grounded in the earth-work, to recall Semper again, then how does temporality manifest itself architecturally? Obviously architecture is not reducible to consumer goods, the homogeneous appeal of which wins over worn-out notions such as singularity and individual taste. In the mainstream of contemporary consumer culture, no one feels at home without access to the cultural products distributed globally. What is involved here has little to do with the nature of some products or others. Rather, it is the excess, both visual and tactile, that orchestrates today's culture of spectacle for which we have no adequate words except to say, "It's cool!" Of all the art forms, movies we watch and buildings we visit, to mention two artworks with close ties to capital and technique, architecture still remains the most controversial mainly because it has the potential to resist but also to be plunged into the contemporary culture of spectacle. The fact is that architecture today has become the site of spectacle, and its temporality is informed by a culture that is primarily image laden. It is, therefore, the task of the critic to uncover the thematic of the culture of the building nestled beneath architecture's spectacle.

The significance of criticism advanced in every chapter of this book has to do with the fact that a paradoxical situation is indeed the destiny of architecture in modernity, a phenomenon tangible for some architects as early as the mid-nineteenth century. This much is clear from Semper's allusion to the essentiality of *fabrication* to the tectonic. What this means is that architecture is construction plus something else, and that the site of excess is not the form or "surface," but the thematic of the culture of building. Without dismissing aesthetic theories that have informed contemporary formalistic approaches to architecture, the argument presented in the following pages wishes to demonstrate how roofing and wrapping, to mention two important tectonic elements, have become topical for a critical analysis of architecture. The word critical here has as much to do with a non-formalistic and aesthetic approach to architecture as it has with the fact that it addresses architecture's dialogical rapport with the present visual spectacle.

If theatricality in architecture, excess, is internal to the lawful embellishment of a constructed form, what then should be the subject matter of criticism when the main source of excess happens to be of a technical nature? This inquiry necessitates discussing the impact of parametric design on architecture. Capitalizing on the difference between theatricality and theatricalization, this book explores architecture's particular apprehension of the aesthetics permeating the cultural today. It also underlines the difference between the present experience of image and the image available during the post-war era when, for the first time, architecture was exposed to contemporary communication technologies and semiotic theories.

The book presents a comprehensive criticism of architecture in a situation where things can be put together in an *ad hoc* manner. Because it does not claim to tell architects how to design, the book presents a critical understanding of the stakes involved in contemporary architecture, and provides a paradigm for historiography that is centered on the thematic of the culture of building rather than subjecting architecture to sociological, aesthetic, or philosophical discourses. Furthermore, the argument presented in the book offers a pedagogical platform, a subject relevant to today's situation where in most schools of architecture technique commands the design, and the teaching of architectural history/theory appears to be divorced from practice.

1

The Crisis of the Object

We belong to the future. We must put ourselves into it, each one at his situation. We must not plant ourselves against the new and attempt to retain a beautiful world, one that must perish. Nor must we try to build, with creative fantasy, a new one that claims to be immune to the ravages of becoming. We have to formulate the recent. But that we can only do if we say yes to it; yet with incompatible heart we have to retain our awareness of all that is destructive and inhuman in it. Our time is given to us as a soil on which we stand, as a task that we have to master.
Romano Guardini

These words of Romano Guardini have not lost their allure even today at the dawn of this new century.[1] Like many other thinkers of his time, Guardini seemingly addresses the sensitive issue of cultural heritage and the ways its foundation should be shaken and readjusted according to the demands of the "time." Contemporary history is full of instances of architects' attempts to rethink architecture in the context of the socio-cultural and technical imperatives of modernity. From the 1914 debate of the Werkbund, concerning architecture of *Sachlichkeit*, to Peter Eisenman's advocacy for the "Futility of Objects,"[2] architecture is relentlessly reformulating itself according to formal and contextual factors. It is the intention of this volume to discuss the theoretical issues pertinent to the crisis of the object, thus historicizing contemporary architectural praxis. Of interest is the thematic shift from construction to surface, a subject central to the advocates of the international style of architecture, but more importantly is the current turn to "surface" in spite or because of the proliferation of media technologies. The project's importance has to do with the early modernist infatuation with the machine, but also the fact that it is not the image of machine any more but the very *technique* itself that determines the processes of design and perhaps the final form of architecture. In spite, or perhaps because of the crisis of the object, the present state of architecture is suggestive of a return to the thematic of the disciplinary history of architecture. Central to the objectives of this book is Gottfried Semper's discourse on theatricality and its theoretical potentiality in offering a different interpretation of the dialogue between construction and "expression" permeating contemporary architecture.

The title of this chapter recalls André Breton's text "The Crisis of the Object" published in 1932.[3] This crisis, some argued, "was brought on in part by recent discoveries in physics and by the new science of psychology, both of which privileged the subjective and relative over the objective and absolute."[4] Against the early modernists' intention to transform artifacts according to the vicissitudes of technology, Breton and other surrealists presented a project of reconstitution of the object that in one way or another would problematize the total and smooth transformation of the traditional object into the "new." Their project also differed from the romanticist nostalgic yearning for craftsmanship and the desire to defuse the drive of mechanization that was shaking the ethics and moralities imbued with the guild system. The weight of the antinomies of modernity did indeed haunt architectural tendencies permeating both the Bauhaus school and the work of architects like Le Corbusier and Adolf Loos, to mention two figures among a few others, whose view of the crisis of the object remained peripheral to the mainstream of the Bauhaus.

The impact of technology on art and architecture is a complex one. Mechanization and industrial production posed problems for artistic activity that had no precedent in the work carried out through the pre-modern production system. The history of the Werkbund School in Germany, the decorative arts in France, and the arts and crafts movement in England present three historical cases each demonstrating the complex and manifold issues involved with the phenomenon of the crisis of the object. To sustain a reasonable trade balance around the turn of the last century, each industrialized nation had to have an answer to the following questions: how to reorganize a system of apprenticeship appropriate to the new educational institutions? Or, how to accommodate design skills developed in the old guilds with the needs and technical skills imposed by the industrial production system? More importantly, how "to resolve the conflict of interest between artists and manufacturers?"[5] And yet, if one broadens his/her scope of industrialization beyond the romanticists and their legitimate concern for dehumanization created by mechanization, then, the relationship between style and production is another issue that should be attributed to the socio-technical difficulties caused by the abolition of the guilds.[6] Many groups involved in the production of industrial commodities had no choice but to collaborate with each other within the newly established institutions. In spite or because of this development, the question concerning the crisis of the object retained its own momentum for the reason that architecture exercises a complex relationship both with its own disciplinary history, and with the technical and programmatic needs unleashed by modernization.

Most European architects, in one way or another, participated in the debate for the new objectivity, i.e., *Neue Sachlichkeit*. In various disciplines, the term *Neue Sachlichkeit* is interpreted and applied differently. G.F. Hartlub used it in its general connotation during an exhibition in Mannheim in 1923. Most participants in the show inclined for formal objectivity and minimal ornamentation.[7] According to Harry Francis Mallgrave, Richard Streiter introduced the word *Sachlichkeit* to architectural discourse, and Hermann Mathesius later reinterpreted it in the context of the 1914 Werkbund debate on norm and innovation in architectural style. While realism in architecture compromises with *Sachlichkeit* in the first decades of the twentieth century, in painting and literature, some scholars have discussed the two terms from a political point of view.[8] Recently, Fredric J. Schwartz has looked at the subject from a fresh point of view. His main thesis is that, by aligning architecture with technology, the Bauhaus of Walter Gropius came short of touching the other side of production, i.e., exchange and consumption. Schwartz sees the theoretical discourse of the Werkbund as the first step towards the formation of a mass culture that debunks the idea of style motivated by historical forms or craft-oriented techniques.[9]

The early modernists sought to dress both the interior space and the exterior body of architecture with a garment that was cut according to the aesthetics of abstraction; a plain form devoid of any ornamentation.[10] Le Corbusier even purposed a new vision of the city to rise above the ashes of the old one. Others, like Mondrian and the De Stijl group, saw the time ripe to integrate architecture with painting and the city. Central to the discourse of these artists and architects is the idea of total design, one implication of which was to make homologies between private and public spaces. Another was to see the project of modernity as embodying ideas and visions that framed ensembles inaccessible to the horizons experienced in the pre-modern life-world. One might go further and suggest that, even Loos's dichotomy between interior and exterior spaces, and his belief that only tombs and monuments deserve the name architecture, were indeed his way of endorsing the nihilism of technology, and the need for a different concept of objectivity.[11]

Modernization forced architects and historians to respond to the unfolding conflict between what, after Fritz Neumeyer's reading of Otto Wagner's architecture,[12] might be called the "culture of stone" and the rising spatial and visual sensibilities invigorated by steel and glass structures. What historians have coined "realist architecture"[13] speaks, among other things, for theoretical transformations responding to the situation induced by techniques of industrialization, but also Semper's discourse on monument, ornament, and the tectonic. Equally important was Carl Bötticher's observation that the spatial potentialities of the so-called "stone culture" were exhausted, and thus the need for architects to explore the artistic and spatial potentialities vested in new structural materials like iron. Unlike Semper "who was not concerned with visually expressing new structural developments, and who condoned the wrapping of the structural frame by a decorative wall system, Bötticher required maximum visibility of the structural/ serial frame."[14] According to Stanford Anderson, Semper "chastised Bötticher for his *Struckturschemen* and his applied symbolic ornament." The difference between these two nineteenth-century German architects becomes more obvious in Anderson's remark that, for Semper, the very artistic dimension of form was itself a derivative of a "production-related concern."[15] For Harry F. Mallgrave, on the other hand, the difference between Semper and Bötticher rests in their approach to Greek architecture: "Semper rejected Bötticher's claim for Greek cultural artistic autonomy, for the creation of these tectonic symbols in stone temples rather than in other prototypical forms." However, he underlines Bötticher's theoretical contribution to Semper.[16] And yet, the abstract forms of the international style, formulated around the 1930s, nullified the dialectical synthesis of tradition and modernity expressed in the realist architecture. Again, the date recalls Breton's article and the surrealists' refusal to see and construct the object merely in terms of the organic or mechanistic paradigms at work since the modernization of the production process.[17] Were there equivalent developments taking place in the discipline of architecture?

Again, Loos comes to mind, whose work, unlike the abstract and homogeneous white architecture of the international style, brings together the architectonic elements of vernacular, modern, and even the classical traditions. In addition to the hybrid nature of his work, equally important is Loos's criticism of the Bauhaus's blind reliance on technology, and the school's theoretical shortcoming in making a distinction between the art object and a utilitarian object.[18] Whereas this aspect of his work discloses the gap separating Loos from the avant-garde architects, it nevertheless does not suggest that there is no place for tradition in Le Corbusier's architecture, for example. At question is the level of abstraction involved in the French architect's early design. Loos's simultaneous esteem for tradition and modernity presents a vision of objectivity in which technology does not reduce the object to its mirror image; it rather assists to save the claim of the past, i.e., the culture of building, without denying the usefulness of modern technology. When this is established then we can underline the centrality of the concept of montage in architecture whose use and implications differ from those of film and the work of surrealists. There is another reason for introducing the concept of montage: it recalls Walter Benjamin's idea of the "wish-image" which, as will be demonstrated shortly, was instrumental in understanding the shortcomings of the project of surrealism and the esteem for *Sachlichkeit*.

That the concept of montage was instrumental for modernism is obvious. What needs to be addressed here is the role montage might play when the act of representation is informed by images of a technical nature.[19] The proliferation of computer technologies has shifted architects' attention from the tectonic of the final product to the surface. For many, the early modernists' concern for the impact of industrial building techniques on architecture is not a formative theme any more. This line of thinking is supported by the belief that the building industry, especially in America, has been unable to introduce new materials and techniques, thus the impossibility of changing architectural "image" beyond that of modernism. From this point of view, the use of glass, steel, and even new synthetic materials in the architecture of the last two decades has not pushed the tectonic thinking beyond what the Dom-ino frame has to offer.[20] Modifying existing techniques, the building industry, however, is slowly accommodating its products and techniques to the architects' esteem for virtual images. Thus the moment of transgression of the postmodernist concept of both/and (narrative montage?) for the architecture of theatricalization the aesthetic of which is in harmony with the virtual fluidity of capital in the present corporate and global world system.

A brief examination of the most publicized architectural work supports the claim that, for some, the architectural form has less to do with construction, let alone it's poetic articulation. What is accountable today is an aesthetic form whose animated body can be associated with Benjamin's idea of phantasmagoria, or the aesthetic of what Karl Marx coined commodity fetishism.[21] This development undermines the object's umbilical cord with the craft of building. Others have gone further claiming that even a Baudrillardian concern for simulacra is not a critical issue anymore.[22] Still, some are less interested in considering concepts such as model, type, or the machine relevant to contemporary practice. Bernard Cache pushes this line of thinking to an extreme. According to him, "the design of the object is no longer subordinated to mechanical geometry; it is the machine that is directly integrated into the technology of a synthetical image." Making a distinction between craftsmanship and mechanical production based on the meaning of "contract," he suggests that digitalization has replaced our understanding of contract based on custom and norm for one centered on the maximization of utility. As a result, "the primary image is no longer the image of the object but the image of the set of constraints at the intersection of which the image is created. This object no longer reproduces a model of imitation, but actualizes a model of simulation."[23] Most recently, the discussion has shifted in favor of "digital tectonics,"[24] reducing the dialogue between structure and dressing to that of surface effect.

Dwelling on the crisis of tectonic and scale, Antoine Picon, on the other hand, maps the vicissitudes of design panorama (architecture and the city) as it unfolds in the age of digital reproductivity.[25] He sees an opportunity in the current technological shift to subvert the system from within. Even though his discussion concerning the historical connectivity between tectonic, memory, and history is convincing, Picon fails to demonstrate the political economy of the current interest in surface and the aesthetic of the spectacular beyond explanatory notes most of which are focused on the operative scope of digital techniques. A technological premise also underpins Lars Spuybroek's advocacy for a "materialist theory of architecture."[26] Starting with Semper's "four elements of architecture," Spuybroek underlines the alleged materialist side of the German architect's theorization of architecture, making a case for digital tectonics. Using available techniques such as modeling and seriality, Spuybroek sees the possibility of moving away from the classical part-to-whole aesthetics to those of the Gothic, if only to highlight the surface continuity by weaving the element of column into the ceiling's ribs. This for him is enough reason to transfer the genesis of aesthetics from the corporeality of the body to the "materiality of structures."[27] Obviously the body and its senses have been changed not only since the time of Semper, but also since the inception of the "culture industry"; they indeed become pervasive in the present commodified culture. In these circumstances, one wonders if criticism should not focus on the historicity of architecture conceived as ornament,[28] and underscore the thematic of the culture of building that informs the index of the contemporary architectural object. Given recent developments that blur "the traditional distinction between infrastructure and buildings,"[29] equally important to highlight is the design work that does not reduce the bodily senses and the tectonic of materiality merely to the digital form. This is not to deny the significance of the changes digitalization has introduced into architectural praxis. However, with lessons from the failed experience of modernism having been learned, it is not enough to frame the scope of criticism to the consolidation of the technical nature of the present visual culture, as if technical inventions and aesthetic sensibilities unfold independently of the production and consumption systems of capitalism. Beyond the idea of the tectonic of theatricality and the critique of the aesthetic of spectacle presented in this book, equally significant is a field of inquiry that concerns *landscape* with connotations beyond what, for the sake of convenience, is termed "built-environment."[30]

The infiltration of digital techniques into the various spheres of production and consumption has left its mark on architectural education. The paperless, or virtual design studio, practiced at many schools of architecture, offers a way of seeing and conceptualizing architecture that is nothing more than a series of truncated perspectives comparable to those of video games. It is an ideal picture of the denial of site and the forces of gravity, no bottom or top, and no more frontality and part-to-whole relations either. Challenging the basics of the classical vision of the object, telecommunication technologies offer a vista through which "play" performs a critical role. Parametric design provides a level of formal exploration unavailable to the traditional techniques of draftsmanship. Explosion of the object ends in a truncated spatial labyrinth that ironically sustains the very basics of the perspectival regime, the Cartesian grid system. Virtual architecture gets around the "thingness" of architecture, reducing the latter to a cinematic experience, though experienced through a "paperless" frame.

The accommodation of architecture to the nihilism of technology has opened a new chapter in the book of the crisis of architecture written since the Renaissance. However, the current rush to internalize technology into every facet of culture is not immune to the ideology of postmodernism that has to sell its architectural vision as an index of progress. The question to ask is of the following nature: whether the present esteem for technology has learned its lessons from the modernists' understanding of the *Zeitgeist*.[31] Equally important is to ask whether the modernists' theorization, aiming at a uniform response to the spirit of the time, eliminated the possibility of linguistic difference or not. Paradoxically, contemporary architectural praxis is over-determined by the very infusion of *Zeitgeist* with linguistic multiplicity. Any attempt to respond to these questions necessitates, in the first place, investigating the historicity of the crisis of the object.

THE MATERIAL OF TECHNIQUE

Written in 1935, Walter Benjamin's essay "The Work of Art in the Age of Mechanical Reproduction" discusses the impact of technology on human perception, a subject already touched on by Heinrich Wölfflin, Alois Riegl, and a number of other German scholars.[32] Presenting the case of montage in film, Benjamin articulated the idea of "wish-images" in conjunction with the loss of aura; that is, the magical and ritualistic origin of the work of art where space and time are intermingled, and a harmony between the desire of the subject and the skills of the hand prevails. On another occasion, Benjamin describes the idea of aura in the following words:

> *in a strange weave of space and time: the unique appearance or resemblance of distance, no matter how close the object may be. While resting on a summer's noon, to trace a range of mountains on the horizon, or branch that throws its shadow on the observer, until the moment or the hour becomes part of their appearance—that is what it means to breathe the aura of those mountains.*[33]

Juxtaposing impressions such as "the unique appearance or resemblance of distance" and "resting on a summer's noon," Benjamin presents the idea of wish-images in analogy to the awakening moments when a distinction between dream and reality is difficult to make. The wish-images are indeed analogous to intoxicated objects with no task except radicalizing the moment of awakening. This was a project where according to Benjamin, surrealists came short of its full realization, and thus, their work remained in the state of intoxication. One might speculate that the idea of wish-images also concerns a state of mind that is purged from historicism: "In the dream in which every epoch sees in images the epoch which is to succeed it," the latter, according to Benjamin, "appears coupled with elements of prehistory—that is to say of a classless society."[34] Distancing himself from historicism, and discussing architecture in reference to the work's tactile and optical dimensions, Benjamin's position both benefits and departs from the discursive horizon of art history, and the Bauhaus interest in the new objectivity.

Benjamin's position is important because his discourse on historical material alludes to a shift from individual to collective experience of a past that is not necessarily embedded in the high art. It rather rests in anonymous works and in the detail. This attention to the marginal was for Benjamin the result of a major methodological discovery laid down by Riegl. According to Benjamin, Riegl's study of *Late Roman Art Industry*, "broke with the theory of 'periods of decline,' and recognized in what had previously been called 'regression into barbarism' a new experience of space, a new artistic volition [*kunstwollen*]."[35] This lengthy attention given here to Riegl and Benjamin has in part to do with my interest in Semper who broke away from the classical wisdom of architecture, locating the origin of monuments in marginal works like the stage-sets for carnivals and skills developed in industries such as textile, carpentry, ceramics, and masonry.[36] Similar to both Semper's and Riegl's interest in applied arts and ornament,[37] Benjamin underlined the importance of the principle of montage as a means to "build up the large constructions out of the smallest, precisely fashioned structural elements. Indeed to detect the crystal of the total event in the analysis of the small, individual moment."[38] While the high art reinforces autonomy, the "insignificant" is apprehended through the recollection and involuntary memory of the collective experience. For Benjamin, the point was not to reiterate those moments of the bygone past, but to underline their function for the intelligibility of the work of art and to comprehend their redemptive power in the light of what is "recent." To see the archaic in the latest technologies, as Benjamin suggested, shows a strategic position that questions the linear idea of progress without dismissing the radical potentialities of the new. What makes Benjamin relevant to the main subject of this book, however, is his insightful approach to technique in modern arts. Equally important is his method, delivering a strategy of criticism unavailable to most critics and historians writing before the post-war era. The importance of "construction" in Benjamin's oeuvre is paramount. An attempt is made in this book to address "construction" within a theoretical paradigm that juxtaposes Benjamin's discourse on the exhibition value of the art and Semper's notion of theatricality.[39]

Benjamin's essay, "The Work of Art in the Age of Mechanical Reproduction," is important on another front: it maps the vicissitudes of the crisis of the object in modernity. Towards the end of the essay Benjamin reflects on architecture though without providing a detailed discussion of the impact of technology on it. Benjamin's belief that buildings are appropriated by habit and tactile experience addresses the complexities involved in the idea of the crisis of the object. For Benjamin, architecture provides a model of reception comparable to film where "the distracted mass absorbs the work of art." This aspect of film "is most obvious with regard to buildings. Architecture has always represented the prototype of a work of art the reception of which is consummated by a collective in a state of distraction."[40] Two conclusions should be drawn from Benjamin's observation. First, the most enduring elements of architecture are those that embrace both constructive and aesthetic aspects of form. This is not to suggest that the historically received forms and typologies should be imitated as if they were written rules. Rather, these formal structures should be recoded by the "handing over" of architectural traditions to the process of modernization. Typological studies are still valid subjects of research if "type" is considered a spatial construct like "corridor," where use and the logic of making are fused into the form of corridor. This understanding of type does not equate it with the ossified forms of the classical language of architecture. An argument can be advanced to suggest that central to the re-articulation of the relationship between seeing and making are the memory and habits that are glued to a particular type. Second, the optical side of architecture is not limited merely to what a building represents, symbolically or otherwise. For Benjamin, "habit determines to a large extent even optical reception." The priority given to habit over optics recalls Loos's belief that architecture "arouses feelings in people. The task of the architect is, therefore, to define what the feelings should be."[41] But, if the habits are not permanent, then, how should we reapproach Loos's statement in the light of distractions generated by film and other forms of art that are, in one way or another, conceived within the perceptual horizon opened by the process of mechanical reproduction? More importantly, how should we evaluate Benjamin's belief that after the loss of aura, the work of art seizes every opportunity to release its exhibitionist value?; an aesthetic sensibility that is formative for the present state of the crisis of the object. From fashion to videotapes, every cultural product of late capitalism stresses the exhibition value of the work. This is true even of architecture, where distraction finds its architectonic form in the fragmentation and juxtaposition of dreamlike forms with familiar tectonics that can be mistaken for Semper's discourse on theatricality.

At this point it is worth speculating that the distraction Benjamin attributed to modern technology is also applicable to Semper's definition of the tectonic. For

Semper, the tectonic is a cosmic art in which the art-form relates to the core-form in "a *structural-symbolic* rather than in a *structural-technical* sense."[42] The perceived duality in the tectonic not only attests to the in-between state of architecture (compared to the opposition between art and craft), but also marks a departure from the classical *techné* by which the homology between the technical, symbolic, and aesthetic of architecture is sustained. What is involved here is the possibility of radicalizing Semper's theory further. One way of advancing it would be to say that after the mechanical reproduction of art, and faced with the contemporary drive for fragmentation, the tectonic should stress the fact that the perceived spatial envelope is, literally, a fabrication: it is a falsehood. When this is established, then the question to ask would be: how and to what end is it useful to advance an argument making a distinction between atectonic and the tectonic?[43]

The distinction between what is essential to architecture and what is excessive or ornamental was not grounded until the functional-rationalists' attempt to separate these architectonic elements from each other.[44] Leon Battista Alberti, for one, saw the relationship between the column and the wall differently. He treated these architectonic elements more like grammatical entities whose particular juxtaposition would connote certain meanings embedded in the metaphysics of humanism. Mies van der Rohe's architecture, to mention just one contemporary example, entertained instead the "structural symbolic" dimension of the column and the wall, and the way these elements wrap and disclose the space where the tectonic, regardless of the building's function, marks a departure from the totalizing content of *techné*. Any clarification of "structural symbolic" requires a discussion of *techné* in the first place.

The Greek word for technology, *techné* connotes the art of making that is fundamental to every activity involved in cultural production. The architectonic implication of *techné* is implied in the Vitruvian triad of *firmitas*, *venustas*, and *utilitas*. The triad characterizes the Greek understanding of an object in the most general connotation of the term. In the Renaissance reading of Vitruvius, however, *techné* was imbued with the values of a culture where "resemblance" was a formative theme.[45] In this context, architecture functioned as a symbol of mediation between the life-world and the mythologies of the divine forces. First, during the Renaissance, a transparent maze surrounded the object through which the masses could perceive something beyond the immediate usefulness of artifacts. Like every icon of Christianity, the object was made to last, and by its very durability it also endorsed the permanence of the world cherished by Christianity. Second, the suggested perception of transparency alludes to the homology that connects the desire of a craftsperson, and the product of that person's skills. These qualities of the object were dramatized by a perspectival regime, the visual cone of which clothed, metaphorically, the durable integrity of an object with the fabric of Christian morality. Thus, for a long time to come, art and architecture would not possess any meaning that was not bathed in the cultural changes wrought by Christianity. We are reminded of the importance of centrality of the cruciform that permeated the design of Renaissance churches. Nevertheless, since the Renaissance, the constructive content of *techné* has been diminished and the word's connotation is reduced to mere intellectual practice, perpetuating an ideal integrity between architecture and society, i.e., architecture as style building, with a compositional character similar to that of language.

The brief historical detour is not meant as a lament for the bygone past. Even Martin Heidegger's recourse to *techné* was not a nostalgic yearning for the Greek way of seeing and making. The nihilism of technology is understood by recalling *techné*, and by demonstrating the potential embedded in technology if the metaphysics are brushed aside. The loss of aura, and the separation of art from technique are historical; thus, today, art and architecture cannot avoid the importance of technique. Therefore, the duality in Semper's tectonic is historical, and yet his discourse on the subject hinges the dialectics between the core-form and the art-form. The tectonic speaks of the materiality of form, construction, and purpose. One implication of this is that the tectonic has the potential to represent values that have no direct connotation with the logos of construction,[46] meaning that, if "purpose" is reduced merely to representing values extraneous to those emanating from construction, then the line between atectonic and tectonic is blurred and architecture is relegated to the realm of the scenographic.

The implied hinge, or joint in Semper's tectonic, is one reason why montage can be presented as a mode of making that relates architecture to the experience of film.[47] This association between film and architecture can be articulated differently from Benjamin's remarks on the subject. Consider this: the etymology of the word tectonic goes back to *tekton* signifying a carpenter.[48] In addition to Semper's emphasis on the essentiality of the experience of carpentry for architecture, most traditional builders were good carpenters in the first place. The analogy between architecture and carpentry can be traced in the importance given to Marc-Antoine Laugier's hut in the development of Greek architecture as discussed in eighteenth-century architectural theories. Quatremère de Quincy, for example, claimed that, "one is able to affirm that the school of carpentry is able to make architecture a rational art." He continued, "in effect it takes little to recognize that the essence of architecture, and in large part the means by which it pleases us, is in raising this agreeable fiction, this ingenious mask, which, in association with the other arts, permits them to appear on its stage and furnishes architecture with an occasion to rival them as well."[49] There is no doubt that film and carpentry are two unrelated professions. However, in addition to the use of raw materials, the fragmented processes of film making involve various cuts and frames and their dramatization through montage and visual effects which together recollect some archaic moments of making that are essential to joinery. A carpenter too makes each part of an object separately; a process that sometimes is carried even to the last stage of the object's artistic embellishment. Only when all the cuts are prepared are the fragmentary pieces assembled together through joints, moulds, and reveals. What makes the analogy between film and carpentry interesting has to do with the fact that in these two *métiers*, technique and artistic embellishment are connected, though serving different purposes: film is a non-objective entity whose virtual nature has leaked into every facet of today's life-world. In contrast, a

1.1   Mies van der Rohe, Barcelona Pavilion, 1929. Photograph by author

work of carpentry not only is a "thing" that occupies space, as does the body, but its products have been good companions to the body in more ways than one.

Kasimir Malevich once said that "a chair, bed and table are not matters of utility but rather, the forms taken by plastic sensations, so the generally-held view that all objects of daily use results from practical considerations is upon false premises."[50] Like weaving and ceramics, carpentry enjoys an ontology bound with the body. More importantly, the aesthetic and technical skills invested in film and joinery are apprehended by the masses through habit and use. And yet, in both montage and the tectonic, technique is embellished through artistic means without reducing one to the other. If the concept of montage is emptied of its artistic dimension, then film is nothing but technical reproduction. Likewise, the tectonic cannot avoid the above-mentioned hinge; that is to say, a chosen structural system imposes certain limitations on artistic embellishment of the constructed form. Mies's Barcelona Pavilion, for example, is erected on a regular steel frame structure (Figure 1.1). The final form, however, appears to be made of horizontal and vertical planes re-interpreting the tectonic dialogue between the column and the wall. Furthermore, the implied duality in the tectonic alludes to the historical fact that by the nineteenth century, techné could not continue its classical poetics. Both the subjective and objective transformations of the time necessitated an architecture whose complexities are worth examining through the idea of wish-images.

WISH-IMAGES: THEN AND NOW

Again, after the Renaissance and through various re-interpretations of classical idioms, architecture had to wait until the early nineteenth century to think of itself as architecture. The century's loud yearning for style alludes to the disintegration

1.2   Eugène Viollet-le-Duc, project for a concert hall, 1866. Image courtesy of the MIT
Press from *Studies in Tectonic Culture*, by Kenneth Frampton, edited by John Cava

of *technè* and architecture's desire for autonomy. The fact that the century's best architecture made room to juxtapose a masonry construction-system with iron-made structural elements should be considered positive. It was a step towards the deconstruction of the metaphysics of *technè*, a transformation that made both romantics and the academicians of the École des Beaux-Arts uncomfortable. According to Neil Levine, "the dematerialization of structure and abstraction of space that has come to characterize modern architecture, along with the consequent transparency of surface and reflexive relationship between exterior and interior, or container and contained, has its sources in that particular object of 19th-century mechanomorphism celebrated by Hugo." He concludes that, this "allowed architecture to break out of the confines of classicism."[51] There were moments in architectural history that are critical for the main theme of this chapter, i.e., an examination of the result of the association of the idea of the wish-images with Semper's discourse on theatricality.

Apart from the arcades, other building types illustrate Benjamin's idea of wish-images. Not every building of the nineteenth century was conceived in the image of classical or Gothic architecture. Many architects attempted to reinterpret the culture of building with an eye to what was going on in the technical field and the ethics promoted through modernization. Consider the tectonic qualities of the visionary projects proposed by Viollet-le-Duc. In the interior of what seems to be a concert hall the stone is cut, not to receive another piece of stone, but to allow for the insertion of a structural iron bar (Figure 1.2). The structural network covering the central space weaves together steel and stone presenting a structural image that provides a link between the memory of a Gothic ribbed vault and the as yet unborn space-frame structures of Buckminster Fuller.

Viollet-le-Duc's architectonic montage was also at work in Henry Labrouste's Bibliothèque Sainte-Geneviève. In the main reading room of the library, the stone pedestals provide a base for iron columns that are shaped and detailed to simulate the flutes used in classical stone columns. More dramatic, as far as the idea of wish-images is concerned, are the cast-iron arches of the main reading room (Figure 1.3). The exposed truss of these arches juxtaposes structural logic with a classical sense of ornamentation: like a burdened row of leaves forming a cyma and abacus, the floral forms, cut out of the fabric of the truss, are meant to increase the inertia of iron. Kenneth Frampton observes that "Labrouste strove for a consistent tectonic expression, one in which the ornamentation would be derived directly from the process of construction."[52] And Robin Middleton notes that, besides its utilitarian use, iron was entertained for symbolic aims. According to him, Labrouste "aimed not just at making evidence the structural system, but to present it as part of a civic décor appropriate to the nineteenth century."[53] Middleton's position recalls Semper's idea of theatricality in architecture discussed in the next chapter. What should be added to

1.3 Henri Labrouste, Bibliothèque Ste-Geneviève, Paris, 1838–50. Reading room. Image courtesy of the MIT Press from *Studies in Tectonic Culture*, by Kenneth Frampton, edited by John Cava

1.4 Auguste Perret, 25 bis rue Franklin, Paris 1902–04. Photograph by author

Middleton's observation, however, is the use, if not the abuse of "nature" in domesticating the new industrial materials. The idea of masking structural members with references to natural forms reappears in Auguste Perret's 25 bis rue Franklin (Figure 1.4). Like a carpet, the concrete structural frame of this building is framed with ceramic sunflower infill, representing the duality between the core-form and the art-form. In these examples, the tectonic speaks for the form derived from construction and the values laid down by the Enlightenment, in particular, the desire to juxtapose history with nature, the outmoded with the new. The intention perhaps was to "return" to a mythic time when the natural world was not separated from the experience of everyday life. The cladding of rue Franklin disguises the frame and, at the same time, expresses the desire for a repressed state of the natural, as depicted in Laugier's hut.

Exploring many other examples from late nineteenth-century architecture, one wonders why the use of iron was confined to the interior spaces that were enclosed by masonry walls. A plausible answer to this question might have to do with the metaphysics of the monument, whose language was for a long time associated with the classical language of architecture. It also confirms Semper's theoretical speculation concerning the lack of corporeality of iron, and thus, its unsuitability for monumental effects. In fact, in an early struggle to redeem architecture from the classical vocabulary, architects were not yet able to articulate the tectonic forms suited to steel and glass without reducing architecture to the dazzling work of engineers, as displayed in the new building types such as exhibition halls and train stations. In this mutation, Peter Behrens's Turbine Factory is an exemplar that demonstrates the centrality of "purposefulness" for any tectonic consideration.[54]

On the one hand, the solid battered corners of the main façade of the AEG Factory are conceived to suggest the masonry wall's non-load-bearing character (Figure 1.5). On the other, the exterior architrave conceals a triangular girder visible from the inside. What is involved here is Behrens's misuse of the tectonic hinge to inject monumental sensibility into the main façade of a factory. The details used in this building show Behrens's awareness of the ways in which steel-frame structures work. But the perception invested in the overall form of the building has less to do with the forms derived from the chosen construction technique. The difference between the front façade and the side elevation, facing the factory's ground, reveals Behrens's understanding of the dichotomy between art and technology, and his

1.5   Peter Behrens, AEG Turbine Factory, Berlin 1908–09. Photograph by author

inclination to turn the dichotomy in favor of traditions of symbolic representation, rather than tectonic culture.[55] In the AEG Factory, most of the detailing, cutting, and putting together of different materials serves ultimately to convey the temple-like image of the main façade. Frampton's reading is convincing: "While accepting the ascendancy of science and industry with pessimistic resignation, Behrens sought to bring the factory under the rubric of the farm—to restore factory production to that sense of common purpose innate in agriculture, a feeling for which the newly urbanized semi-skilled labour of Berlin would supposedly still have a certain nostalgia."[56] As discussed before, when the horizon of "purpose" is limited to representation of a kind that has nothing to do with the expressive potentialities of construction, then, not only the line between atectonic and tectonic is blurred, but also the complexities invested in wish-images are compromised with historicism. To shed critical light on some aspects of modern architecture, the observation should be extended to a discussion that centers on the difference between theatricality and theatricalization.

The early history of modern architecture demonstrates the fact that architects were forced to revise the classical discourse of construction. While the historicists covered construction by historical styles and pumped new blood into humanism, the Jugendstil, for example, used artistic freedom to advocate a modern vision that goes beyond the ordering principles dictated by the machine and mechanization. A few architects who wanted to resist the forces unleashed by technology sought refuge in primitive art. An ancient sculpture or a vase, for instance, was admired either for its unspoiled expressive qualities, or for the material and technical aspects that were seen unseparated from the myth surrounding primitivism. Joseph Masheck associates the first inclination with German expressionism and the widespread interest in themes such as empathy and expression discussed by Wilhelm Worringer and others.[57] The second line of thinking might be traced in Semper, William Morris, and G.V. Plekhanov, a group that, in one way or another underlined the importance of labor and material over "play."[58] In addition, upon the arrival of modernity, the century was already divided into revivalist camps in favor of the Renaissance humanism or the Gothic transcendentalism. Both movements offered alternatives to modernity's will to disintegrate totalities of every kind. The salvation was seen in the sensuous beauty of classical architecture, and/or in the power of expression attributed to Gothic architecture.

In the context of this polarity of ideas, Semper's aspiration for both Renaissance architecture and primeval arts seems rather intriguing. Central to Semper's theory is the way that material and technical experience used in the four industries of carpentry, ceramics, masonry, and weaving contributes to the art-form of architecture. Even Worringer, who disliked Semper's views on Gothic architecture, claimed that Gothic sculptural modeling belongs "not to the history of art, but to the history of handicraft."[59] Here Worringer sounds a Semperian materialist. However, what Semper saw in Renaissance architecture was structural flexibility, providing more options to carry primitive motives from their craft-based roots into a "higher" order, i.e., architecture. This may have been his way of saving past traditions and juxtaposing the new with the old. That Gothic architecture was a tectonic form did not concern Semper. It was rather the absence of duality between the core-form and the art-form that made him skeptical of the tectonic potentialities of Gothic architecture. The lack of flexibility in Gothic form robs stonewall of its expressive potential, and minimizes the tectonic expression of enclosure, an essential aspect of Semper's theory of theatricality.

The duality in the tectonic pondered here has to do with the need for a flexible relationship between the art-form and the core-form, and thus the possibility of the "lawful" articulation of a chosen construction method. The duality also alludes to the historical fact that, although by the nineteenth century the gap between theory and practice was institutionalized, architects were still able to consider construction the sole domain of "artistic design."[60] Now we should ask if the tectonic is attainable only when the duality between structure and the skin is established. Should we associate Semper's distinction between the core-form and the art-form with the historical division between the object and the subject? For it turns out that in monolithic structures the tectonic does not necessarily reveal its poetics through an actual separation of the load-bearing members from the enclosure. Paradoxically, in Semper's discussion of the evolution of the Assyrian column, we are reminded that, at one point, the wooden shaft (the core-form) disappears and the metal sheathing is used to function for both the core-form and the art-form.[61] The case can be made for arguing that the embellishment of the art-form might, at some point, attain a degree of autonomy that, without referring to its initial dualistic origin, can still stand for the tectonic. If this is so, then, are there moments in modern architecture when construction was conceived as "self-illuminating" form?

An argument can be advanced to suggest that contemporary interest in displaced objects of surrealism, and the work of some Russian constructivist architects is partly due to the work's anonymous rapport with an archaic past. Interestingly enough, according to Benjamin, constructivism and surrealism "accepted the antinomy of bourgeois thought (not identical with being), the subject-object division—in order later to protest against it even extremely sharply." Precisely for that reason, expressionism and the Neue Sachlichkeit, according to Benjamin, "could not produce any artistic result but a pathological insight or a dry abstraction."[62] This observation is critical not only because it maintains the importance of technology for early modern architecture, but because it offers a paradigm to postulate the centrality of wish-images in Russian constructivist architecture.

There is the tendency to discuss Russian constructivism to conflate its achievements with the international constructivists, or else to value their work strictly in terms of technology. We are reminded of Manfredo Tafuri and Hubertus Gassner who highlight the historical avant-garde's huge investment in technology.[63] The criticism of these two scholars is valid if the subject matter is seen strictly from the historical perspective of the project of modernity, and if the inevitability of accepting modernization as an alternative to expressionism and historicism is established. The question to ask then is how we should assess the project of modernity if it is necessary to make a distinction between art and architecture without reducing diverse tendencies within constructivism to formalism? According to Christian Lodder, even in the Russia of 1917–22 "there were important differences between Gabo's constructions with their rather mathematical approach to form and the more empathically textual, abstract work of Tatlin."[64] Indeed, the constructivism permeating Vladimir Tatlin's reliefs and counter-reliefs, and his numerous kiosks and stage-set designs were primarily inspired by the iconological tradition of pre-modern Russia, and a vision of primitivism that would emphasize the texture of material (faktura), use of simple techniques, and disdain for "artistic design."[65]

At the conceptual level, however, even Boris Arvatov's stress on technology differed from the Bauhaus attempt to reduce art and architecture to the modalities of technological transformation. The fact is that, from its inception, the Bauhaus had close ties with the leaders and representatives of industrial institutions. This was not the case with the constructivists: after the revolution, not only did Russia have no organized industrial representatives; the constructivists' collaboration with the educational institutions enjoyed a degree of autonomy that lasted at least until 1922. Moreover, the advocates of the *Neue Sachlichkeit* considered technology belonging to the sphere of production, with no major relevance to the realm of values, i.e., the realm of "everyday things."[66] For constructivists, instead, theoretical comprehension of the dialectics between production and consumption was critical in any consideration of technology as part of "material culture." It is indeed in the realm of consumption where according to Arvatov:

> The ability to pick up a cigarette-case, to smoke a cigarette, to put on an overcoat, to wear a cap, to open a door, all these "trivialities," acquire their qualification, their not unimportant "culture," which find their meaning in the maximization of economy and precision, in maximum cohesion with the things and their purpose.[67]

Here technology is presented as an engine of collectivization of culture in the broadest meaning of the term.

The position put forward by Arvatov and others was not meant as a denial of the past; to subdue the object with explicit references to vernacular elements of the kind used in Walter Gropius's Sommerfeld House, for example. The stone base and symmetrical composition of Gropius's design frames a romantic vision of architecture whose form is derived from the nature of material. The uniform use of wooden structural elements in Alexander Rodchenko's constructs, and in Konstantin Melnikov's design for the Russian Pavilion in Paris, on the other hand, does not mimic the rational organization of the world of technology. Here the rawness of metal and wood are embellished beyond the utilitarian attributes of material and those pumped into the design by the artist. These constructs demonstrate the ur-form of the work and its latent potential to resist the reduction of the world of consumption to mere commodities. When nostalgia for the past forms and sentimental appreciation of material are suspended, then even the most archaic has the possibility of redemption through ur-images, i.e., when technological nature "flashes together with the old in an anticipatory image of humanity and nature reconciled." Here Susan Buck-Morss relates Benjamin's utopia assessment in the Passage-Werk to communist goals stated by Karl Marx, suggesting that, "It is with the new, technological nature that human beings must be reconciled … " The paradox of such reconciliation is that one has to give up "nostalgic mimicking of the past and paying strict attention to the new nature, the ur-images are reanimated. Such is the logic of historical images, in which collective wish-images are negated, surpassed, and at the same time dialectically redeemed."[68] One is tempted to claim that, the European avant-gardes stopped short of entertaining the wish-image quality of constructivist objects. This is not to disregard the fact that this quality lost its critical edge as soon as the ideological apparatus of the Soviet state asked artists/architects to produce practical objects; the move slowly diminished the aura of revolution and reduced architecture to a normative practice. Not long afterwards, Stalin forced architects to abandon every norm except those represented by the classical language of architecture. This was an uncanny return to the "natural" state of the object, an ideological rebuff to the crisis of the object indeed!

In associating "wish-images" with Russian constructivists, the intention is not to ignore Benjamin's interest in the work of Le Corbusier, Loos, and Paul Scheerbart. One is reminded of John McCole's reading of Benjamin's discourse on technology in what he calls "anthropological materialism." The latter traces the "bodily collective" in the outcropping of images depicted by surrealists and by Proust, and "a bodily sphere (*Leibrarum*), which was beginning to come into its own through recent developments in technology."[69] According to McCole, Benjamin's understanding of the place of technology in culture was closer to Loos and Le Corbusier than the advocates of the *Neue Sachlichkeit*. In different ways most architects of the early last century rocked the foundation of traditions, making room for an architecture that was relevant to the experience of modernity. What should be underlined here is that constructivists neither pursued the Bauhaus project, nor used technology merely for aesthetic purposes. For constructivists, technique was a derivative of material, and both were perceived to be at the service of material culture. *Tecktonica*, *factura*, and construction, discussed by Aleksei Gan, presented a conceptual triad capable of charging the object with various semiotic layers in accordance with an optimistic ambience informed by the tide of revolution.

The tendency to tie technique with raw material and purpose is epitomized in Tatlin's Monument to the Third International, and in Lyubov Popova's stage-set designs. These works were perceived and constructed using the simple techniques and skills of the Russian craft of log cabin making. Consider Tatlin's Monument to the Third International, where three different volumes, made of glass and wrapped by steel structures, represented the constructive dimension of the October Revolution. "My monument is a symbol of the epoch. Unifying in it artistic and utilitarian forms, I created a kind of synthesis of art and life."[70] Tatlin's explanation recalls the ready-made objects of his counter-reliefs, a montage of material, technique, and purpose. There is another filmic side to Tatlin's monument: renouncing every additional element from the body of architecture, his tectonic articulation intends to transform human perceptibility. Like Dziga Vertov's Kino-Eye, Tatlin's monument upholds the world "without a mask as a world of naked truth,"[71] and avoids using shock effects of the kind entertained by the formalist avant-gardes. The same nakedness energizes Popova's stage-set design: these simple wooden constructs set the stage free for the "event" to unravel. If architecture was meant to be a socio-political agent for modernism, then the minimalism and lightness of constructivist architecture mark a departure from any longing for "silence" and redemption, themes essential for European constructivists' tragic encounter with the project of modernity.

Furthermore, the monism implied in *tecktonica*, *factura*, and construction does indeed undermine the duality between the core-form and the art-form of any tectonic form. Constructivist architecture might be considered to produce monolithic structures not of the kind that would use symbolic geometry, as was the case with the architecture of the French Revolutionary architects. Like a filmic frame, constructivist work demonstrates the infusion of "idea" with technique, stressing the materiality of the object. The animated body of such architecture enchants the viewer, as do the images perceived at the moment of awakening from sleep, that momentary pause when construction recalls the dormant and forgotten experiences residing in the subconscious.

Consider A. Leonid and Victor Vesnin's design for the "Pravda Building," Ivan Leonidov's "Lenin Institute," Konstantin Melnikov's "Commissarial of Heavy Industry," and, more importantly, Ikaov Chernikhov's "Architectural Fantasies." These projects bring together the pre-historic sense of construction with the aesthetics of machine technology. In "Industrial Tales," for example, we are confronted by an architecture that is devoid of applied decoration, and yet the final object is represented as an ornament *per se*. Chernikhov's architectural drawings are comparable to Piranesi's engravings where technique becomes, to use a Semperian phrase, "self-illuminating symbols," directing the spectator's eye to the particularities of construction.[72] More importantly, his drawings address the problematic theme of the frame and cladding that has been at work since the nineteenth century. Conceiving construction as an artistic design, Chernikhov's work unleashed the fear Sigfried Giedion had observed lurking beneath the historicists' masking of construction. According to Giedion, "Construction in the nineteenth century plays the role of the subconscious. Outwardly, construction still boasts the old pathos; underneath, concealed behind facades, the basis of our present existence is taking place."[73] While Giedion was making rather radical remarks in connection to the early architecture of Le Corbusier, Russian constructivists were weaving the anticipatory potentialities of technology with the collective practice, grafting revolutionary sentiments into the linguistic potentialities of architecture.

Now, putting behind the architecture of the machine age, the question to ask is what the implications are of the idea of wish-images for contemporary architecture. More specifically, how should we discuss the neo-avant-gardes' apparent esteem for an expressionism that is motivated either by computer technologies, or by the hybrid formulation of an abstract and yet vigorous form that might be associated with constructivism?

If the distraction Benjamin alludes to is caused by the everyday experience of the metropolis, then architecture stands outside of such experience, and paradoxically, architecture has no choice but to internalize some aspects of that very experience. It might be claimed that architecture is the art of construction of the conditions of life: the integrity of architecture with life is intense enough to suggest that one cannot separate it from the habits developed through collective experience. On this subject, Sándor Radnóti says:

> Every transformation, every reform of aesthetics is accompanied by a paradigm shift ... Even more than drama, Benjamin links more closely with the social mission and effect of collective art than all other arts. Even the collective, social possibilities which find expression in a technical culture are manifested with striking transparency in the technical foundations of architecture.[74]

The complex picture presented here of architecture's relation to ideology is the crux of current theoretical debates and is expressed through discussions concerning the relevance of themes such as ornament, construction, and cladding. It is the intention of this book to address these issues in the light of Semper's theory of theatricality.

Central to the idea of theatricality is the communicative dimension of architecture.[75] As will be discussed in the following chapters, the tectonic represents the art-form in relation to the core-form by relating architecture to the vastness of a given cultural experience. What is involved in the "relation" has to do with Semper's idea of *Stoffwechsel*;[76] where skills and techniques immanent in the art of building play a significant role in transforming and modifying motifs from the domain of cultural productivity into that of architecture. The modification is carried out by techniques that are architectural. Only in this way can we discuss the aesthetic dimension of the tectonic and avoid attributing the poetics of construction to the artist genius, and/or attempt a superficial understanding of the import of aesthetics for the tectonic. There is a historical dimension to this claim: the nineteenth-century style debate, especially in German-speaking countries, was instrumental in generating aesthetic discourses (such as the theories of empathy and the place of the beholder in the work of art) that were not mere abstract speculations, but aimed at orchestrating a visual culture that was not accessible to previous generations.[77] To put it differently, what was considered to be "dream-work" in the nineteenth century had turned into the "real." Therefore, one of the main theoretical objectives of this book is to show the centrality of the nineteenth-century dream of theatricality (Nietzsche and Richard Wagner, as well as Semper[78]) for neo-avant-garde architecture, and to present a different interpretation of the current state of architecture. The intention is not to approach contemporary architecture based on Semper's theory; it rather says that one reason why Semper has been topical for the past couple of decades has to do with the historical coincidence between his concept of theatricality and the spectacle permeating the visual culture of late capitalism.[79] One might go further and argue that *technique*, as subtext, is what makes Semper so interesting a figure for contemporary architecture. The present turn to Semper is also informed by electronic technologies and perceptual horizons that are endemic to a different way of seeing and making.

At this point it is necessary to caution the reader with two problems concerning the idea of theatricality. First, the esteem for totality implied in Semper's theory might be seen as responding to both the tragic dimension of modernity, i.e., the deterritorialization of all kinds of totalities, including cultural homogeneity of pre-modern communities,[80] and the broken connection between the classical language of architecture and the ethics and moralities of the theological world that had existed since the Renaissance. However, in the context of postmodernity and the globalization of capital and the information industry, any attempt to restore the communicative dimension of architecture might fall in the populism of "learning from Las Vegas," if not the spectacle as such.[81] Even if this might not be the case with the entirety of today's architectural practice, it could still be argued that the present situation, marked by the saturation of the life-world with techniques of image-making demands a reading of neo-avant-garde architecture in association with the impact of technology on disciplinary history, rather than theorizing architecture through concepts borrowed from other disciplines. Each chapter in this book attempts to discuss contemporary architecture through tropes such as roofing, wrapping, and the tectonics of skin and structure.

Second, to read Semper's concept of theatricality and to restore the past traditions of architecture is one thing; to read him in the light of Benjamin's discourse on wish-images and the exhibition value is another. Benjamin also suggested, "The camera introduces us to unconscious optics as does psychoanalysis to unconscious impulses."[82] Thus we have the argument that beneath the visible, self-referential, and yet playful forms of neo-avant-garde architecture lies the unconscious dimension of a modernist experience of the object/subject relationship, which in postmodernity is inflected by the aesthetic of commodity-form. Reviewing Peter Eisenman's work at a 1985 Exhibition of the Architectural Association, London, Robin Evans wrote, "if we are still sometimes touched by the ancient idea that rocks are animate, we ourselves are in the grip of a similar sentiment amplified by language when we think of building as *animated*." He continued, animation in its modern form has less to do "with the wilful breathing of life into inert objects." Rather, "it has more to do with a willful unrealization of them: the hallucination of a transcendental yet entirely corporeal world is involved."[83] In this context, the tectonic embellishment of the thematic of the culture of building possesses the seeds of critical practice if the art-form is not informed by the exhibition value permeating contemporary visual culture. The communicative side of architecture demands that architecture be approached through a web of ideas and concepts generated by various activities of production and consumption. Central to the idea of theatricality is the ability to embellish the constructed form to a point where the art-form remains anonymous; anonymous because the final form is not tied to the conceptual process of design. When this is established, a distinction can be made between the concepts of the theatricality and theatricalization of architecture. Central to this differentiation is the criticism of the aesthetic of the commodity-form and its impact on architecture.

The idea of theatricality discussed throughout this volume, and the stress put on the recollection of the culture of building also dismisses the argument which claims that, at the theoretical level, the tectonic aims to "confer unity on the disparate procedures of design and construction" or, for that matter, a hermeneutic interest in the past.[84] The architecture of theatricality communicates through the tectonic of the art-form and core-form that it has the capacity to retain that which is immanent to architecture; meaning that, architecture is not a direct product of construction, and yet the core-form, the physical material of building, inevitably puts architecture on the track of technological transformations and scientific innovations. The same might be said about the art-form; in suspending the romantic idea of genius, the art-form remains the only means by which architecture is charged with aesthetic sensibilities that, interestingly enough, are informed both by perceptual horizons offered by the world of technology, and by the tactile and spatial sensibilities deeply rooted in the disciplinary history of architecture. Therefore, while the core-form assures architecture's rapport with the many changes taking place in the *technique* of construction, the art-form remains the sole domain where the architect might choose to impinge on the core-form with those aspects of the culture of building that might sidetrack the formal and aesthetic consequences of commodification essential to the cultural production of late capitalism, and yet embrace the latest technological developments.

Moreover, the introduction of digital programming (parametric) as a determining factor in the formal potentialities of the final object questions the classical discourse of the object beyond the modernists' intentions. Influenced by Gilles Deleuze's idea of the "fold," Bernard Cache, for one, presents an idea of image that is a by-product of a second-generation of computer-assisted design in which "objects are no longer designed but calculated." We can agree with his advocacy for a sense of lightness in design and his observations that our experience of weightlessness "was aesthetic before it became technological." Also noteworthy is his reflection on the relationship between fold and structure, concluding that "Two architectural principles thus confront one another: the principle of structure and that of the skin. Modern architecture could be described as the site of confrontation between these two principles." According to Cache, if Le Corbusier and Gropius invoke the primacy of structure, Loos, following Semper, stresses the primacy of skin.[85] Nevertheless, digitally rendered forms take the distinction between the *Kernform* and *Kunstform* for granted, and charge the art-form with a degree of autonomy that has the potential to represent any icon, including those of the mainstream of commercial culture. Unlike industrial techniques, telecommunication technologies have no direct impact on the construction process, and yet their impact on one's perception of the object is enormous. Once this is established, the task is to explore strategies by which one might cultivate the nihilism of technology, and animate the duality between structure and clothing, for example, beyond the tradition of lineaments and the modernist engagement with the free façade (surface?). It is important to mention once again that a thin line separates the Semperian idea of theatricality from theatricalization induced by the culture of spectacle. It is the aim of this book to capitalize on the difference by discussing selected projects from neo-avant-garde architects.

Finally, the increasing pressure of commodity-form on architecture demands recoding themes such as monument, ornament and the tectonic beyond and yet within the disciplinary history of architecture. There are two reasons for this quest. First, even a cursory examination of present architectural practice supports the claim that form has little to do with construction, let alone artistic re-presentation. The animated body of neo-avant-garde architecture intends to cut the cord that links the object to the culture of building. Even if metaphysics is the main subject matter of deconstruction architecture, we can still ask if it is possible to dismiss the ontological dimension of the culture of building. This is not a call to return to historical models and types, nor even a leaning towards postmodern eclecticism. The infatuation of early modern architecture with the question concerning technology, and the attempt to see architecture as a by-product of a machine should be rethought as architecture enters the virtual world of telecommunication technologies. If Mies van der Rohe, for example, was able to charge the steel-frame structure with the aesthetics of monumentality, and if Le Corbusier could ponder the impossibility of poetry without technology, then is it not the time to claim that the late 1950s concern for civic architecture has evaporated, and that computer-programming is capable of charging architecture with an excess that makes one wonder if the idea of monument has not become ornament *per se*?[86] Second, by reducing the matrix of an architectural object to the images invoked by computer technology, neo-avant-garde architecture has opened architectural discourse to literary criticism and philosophy. It is true that Vitruvius recommended architects arm themselves with the vast available knowledge of wind and earth as well as philosophy; nevertheless, the inclusion of architectural topics in recent philosophical texts indicates that metaphysics can't erect its own "ground" without concurrent deconstruction of architecture's foundation. The missing point in the writing, teaching, and even the built work of today's mainstream architecture is "the intrinsic nature of the building art,"[87] the thematic of which is essential to the argument advanced in this volume.

The theoretical underpinning of the next chapter aims at presenting an in-depth analysis of the specificity of Semper's idea of theatricality in the purview of the spectacle of late capitalism. The argument benefits from Benjamin's discourse on "exhibition value," and takes into consideration the appropriation of "theatricality" in poetry and painting discussed by Charles Bernstein and Michael Fried respectively. Differentiating Semper's idea of theatricality from theatricalization, the intention is to make analogies between the sense of totalization that is embedded in what Semper, Wagner, and Nietzsche saw in the Greek theater, and that of the culture of spectacle unfolding globally today. To do this, the discussion centers on the disciplinary history of architecture, presenting a critical understanding of "excess" in contemporary architecture. Chapters 3 through 8 provide an in-depth discussion of selected buildings and projects by Peter Eisenman, Bernard Tschumi, Rem Koolhaas, Zaha Hadid, Frank Gehry, and Steven Holl. There are three reasons for the selection. Firstly, the intention is to historicize the traces of traditions of modernism in the work of these architects: the re-visitation of the radical facets of formalism in Eisenman; the re-activation of themes drawn from constructivism in Koolhaas and Hadid; the revisitation of "objectivity" in Tschumi; Holl's phenomenologization of architecture after Le Corbusier's meditation on nature and his tendency to anchor the human body into the world. And finally, the importance of regionalism in the early work of Gehry, and its metamorphosis into the architecture of theatricalization. The argument wishes to demonstrate the impossibility of stepping out of the historicity of modern architecture, let alone the culture of building. Moreover, the playful dialogue that Gehry establishes between the element of wrapping and the roof recalls this author's previous remarks about the problematic nature of theatricality today, and the relevance of the culture of building not only in Gehry's work, but in that of many other contemporary architects, briefly discussed throughout this book. Secondly, the work of the selected architects is important because their theoretical ruminations have put a cap on the scope of any constructive criticism of their architecture. Most inspiring criticism of these architects' work, and one might extend this observation to the significant work produced during the last two decades, is haunted by the weight of contemporary philosophical ideas. One consequence is to turn architecture into a text mirroring epistemological debates,[88] or else, as mentioned before, to suggest a one-to-one correspondence between design theory and the work itself. Thirdly, the selection concerns contemporary architecture's dialogue with the *Zeitgeist*: while Eisenman attempts to transgress the issue, Tschumi problematizes it by recoding the concept of "objectivity," a theme central to the very in-completeness of modernism of the 1920s. Whereas Koolhaas and Hadid make and attempt to suspend the contemporaneity of time as such, Holl's architecture mediates between the worldliness of time and the body's perceptual experience of space. Gehry, instead, maintains a non-critical position *vis-à-vis* the cultural logic of late capitalism, to recall Fredric Jameson, allowing "design" to be inflated by the present spectacle. Still there are aspects of temporality in the work of these architects that allows us to consider theatricality as a useful tool for checking each individual work's appropriation of the visual spectacle of late capitalism. In addressing these issues the author wishes to raise questions that concern the state of architecture in the new millennium. To this end the final chapter wishes to demonstrate that the current proliferation of the tectonic rapport between the two elements of roof and enclosure is informed by the conflation of architecture's interiority with digital techniques. Once a semi-autonomous understanding of architecture is established, the argument takes up a number of diverse architects' work, advancing an argument that plots the recent interest in "surface" in analogy to the tectonics of topology. The binary underpinning of this comparison is problematized when Greg Lynn's views on the tectonics of blob is included in the fuzzy picture of current architectural practice.

The argument presented throughout the book intends to raise many questions, including: Is the accommodation of architecture to the nihilism of technology adding a new chapter to the book of the crisis of architecture? In what ways can the dialectics between modernity and tradition be nurtured beyond what has already been done by the protagonists of modern architecture? What is the place of history in architecture at a time when abstraction gets around the "thingness" of architecture, reducing it to a textual phenomenon? And last, but not least, while the point has surpassed where one could associate the monument with the classical language of architecture, in what ways does the enduring aspect of architecture speak not only for the simultaneity of ornament and structure, but for a marginal truth, as Heidegger would have said?

What are the fruits of this rather bleak vision compared to the celebratory approach of postmodernism? Instead of pursuing the *Zeitgeist* in current architectural practice; to become enchanted, if not intoxicated, by what telecommunication technologies could do for architecture; to avoid the culture of building and discuss architecture as a text among other interdisciplinary texts. The following chapters intend to discuss architecture from the point of view of themes that have been developed through the history of architectural theories and practice. Particular attention is given to the place of theatricality, monument, and ornament and their relevance for contemporary architecture. This book attempts to show how the neo-avant-garde's strategic position, of continuing the dream of the project of the historical avant-gardes, turns out to be no more than another *technique* towards the implementation and expansion of the horizon of instrumental reason. To demystify neo-avant-garde architecture is not to flatten its achievements. The aim rather is to historicize, to show the material presence of the past and to re-empower the thematic of the culture of building even at the dawn of this new century when the commodification of culture is almost total and the historical energies of the project of modernity are seemingly exhausted.

NOTES

1   According to Fritz Neumeyer, Mies van der Rohe was influenced by Romano Guardini's thought, in general, and his ambivalent approach to technology, in particular. Fritz Neumeyer, *The Artless Word* (Cambridge, MA: The MIT Press, 1991). Neumeyer writes: "Thus Guardini called for something with which Mies was in profound agreement: another, new, but not unilateral modernism in which subjective forces were restrained by objective limits, but, in which, conversely, the potentially threatening objective powers inherent in technology were subordinated to the subject, to man and his life" (Neumeyer, 1991, 201). The dichotomy between the will of technology and the state of cultural products and architecture is relevant today when telecommunication technologies are influencing every facet of one's daily experience.

2   Peter Eisenman, "The Futility of Objects," *Harvard Architecture Review* 3 (winter 1984): 65–82.

3   Haim N. Finkelstein, *Surrealism and the Crisis of the Object* (Ann Arbor, MI: University Microfilms International, 1979).

4   Daniel Naegele, "Object, Image, Aura," *Harvard Design Magazine* (fall 1998): 38.

5   Nancy J. Troy, *Modernism and the Decorative Arts in France* (New Haven, CT: Yale University Press, 1991), 52.

6   For a concise discussion of this subject in the circles of German Werkbund, see Fredric J. Schwartz, *Werkbund: Design Theory and Mass Culture before the First World War* (New Haven, CT: Yale University Press, 1996), especially the section on "Individuality," 151–63. See also Walter Curt Behrendt in footnote 9 below.

7   See Fritz Schmalenbach, "The Term *Neue Sachlichkeit*," *Art Bulletin* 22, 3 (1940): 155–65. See also Weiland Schmied, *Neue Sachlichkeit and the German Realism of the Twenties* (London: Hayward Gallery, 1979), 7–32.

8   H.F. Mallgrave, "From Realism to *Sachlichkeit*: The Polemics of Architectural Modernity in the 1890s," in H.F. Mallgrave, ed., *Otto Wagner* (Santa Monica, CA: The Getty Center for the History of Art and the Humanities, 1993), 281–322.

9   Detlef Martins has contextualized the 1920s discourse in German architecture in his introduction to Walter Curt Behrendt, *The Victory of the New Building Style*, trans. H.F. Mallgrave (Los Angeles, CA: The Getty Research Institute, 2000), 1–86.

10 For a full account of the implication of fashion and dressing for modern architecture see, Mark Wigley, *White Walls, Designer Dresses* (Cambridge, MA: The MIT Press, 1995).

11 For an extended discussion of Adolf Loos, see Gevork Hartoonian, "Adolf Loos: The Awakening Moments of Tradition in Modern Architecture," in *Ontology of Construction* (Cambridge: Cambridge University Press, 1994), 43–55.

12 Fritz Neumeyer, "Iron and Stone: The Architecture of the Grobstadt," in H.F. Mallgrave, ed., *Otto Wagner*, 1993, 115–56.

13   On this subject, see the entire "Part III," in H.F. Mallgrave, ed., *Otto Wagner*, 1993.

14   Mitchell Schwarzer, "Freedom and Tectonics," in *German Architectural Theory and the Search for Modern Identity* (Cambridge: Cambridge University Press, 1995), especially 189–200. A comprehensive study of the differences between Gottfried Semper and Karl Bötticher on the concept of tectonic is still waiting.

15   Stanford Anderson, *Peter Behrens* (Cambridge, MA: The MIT Press, 2000), 117.

16   H.F. Mallgrave, *Gottfried Semper: Architect of the Nineteenth Century* (New Haven, CT: Yale University Press, 1996), 222.

17   On this subject, see Hal Foster, "Exquisite Corpses," in *Compulsive Beauty* (Cambridge, MA: The MIT Press, 1993), 125–53.

18   For a fresh reading of these aspects of Adolf Loos, see Hal Foster, *Design and Crime* (London: Verso, 2002), 16.

19   This observation precedes Hal Foster's seminal essay "Image Building," first published in *Artforum* 43, 2 (October 2004), 270–73; 310–11.

20   For a discussion of the history of frame-structure, see Colin Rowe, "Chicago Frame," in *The Mathematics of the Ideal Villa and Other Essays* (Cambridge, MA: The MIT Press, 1982), 89–118. For the aesthetic, but also the political implications of the contemporary use of glass and steel frame architecture, see Annette Fierro, *The Glass State: The Technology of Spectacle, Paris, 1981–1998* (Cambridge, MA: The MIT Press, 2003).

21   A commodity is for Marx "a mysterious thing simply because in it the social character of men's labor appears to them as an objective character stamped upon the product of that labor" (Karl Marx, *Capital* vol. 1 [New York: International Publishers, 1967], 35–93). For Marx, fetish is a subjectified object that facilitates the return of the familiar in a different appearance. The implied confusion recalls "the misty realm of religion" where "the products of the human brain appear as autonomous figures endowed with a life of their own" (Marx, 1967, 165).

22   Jean Baudrillard, *Simulations* (New York: Semiotext(e), 1983).

23   Bernard Cache, *Earth Moves* (Cambridge, MA: The MIT Press, 1995), 87–94, 96.

24   In Neil Leach, David Turnbull and Chris Williams, eds, *Digital Tectonics* (London: Wiley-Academy, 2004).

25   Antoine Picon, *Digital Culture in Architecture: An Introduction for the Design Professions* (Basel: Blrkhauser, 2010).

26   Lars Spuybroek, *The Architecture of Continuity* (Rotterdam: V2 Publishing, 2008), 19.

27   For a contesting view, see H.F. Mallgrave, *Architect's Brain: Neuroscience, Creativity, and Architecture* (London: Wiley-Blackwell, 2010).

28   On this subject see the last chapter in Gevork Hartoonian, *Ontology of Construction* (Cambridge: Cambridge University Press, 1994).

29   Antoine Picon, *Digital Culture*, 2010, 124.

30   I am reminded of Kenneth Frampton's *Megaform as Urban Landscape* (Ann Arbor, MI: The University of Michigan Press, 1999), and Slavoj Žižek, "The Architectural Parallax," in *Living in the End Times* (London: Verso, 2011), 244–78.

31   See Patrick Schumacher's remark on style discussed in Chapter 6.

32   The nineteenth century is famous for its positivistic approach to history. In Germanic countries, however, the importance of aesthetics for art and architecture, as well as the

ways we appreciate and enjoy form and space were discussed in terms of perception, empathy, and style. See H.F. Mallgrave's introduction to *Empathy, Form, and Space* (Santa Monica, CA: The Getty Center for the History of Art and the Humanities, 1994). The book compiles essays by many authors including Heinrich Wölfflin and Alois Riegl, among others, where the theme of aesthetics in art and architecture are discussed from different perspectives.

33   Walter Benjamin, *One-Way Street* (London: New Left Books, 1979), 250.

34   Walter Benjamin, "Paris: The Capital of the Nineteenth Century," in *Charles Baudelaire: A Lyric Poet in the Era of High Capitalism* (London: Verso, 1983), 159.

35   Quoted in Thomas Y. Levin, "Walter Benjamin and the Theory of Art History," *October* 47 (winter 1988): 80.

36   See Gevork Hartoonian, *Ontology of Construction*, 1994.

37   On Alois Riegl's reflection on Gottfried Semper, see H.F. Mallgrave, "Epilogue," in *Gottfried Semper*, 1996. See also, Alois Riegl, in trans. J.E. Jung, *Historical Grammar of the Visual Arts* (New York: Zone Books, 2004), 355–81.

38   Walter Benjamin, "N [Re the Theory of Knowledge, Theory of Progress]," in Gary Smith, ed., *Benjamin: Philosophy, Aesthetics, History* (Chicago, IL: University of Chicago Press, 1989), 48.

39   I have taken up this subject in "Looking Backward, Looking Forward: Delightful Delays," in Gevork Hartoonian, ed., *Walter Benjamin and Architecture* (London: Routledge, 2010), 23–38.

40   Walter Benjamin, "The Work of Art in the Age of Mechanical Reproduction," in Hannah Arendt, ed., *Illuminations* (New York: Schocken Books, 1969), 239. Rosemarie Haag Bletter reminds us of Adolf Behne's discussion in "*Das reproduktive Zeitalter*" [The Reproductive Era] that prefigured Benjamin's thesis "about the effect of mass produced images on art." The association was first noted by Arn Bohm in an essay published in *The Germanic Review* 68, 4 (1993): 146–55. See Bletter, "Introduction" to Adolf Behne's *The Modern Functional Building* (Santa Monica, CA: The Getty Research Institute for History of Art and the Humanities, 1996), 5.

41   Adolf Loos, "Architecture" (1910), in Charlotte Benton and Dennis Sharp, eds, *Architecture and Design: 1890–1939* (New York: Watson-Guptill Publications, 1975), 45.

42   This aspect of the tectonic is indeed the theoretical underpinning of Gottfried Semper's theory of style. For a comprehensive understanding of Semper's theory of architecture, see Gottfried Semper, *Style in the Technical and Tectonic Arts; or Practical Aesthetics*, introduction by H.F. Mallgrave, trans. H.F. Mallgrave and M. Robinson (Santa Monica, CA: Texts and Documents, The Getty Research Institute, 2004).

43   The distinction is essential for Kenneth Frampton's discourse in *Studies in Tectonic Culture* (Cambridge, MA: The MIT Press, 1995).

44   See Anne-Marie Sankovitch's comprehensive work on the subject in "Structure/ Ornament and the Modern Figuration of Architecture," *The Art Bulletin* 80, 4 (December 1998): 687–717.

45   I am thinking of Michel Foucault's claim that up to the end of the sixteenth century, resemblance played a constructive role in the discursive formation of Western culture when "the universe was folded in upon itself: the earth echoing the sky, faces seeing themselves reflected in the stars …" (Foucault, *The Order of Things* [New York: Vintage Books, 1973], 17).

46   See H.F. Mallgrave's introduction to Kenneth Frampton, *Studies in Tectonic Culture*, 1995, ix–xi.

47   See Gevork Hartoonian, "Montage: Recoding the Tectonic," in *Ontology of Construction*, 1994, 5–28.

48   See Kenneth Frampton, "Introduction: Reflections on the Scope of the Tectonic," in *Studies in Tectonic Culture*, 1995, 1–28. See also Indra Kagis McEwen, "Daedalus and the Discovery of Order," in *Socrates' Ancestor* (Cambridge, MA: The MIT Press, 1993), 41–78.

49   Quoted in H.F. Mallgrave, *Modern Architectural Theory: A Historical Survey, 1673–1968* (Cambridge: Cambridge University Press, 2005), 73.

50   Kasimir Malevich, *The Non-Objective World* (Chicago, IL: Paul Theobald Company, 1959), 98.

51   Neil Levin, "The Book and the Building: Hugo's Theory of Architecture and Labrouste's Bibliothèque Ste-Genevieve," in Robin Middleton, ed., *The Beaux-Arts and 19th Century French Architecture* (Cambridge, MA: The MIT Press, 1982), 173.

52   Kenneth Frampton, *Studies in Tectonic Culture*, 1995, 45.

53   Robin Middleton, "The Iron Structures of the Bibliothèque Saint-Genevieve as the Basis of a Civic Décor," *AA Files* 40 (2000): 33–52.

54   This building was discussed by many scholars among whom the following are suggested: Stanford Anderson, "Modern Architecture and Industry: Peter Behrens and the Cultural Policy of Historical Determinism," *Oppositions* 11 (winter 1977): 52–71; Mechtild Heuser, "La Finestra Sul Cortile Behrens M. Rohe: AEG-Turbinehalle, Berlin," *Casabella* 65 (January 1998). My interest in this subject was inspired by Fritz Neumeyer's discussion in, "Iron and Stone," 1996, 115–53.

55   According to Stanford Anderson, "Behrens designed the public, street facades of the building, incorporating modern engineering construction into forms which he conceived through the adaptation of established architectural conventions to the new problem of representing modern industrial enterprise …" (Anderson, "Modern Architecture and Industry," 1977, 68).

56   Kenneth Frampton, *Modern Architecture: A Critical History* (New York: Oxford University Press, 1980), 112.

57   On this subject see H.F. Mallgrave's introduction to *Empathy, Form, and Space*, 1994.

58   Joseph Masheck, "Raw Art: 'Primitive' Authenticity and German Expressionism," *Res* 4 (autumn 1982): 93–116. In this article Masheck sides with the expressionist reading of primitive works of art and seemingly misses both Joseph Rykwert's and Harry F. Mallgrave's discharge of the crude materialist content of Gottfried Semper's discourse. See Mallgrave's *Gottfried Semper*, 1996, especially the final chapter. On the subject of empathy, see trans. H.F. Mallgrave and Eleftherios Ikonomou, *Empathy, Form, and Space*, 1994. However, whether it was the influence of Darwinism or the result of archeological research, some similarities can be seen between Semper's emphasis on the importance of practical arts for aesthetic laws and G.V. Plekhnov's argument that the origin of ornament goes back to hunting, and how the early wooden elements incised into the body would later become the source of ornaments made out of metal. See G.V. Plekhanov, "Labour, Play and Art," and "Art and Utility," in *Art and Social Life* (London: Lawrence and Wishart, 1953), 75–129. For Semper's idea of *Stoffwechsel*, "the carrying over of visual motives from one material to another," see Wolfgang Hermann, *Gottfried Semper: In Search of Architecture* (Cambridge, MA: The MIT Press, 1984), 86. And Gottfried Semper, *Style*, 2004.

59   Quoted in Joseph Masheck, "Raw Art," 1982, 96.

60   For a discussion of the tectonic in contemporary architecture and Gottfried Semper's discourse on what he called the core-form and the art-form, see Gevork Hartoonian, *Ontology of Construction*, 1994, and Kenneth Frampton, *Studies in Tectonic Culture*, 1995.

61   See H.F. Mallgrave and Wolfgang Herrmann, *Gottfried Semper: The Four Elements of Architecture and Other Writings* (Cambridge: Cambridge University Press, 1989), 38.

62   Sándor Radnóti, "Benjamin's Dialectics of Art and Society," in Gary Smith, ed., *Benjamin: Philosophy, Aesthetics, History*, 1989, 146.

63   See Manfredo Tafuri, "U.S.S.R.-Berlin,1922: From Populism to 'Constructivist International'," in Joan Ockman, ed., *Architecture Criticism Ideology* (Princeton, NJ: Princeton Architectural Press, 1985), 121–81. See also Huertus Gassner, "The Constructivists: Modernism on the Way to Modernization," in *The Great Utopia: The Russian and Soviet Avant-Garde, 1915–1932* (New York: Guggenheim Museum Publications, 1994), 298–319. Exploring various utopian manifestations of German humanitarian populism and expressionism, Tafuri sees the impact of the 1922 exhibition of Russian artists in the politicization of dada, and the introduction of constructivist utopia, which was based on technical organization of the real. Tafuri concludes that "the Soviet avant-garde, … found itself objectively carrying out the task of revealing that the only 'politicalness' possible for the avant-garde was that of announcing the advent of a universe of *non-values, amoral, elementary*: exactly the technological universe of the organized development of great capital denounced by Grosz as a terrifying universe 'without value'" (Tafuri, "U.S.S.R.-Berlin,1922," 1985, 179). Whereas Tafuri underlines the inevitability of the failure of any project within the problematic history of modernity, Gassner instead sees in suprematicism and other more subjective oriented tendencies the missing chance to oppose the turn of Russian modernism towards the total modernization of life and art.

64   Christian Lodder, *Russian Constructivism* (New Haven, CT: Yale University Press, 1983), 38.

65   In addition to the influence of Picasso and futurism, Christian Lodder stresses the importance of "native Russian artistic traditions and Primitivism as manifest in peasant and children's art, employing icons, …" for Vladimir Tatlin and the Russian futurist movement (Lodder, *Russian Constructivism*, 1983, 11). In a remarkable essay, Kenneth Frampton discusses the importance of primitivism and its importance to "preserve the inherent material quality of the transformed substance and, at the same time, to express directly the nature of its transformation." He also highlights the sensibility derived from the use of simple techniques and raw materials, advocated by filmmakers like Dziga Vertov, for productivism. See Frampton, "Constructivism: the Pursuit of an Elusive Sensibility," *Oppositions* 6 (fall 1976): 26–44.

66   Boris Arvatov, "Everyday Life and the Culture of Thing (Toward the Formulation of the Question)," in trans. Christina Kiaer, *October* 81 (1997): 120. For Arvatov's ideas, see Christian Lodder, *Russian Constructivism*, 1983, 105–8.

67   Christina Kiaer, "Boris Arvatov's Socialist Objects," *October* 81 (1997): 126. The author associates Arvatov's vision with Benjamin's belief in the possibility to "redeem the past" through wish-images (see Kiaer, 1997, 105–18).

68   Susan Buck-Morss, *The Dialectics of Seeing* (Cambridge, MA: The MIT Press, 1989), 146.

69   John McCole, *Walter Benjamin and the Antinomies of Tradition* (Ithaca, NY: Cornell University Press, 1993), 172. For a brief and concise documentation of Benjamin's

attraction to the work of modern architects, especially Le Corbusier and Scheerbart, see Detlef Mertins, "The Enticing and Threatening Face of Prehistory: Walter Benjamin and the Utopia of Glass," *Assemblage* 29 (April 1996), 6–23.

70 See Christian Lodder, *Russian Constructivism*, 1983, 65. In regard to the intuitive dimension of Tatlin's work, Lodder sees the presence of "an almost mystical element, which is related to the messianic conception of the artist's role" as creator and interpreter of a given environment (Lodder, 1983, 66).

71 Annette Michelson, "The Man with the Movie Camera: From Magician to Epistemologist," *Artforum* (March 1972): 60–71.

72 For an extensive elaboration of the concept of theatricality in Gottfried Semper's discourse, see H.F. Mallgrave, *Gottfried Semper*, 1996; and Gevork Hartoonian, *Ontology of Construction*, 1994, especially the final chapter.

73 Sigfried Giedion, *Building in France, Building in Iron, Building in Ferroconcrete* (Santa Monica, CA: The Getty Center for the History of Art and the Humanities, 1995), 87. Giedion's statement stimulated Walter Benjamin to invest in technology, considering it the source of new collective needs. Upon receiving a copy of Giedion's book Benjamin admired Giedion in the following words: "I am studying in your book ... the differences between radical conviction and radical knowledge that refresh the heart. You possess the latter, and therefore you are able to illustrate, or rather to uncover, the tradition by observing the present" (Giedion, 1995, 53).

74 Sándor Radnóti, "Benjamin's Dialectic of Art and Society," 1989, 142.

75 Here I am benefiting from Harry Francis Mallgrave's translation/interpretation of "theatricality" in Semper's theory of architecture. See Mallgrave, *Gottfried Semper*, 1996. For further references on the subject of theatricality, see Chapter 2 in this volume.

76 In his theory of architecture, Gottfried Semper reminds us of how much architecture throughout history has benefited from the formal achievements of the applied arts. On the concept of *Stoffwechsel* see H.F. Mallgrave, *Gottfried Semper*, 1996, 284–6.

77 In H.F. Mallgrave and Eleftherios Ikonomou, trans. *Empathy, Form, and Space*, 1994.

78 The desire to see modernity in analogy to antiquity was widespread among architects and thinkers of the nineteenth century. Perhaps the schism between the cultural and technical was an incentive to think about an integrated culture. For the relevance of theater as an analogue for bringing art and life together, see Stanford Anderson, *Peter Behrens*, 2000, especially chapter 3. On the importance of the theme of theater in early avant-garde, see Manfredo Tafuri, "The Stage as 'Virtual City': From Fuchs to the Total Theater," in *The Sphere and Labyrinth* (Cambridge, MA: The MIT Press, 1987), 95–112. Discussing the optics of Walter Benjamin, Donald Preziosi reminds us of Alois Riegl's contribution in perpetuating an "immanentist organicism," into the historicist project of modernity. For him, "Riegl's art history occupied a significant juncture in the playing out of this problem, and his theory of art and history constituted an attempt to articulate an organic historicism capable of addressing both facets of this problem" (Preziosi, "The Crystalline Veil and the Phallomorphic Imaginary: Walter Benjamin's Pantographic Riegl," in Alex Coles, ed., *The Optic of Walter Benjamin* [London: Black Dog Publishing, 1999], 131).

79 On this subject see Hal Foster, *Design and Crime*, 2002.

80 I am thinking of what is characterized as the tragic dimension of modernity. See Harry Lieberson, *Fate and Utopia in German Sociology, 1870–1923* (Cambridge, MA: The MIT Press, 1988).

81   Obviously I am reminded of Robert Venturi, Denise Scott Brown, and Steven Izenour in *Learning from Las Vegas* (Cambridge, MA: The MIT Press, 1972). For Kenneth Frampton's response, see "America 1960–1970: Notes on Urban Images and Theory," *Casabella* 359–60, 25 (1971): 24–38. For a contextualization of their debate in the America of the post-war period, see Deborah Fausch, "She Said, He Said," *Footprint* (spring 2011): 77–89. See also Neil Leach, *The Anaesthetics of Architecture* (Cambridge, MA: The MIT Press, 1999). Leach presents a comprehensive view of architecture and the place of mass culture and the populist vision of the Independent Group, London, and its implication for architecture as an urgent demand in the historiography of contemporary architecture. For more recent views of Venturi, see the architect's introduction to *Iconography and Electronics upon a Generic Architecture* (Cambridge, MA: The MIT Press, 1996). Guy Debord discusses the notion of "spectacle" on many different occasions. Consider this one: "The spectacle is not a collection of images; rather, it is a social relationship between people that is mediated by images" (Debord, *The Society of Spectacle* [New York: Zone Books, 1994], 12).

82   Walter Benjamin, "The Work of Art in the Age of Mechanical Reproduction," 1969, 237. On the optic aspect of Benjamin's work on technology, see Detlef Martins, "Walter Benjamin and the Tectonic Unconscious: Using Architecture as an Optical Instrument," in Alex Coles, ed., *The Optic of Walter Benjamin*, 1999, 196–225. Fredric Jameson has discussed the impact of rationalization and capital on the senses in *The Political Unconscious* (Ithaca, NY: Cornell University Press, 1981). Rosalind Krauss has also demonstrated the inevitable presence of "contradictions produced within the real field of history" in a structuralist understanding of art. See Krauss, *The Optical Unconscious* (Cambridge, MA: The MIT Press, 1993).

83   Robin Evans, "Not to be Used for Wrapping Purposes," *AA Files* 10 (1985): 68–78.

84   Stan Allen "Introduction," in *Practice, Architecture, Technique and Representation* (Amsterdam: G+Arts, 2000), XV. What is missing in Allen's correct stress on the dialectics between theory/practice is his aspiration for a pragmatism that dismisses "alienation," perhaps a worn-out subject these days. Putting aside Allan's "post-ideological turn," he presents insightful discussion concerning the relationship between drawing and construction. His emphasis on the physical body of building opens a different window onto architectural criticism that was not available to poststructuralism.

85   Bernard Cache, *Earth Moves*, 1995, 70–87.

86   For a theoretical discussion of this subject, see Gianni Vattimo, "Ornament/Monument," in *The End of Modernity* (Baltimore, MD: Johns Hopkins University Press, 1985), 79–89.

87   On this subject see Fritz Neumeyer, "The View into the Intrinsic," in *The Artless Word*, 1991, 30–35.

88   I am drawing from my remarks in *Modernity and Its Other* (College Station, TX: Texas A&M University Press, 1997), 46–7.

2

Theatricality: The Structure of the Tectonic

Several questions provide an opening for a discussion of Gottfried Semper's idea of theatricality. Is there room for excess within elements basic to a constructed space? How does excess sneak into the purpose of the object and legitimize itself beyond recognition? Is our fascination with structures like the Eiffel Tower and the work of engineers at the turn of the last century, and even the recent structures conceived and built by Santiago Calatrava and Cecil Balmond due to the absence of excess? Or, contrary to our expectation, is it excess in its full representation? And, finally, what does excess have to do with the tectonic? For a positive response to these questions it is enough to recall Semper's idea of constructed-form as "self-illumination" of technique, or look at Carlo Scarpa's architecture and drop the subject right here! Scarpa's work is an exemplar of the tectonic of theatricality at two levels. On the one hand, his entire oeuvre can be classified, metaphorically, as a montage of fragments each articulated tectonically. On the other, his engagement with detailing and materiality is so compelling that each building is seemingly designed just to reveal its artificiality; meaning that it is just a fabrication. We will return to the Italian architect at another occasion in this book. For now we should focus on the neo-avant-garde architecture and the excessive theatricality (theatricalization) in their work that is usually theorized along Gilles Deleuze's discourse on "fold."[1]

Drawing from Heinrich Wölfflin's reflection on Baroque architecture, and W. Leibniz's philosophy, Deleuze presents the idea of fold in analogy to a house with two tiers, one is stretched horizontally and the other vertically. One is adorned with the pleats of matter and the other, like a soul, is opaque and windowless. These two levels (floors?) are distinct from each other and yet remain in harmony with each other. The harmony is held in place by the "point of inflection" where one fold opens out into another. In this act of inclusion or enveloping, the relational correspondences between outside/inside, and/or other metaphysical dualities are eliminated. Deleuze's discourse has appealed to most contemporary architects wanting to deconstruct the presumed one-to-one correspondence between the metaphysics of humanism and the architecture of modernism. As I have discussed elsewhere, the problem with Deleuzianism in architecture can be summarized in the following words.[2] Reflecting on Kafka, Deleuze and Guattari suggested that a minor language does not operate outside of an existing major one. Rather, it uses the major language's potentialities for purposes other than one would expect. According to them, such an act of problematization of language could result either in reterritorialization (James Joyce) or deterritorialization of a given hegemonic language (Kafka).[3] In line with this consideration of what can be called critical practice, we could suggest that multicentralities of Baroque architecture reterritorialized the Renaissance language and sustained the persistence of humanist values, whereas Piranesi's engravings deterritorialized the *raison d'être* of the classical language of architecture, shaking the coherent totality of those values. It is the reductive nature of Deleuzian-architect's association between philosophy and architectural praxis that this chapter wants to address. Cultivating the critical dimension of Semper's discourse on theatricality, the following pages also set the theoretical premises for critiquing the spectacle permeating neo-avant-garde architecture.

The subject of theatricality is important not only because it was first introduced to architecture by Semper, but also because of the communicative dimension of architecture: the way a person relates to architecture by experiencing a building's space as well as appropriating its form. The communicative dimension of architecture, however, has changed since the crisis of the object induced by modernization and the introduction of new technologies into the process of architectural production. We no longer understand the classical language of architecture as pre-modern architects did; nor do we understand a building as an integral part of a given totality. Modernization disintegrated every kind of totality underlining the process of making artifacts as a formative theme for architecture. As will be demonstrated shortly, Semper's discussion of theatricality is indeed the highlight of his discourse on the tectonic: how the revealed poetics of construction becomes part of a larger cultural milieu while architecture appropriates available technical means and concepts developed in the realm of aesthetics.

THEATRICALITY, ART, AND ARCHITECTURE

The intention of this chapter is to explore the developmental tendencies of the culture of spectacle, and to examine its implications for rethinking the idea of theatricality. The point is not to prove the presence of "excess" in Semper's discussion of the tectonic, but to probe the idea of theatricality in a situation when spectacle is the only common visual and spatial experience available to the citizens of most metropolitan cities. The total commodification of everyday life did not emerge overnight. It was, according to Hal Foster, the third stage of a process that started with the radio days of the 1920s, followed by the communication technologies of the postwar era, and taking on a new scale and velocity through the digital techniques of reproduction.[4] Foster might be capitalizing on a state of technological determinism wherein the idea of "image building" is seen as central to the entire development of architecture unfolding since the postwar period.[5] The development is yet of interest because a sense of delirium has overshadowed modernism's tendency for abstraction and the rhetorical mood informing the postmodern eclecticism. It is, therefore, important to discuss the issue of appropriation of art and architecture and the object's potential for absorption. Before discussing Semper's idea of theatricality, however, it is useful to address the way the subject is considered in poetry and painting. Later in the text I will introduce Walter Benjamin's discourse on the exhibition value of the work, if only to expand the historicality of Semper's discussion of the tectonic of theatricality.

Charles Bernstein discusses theatricality and differentiates poetry from other forms of writing.[6] According to him, an ordinary written text communicates with the reader by transparency of the information delivered. However, a poem transcends such textual transparency by utilizing formal and technical means intrinsic or external to poetry. The result is an artifice, a textual fabrication, whose relationship with the reader mutates between two poles of absorption and impermeability. By absorption Bernstein means "engrossing, engulfing completely, attention, arresting attention … " By impermeability, on the other hand, he means "… distraction, digression, transgressive, baroque … "[7] Some of his suggested techniques for absorption were utilized by the architecture and literature of the nineteenth century. One is reminded of the romanticists' quest to integrate architecture into a picturesque environment. For impermeability, we should look instead for techniques such as shock, transgression, and defamiliarization that were employed by dadaists and surrealists. Providing examples from various art forms, Bernstein makes the case that, by combining techniques of absorption and impermeability, a poem or any other work of art can reach the level of theatricality; a state of artistic deliverance by which the reader or the spectator is attracted to the work even when an artist uses non-absorptive techniques. The point is not to press down the quality of the work calculating what kind of means would generate certain expected impressions on the reader or beholder. Such an intention, according to Bernstein, "is in a certain sense simulation, theatricalization. That's what the commodifcation of product is."[8] Theatricality, instead, cloaks poetry with anonymity: the message is understood in an indirect way through the manifold play of the visible and the invisible. Reflecting on visibility and touch, Maurice Merleau-Ponty suggests: "It is that the thickness of flesh between the seer and the thing is constitutive for the thing of its visibility as for the seer of his corporeity; it is not an obstacle between them, it is their means of communication."[9] Following Merleau-Ponty, Bernstein suggests that, "absorption and impermeability are the warp and woof of poetic composition—an intertwining or chasm whose locus is the flesh of the word."[10] Transcending the idealist and empiricist discourse, Merleau-Ponty presents a concept of "object" that does not stand on its own, but is rather woven into many-fold horizons of a given culture. His position is intriguing in the context of the current shift from the object to the text. It can be argued that theatricality is the flesh of construction whose thickness speaks for the invisible presence of the dialectics of seeing and making, that is the way a building relates to its site, framing a constructed space and opening it to the many horizons of today's culture.

Theatricality is also present in dance and music, the two artistic products that Semper considered closer to architecture than painting. Semper's view on the subject will be discussed shortly. What should be brought to the reader's attention is Michael Fried's discourse on theatricality and absorption that precedes Bernstein.

In *Courbet's Realism*, Fried discusses the dialogue between absorption and theatricality in mid-eighteenth-century painting and pursues the subject's importance for contemporary abstract art. According to him, Denis Diderot's writings on drama and his disdain for theatricality or gestural expression put the French painters in a difficult position. How to seal off the beholder from the world of painting became a rather critical task for painters, especially when the subject was a dramatic mood, such as death in Jean-Baptiste Greuze's *Filial Piety* (1763), or "farewell," as depicted in Jacques-Louis David's *Oath of the Horatii* (1785). It is indeed in David's history paintings that Fried sees the seeds of de-dramatization of action, especially in David's *Intervention of the Sabine Women* (1799), in the "sleek-limbed figure of Romulus posed to throw his spear." The idea is also at work in the crowding of the pictorial field with innumerable personages at different distances from the viewer … "[11] According to Fried, two developments were essential for Courbet's realism to take place. First, a change in the subject matter of painting, i.e., a move from historical subjects and court personages to simple human beings and their habits. Following Jean-François Millet, Courbet depicted movement, action, and dramatic scenes by focusing on various aspects of everyday life, such as peasants working in the field. Second, an awareness of the sense of embodiment and its effect on perception enticed the body (and in this case Courbet's body) to emerge, initiating a unique dialogue between absorption and theatricality. To depart from Diderot's concern for theatricalization, Courbet not only made the beholder imagine that he or she had entered into the depicted world, but he painted the "literal merger of himself as a painter-beholder with the painting on which he was working."[12] Introduction of corporeality into the field of painting prevents gestural expression and blurs the line separating absorption from theatricality.

Fried also reminds us of another development that shed a different light on the subject of theatricality. The invention of daguerreotype in the mid-nineteenth century—a mechanical means of representing aspects of the world—encouraged some writers to see the invention of photography as a major motivation for Courbet's realism. Even in Cubism's transition from analysis to synthesis, one important subject of discussion was how to leave the "superficial realism of Courbet" for Paul Cézanne, who combined the empiricism of the senses with the conceptualization of the mind.[13] Disputing these ideas, Fried observes that, "the issue of theatricality turns out not only to have been relevant to photographic practice but to have been given a particular inflection by the powerfully veristic character of the photographic medium."[14] Which is to say that a person posing in front of a camera is unconsciously aware of the gestural act and the theatricality of the effect. Such a theatrical atmosphere does not exist in representational painting where a presumed organic coherency between the subject matter and the final work overrides any unconscious impulses.

Fried's criticism of theatricality was first articulated in his "Art and Objecthood" essay published in *Artforum*, June 1976. Citing a series of works called "literalist" arts or minimalism, Fried upheld the modernist drive in dismantling the object, and thus the creation of a situation where the beholder was absorbed by the work. In minimalism, instead, the work is understood not so much by what it shows, but in an apprehension that comes through the beholder's movement around it. Obviously this was not the case with classical and modernist art where it was explored "face to face." The breach with modernist art was partly, as noted earlier, initiated by the phenomenological priority given to perception. Fried wrote, "literalist sensibility is theatrical because, to begin with, it is concerned with the actual circumstances in which the beholder encounters literalist work."[15] Richard Serra's sculpture, "House of Cardboard," comes to mind where four equally dimensioned steel plates are loosely connected together to present an object with a void within. The sculpture's fragile look, we are told, is one source of theatricality. Another is expressed in the way that the work occupies the display space, a phenomenon that according to Fried forces the spectator to be conscious of the object's size, its materiality, and the void, as he or she contemplates the sculpture from different angles and positions.

Most recently, Fried has taken the case of photography and made a distinction between theatricality and absorption and also what is called to-be-seenness.[16] Central to this differentiation is the position of the beholder and the state of the subject matter (the object) in a photographic image. In the case of absorption, the image usually contains a figure(s) that is so absorbed in an action that he/she is oblivious to being watched or not. The image becomes theatrical when the figure (the person being photographed) is posed to attract the beholder's attention. Fried goes further and presents examples of portrait photography where the figure's gesture does not address the beholder directly, and yet, the image seems to show an awareness of being watched. The dialectics between the object and the subject has another facet to it. Explaining the new Institute of Contemporary Art (ICA) in Boston, Elizabeth Diller and Ricardo Scofolio suggest that the building is both "a self-conscious object that … wants to be looked at" and "a machine for looking."[17] While the analogy between architecture and machine recalls the modernist paradigm, the architects' statement, according to Hal Foster, points to a "postmodernist turn of mind that imagines architecture as a prosthetic subject, one possessed here of expressionistic and voyeuristic proclivities (it 'wants' to be looked at and to look)."[18]

Still if the surface articulation of postmodern architecture was sought in reference to the beholder's memory of various historicist languages, the abstract forms of modern architecture can be associated with a photographic image that shows a landscape, for example, with motionless compositional elements. This so-called stillness is presented as a special case where the image completely excludes the factor of the beholder. The exclusion, according to Fried, underscores the presence of things in their singularity. We can take this exclusion of the beholder for a state of modernist objectivity the central concern of which was the functional, how the form was expected to be seen, rather than the move to create theatrical gestures. This differentiation between modern and postmodern obviously excludes both the architecture of expressionism and the theatrical forms of constructivism. However, it offers a useful strategy for associating postmodern architecture with theatricalization, recent manifestations of which are discussed later in this book's chapters. And yet, throughout the following pages, the opportunity has been taken to present architects whose work tends to exclude the beholder. In a broader consideration of the state of contemporary architecture, we might observe that most of the architecture of Renzo Piano and Tadao Ando avoids taking on the duality of structure and appearance for creating playful formal gestures. Again, a Semperian understanding of the tectonic is by definition theatrical, and yet the work could move towards theatricalization when the appearance is embellished, consciously or unconsciously, for the visual delight of the beholder. This is evident in the architecture of postmodern historicism, and in most of Frank Gehry's recent projects, and also the design work identified with the parametric.

The significance of the idea of theatricality in architecture has to do with Semper's denunciation of architecture as an imitative art and the sense of spatiality embedded in his theoretical departure from the Vitruvian triad. Semper formulated an architectural discourse whose main themes are derived from skills and perception developed in other cultural activities. For him the original motives of architecture reside in the production process of the four industries of textiles, carpentry, ceramics, and masonry. Exercising such radicalism in political life cost him several years of exile and poverty during the period when he wrote most of his theoretical work. While in London, Semper had the chance to follow closely the debates stirred up by John Paxton's design for the Crystal Palace. Against his British colleagues, who argued for the duality of construction and ornament—as implied in the historicist tendency for ornamenting construction, as well as in modernist zeal for the construction of ornament—Semper mapped the subject from the perspective of the cultural anomalies of capitalism. He wrote: "This process of disintegrating existing art types must be completed by industry, by production, and by applied science before something good and new can result."[19] Reading these lines in the context of the current nihilism of technology and commodification of culture leads us to draw some analogies between Semper's discourse on theatricality and the mystique of commodities that has enforced fad and fashion as the ultimate new. This is convincing not because of Semper's architecture, whose theatricality was suggested by iconographic references, but because of his belief in the criticality of architecture for cultural communication and for his idea that art, even when expressing tragedy, should break up tragic elements "in such a way that one could extract enjoyment even from its most affecting parts."[20] The implied theatricality in Semper's statement could be taken for theatricalization if we fail to recall Carl Bötticher's assertion that in a tectonic form the symbolic dressing is simultaneously juxtaposed with the structural function. Both Semper and Bötticher stressed the dialogical relation between a structural system and the expected sensations evoked by the dressing. Addressing this subject, Bötticher reminds us,

> The aim is to grasp the principle of the statics and construction and the law and form of each part of the structural system that characterizes the style in question. Once this is understood, then the key is found to the riddle of the art-forms that have been applied to these parts as a kind of explanatory layer. Since these parts have been made for the sole purpose of creating a spatial structure, any forms applied to them that do not serve this material purpose can only have been

*intended to symbolize this function and to make visible the concept of structure
and space that in its purely structural state cannot be perceived.*[21]

To put it in Semper's words, adornments are "structural-symbolic" when the art-form, in essence, enhances the structural values of the core-form through dressing.[22] By making it clear that the final form of architecture should not correspond to its structural system directly, Bötticher charges the tectonic with an excess, the art-form, that is robbed by eclecticists and formalists alike. The difference between Semper and Bötticher will be addressed shortly. What needs to be added here is that Semper's theory proposes two issues important to modern architecture. First, that as far as the notion of *Stoffwechsel* (the transformation of motifs from one industry to another) is concerned, technique is not in itself accountable for the art-form, an idea that casts doubt on the monumental potentiality of iron structures permeating the nineteenth century. It also puts most of contemporary architecture's use and abuse of steel-frame structure in a difficult position. As will be demonstrated throughout this book, beneath the biomorphic forms of contemporary architecture we cannot but notice the Dom-ino frame, a structural concept that not only helped Le Corbusier to articulate the idea of the free-façade, but also assisted the postmodernists like Robert Venturi to give a radical twist to the discourse of historicism. This is important because Semper's theorization of style relies heavily on the principle of dressing and the role of the element of wall in monumental effects. Second, attention should be paid to his criticism of historicism, and that branch of formalism whose "tendentious nature" has little to do with "purpose" and "construction" themes central to Semper's discourse on the tectonic of theatricality. Again, what should be underlined is the principle of dressing through which "tectonic structures achieve monumentality," and that this transformation takes place "only through emancipation from structural-material realism, through a symbolic spiritualization of their functional expression."[23]

Harry Francis Mallgrave is one of the few scholars to have explored the idea of theatricality, and his book on Gottfried Semper is a fine supplement to the current proliferation of Semper's oeuvre. Besides the early translations of Semper's major texts, in the last two years, several publications have made important contributions shedding light on various aspects of Semper's discourse.[24] These books explore themes such as the tectonic, *bekleidung* (the principle of dressing), and *stoffwechsel* (transforming motifs from one production activity into another). Mallgrave's work, however, stands out for its fine and detailed biographical account and the way he weaves the formative themes of Semper's architectural theory with the socio-political, cultural, and technological developments characterizing the heroic period of the early experience of modernity. Of particular interest is the association he makes with the thought of two other giants of Semper's days, Friedrich Nietzsche and Richard Wagner. According to him, one reason why "a limited biographical format is called for in the case of Semper, is the importance his theory and built works possess for more broadly based cultural studies. The Semper-Wagner-Nietzsche triangle of ideas alluded to above underscores the centrality of Semper's thought to the nineteenth century, but it is a presence yet to be adequately perceived and assessed."[25] This last point deserves attention not only because of the association that might be made between the uncertainties surrounding the last decades of the twentieth century with those of the end of the nineteenth but also because of the formativeness of the theme of surface and a perception of theatricality that is stirred up by digital techniques. Moreover, current diversities in theories of architecture perpetuate a state of confusion equal to the nineteenth century's quest for style.

Mallgrave depicts Friedrich Schinkel as the forerunner of the concept of theatricality through which Semper saw an alternative to the crisis of architectural historicism in Germany. Schinkel sought to resolve the contemporary architects' fluctuation between utility and imitation by what he termed the "refinement of feeling," anticipating Adolf Loos's belief that the task of an architect is to arouse feeling and sensation in the beholder. Traveling around historical sites, Schinkel was absorbed by the formal aspects of the buildings he visited. He was equally attracted to a sense of theatricality caused by modifications needed to accommodate an ideal form to a given landscape and its topography.[26] According to Barry Bergdoll, the true heir to Schinkel's architectural vision is Friedrich Gilly whose design "drew on more than the latest archaeological knowledge. It embodied the contemporary theory that through the manipulation of mass and proportion, light and shade, rhythm and texture, architecture constituted a formal language that spoke more directly to the senses than even speech."[27] And yet, Schinkel's interest in stage-set design, panorama, and landscape sets him apart from those architects who sought the abstraction and denunciation of history as a way to overcome the complexities, if not anxieties, generated by modernity. In defiance of the fallacies of an arbitrary simulation of history and architecture's reduction to utility and construction, Schinkel believed that the tectonic should express a building's purpose artistically. For Mallgrave, the Berlin Altes Museum (1823–30) demonstrates the architect's willingness "to draw from the historical treasury and forms but at the same time to modify these motifs in an original manner, taking into account contemporary ideals and conditions."[28] Presenting the nineteenth-century philosophical debates on realism and idealism, Mitchell Schwarzer suggests that like Kant, "Schinkel accepted semi-independence processes for architectural materiality and ideality." Unlike Kant, however, Schinkel believed that, "nature, not the subjective mind, contained the essence of architecture."[29] In addition to new building techniques and materials, what was contemporary for Semper and others of his school of thought was the unfolding of a different experience of time and space, and the latter's tectonic expression. According to Kurt W. Forster, "Schinkel recognized in the human imagination a native tendency to extend the transformation of nature into history beyond its time-bound order, to expand the process into the internal realm of desire."[30] Drawing on drama and stage-set design, both Schinkel and Semper saw architecture as a frame accommodating human experience. The tectonic of such a "frame" should absorb the beholder first and then direct his/her attention to the drama of life.

Schinkel's theory also alludes to a shift of paradigm at work in eighteenth-century French architecture. Those known as the "revolutionary architects" did indeed depart from a sense of beauty associated with the proportions of the body for the aesthetic of the sublime. In the context of the experience of modernity, the sublime was charged with psychological feelings of both joy and sorrow. A feeling for "play" was also invested in the aesthetic writings of the century, whose original intrusion into the world of art might have to do with the primeval struggle against the not-yet-tamed nature. Echoing the romantic tradition, Semper would "set up play as the basis of the aesthetic drive, and the means by which man confronts an often hostile world and deals with its imperfections." For Semper "play is humanity's 'cosmogonic instinct' through which he creates his own 'tiny world' (lawful and decorative) and mediates his contact with the world."[31] In recapitulating these words, it seems fair to suggest that play and fancying with mask and tattoo was indeed a reaction to the anxieties generated by modernization. This is where Wagner's music and Nietzsche's *The Birth of Tragedy* enter the complex picture of Semper's life and architecture.

Aware of Wagner's problematic concept of *Gesamtkunstwerk*, Mallgrave underlines the similarities between Semper's understanding of theatricality and Wagner's zeal for dramatization and the architecture of theater if only to illustrate the ultimate unison of all the arts. Nietzsche also underlined the understanding of art in association with the Greek chorus as a way out of the will to knowledge. For Nietzsche, music was the art that overcomes its material basis, and by intensification its melody could also surpass the domain of the "will to power." There is a sense of formlessness in music that architecture could achieve only by denying the forces of gravity. Tilmann Buddensieg reminds us of Nietzsche's speculation on music's possible belonging "to a culture in which the dominion of men of power, of every kind, has already come to an end."[32] These kinds of reflection point to Nietzsche's interest in an architecture that could eliminate the symbolic and religious burden of classical revivalism permeating the late nineteenth century. It was indeed the non-visual and plastic qualities of music that enticed him, Wagner, and Semper to emphasize the dramatic potential of architecture that were at work in the festive ensembles of Greek and other early civilizations. As Semper put it, and according to Mallgrave, Nietzsche gleaned from him "the haze of carnival candles is the true atmosphere of art." In a footnote to his theory of style, Semper continues, "The denial of reality, of the material, is necessary if form is to emerge as a meaningful symbol, as an autonomous creation of man."[33]

What is intriguing in Semper's idea of theatricality is his continuous attempt to weave adornment with the lawful execution of material and technical means. Furthermore, his reflection on theatricality is full of allusions to drama, theater, carnival, and mask. In the earlier cited footnote we read, "The spirit of masks breathes in Shakespeare's dramas; we meet the humor of masks and the haze of candles, the carnival sentiment (which truly is not always joyous) in Mozart's *Don Juan*. For even music needs a means to deny reality. Hecuba also means nothing to the musician— or should mean nothing." And in order to prevent any misunderstanding of his stress on the necessity for architecture to deny reality (theatricality), Semper advises that "Masking does not help, however, when *behind* the mask the thing is false or the mask is no good." He continues; "In order that the material, the indispensable (in the usual sense of the expression) be completely denied in the artistic creation, its complete mastery is the imperative precondition."[34] Implied in this statement of

Semper's is the importance of the tectonic for any discussion of "dressing" or the mask in architecture. Without relating the mask to the tectonic, one might end up negating the importance of construction for the dialectics of theory and practice. Perhaps, aware of this risk, Kenneth Frampton was hesitant to touch the idea of theatricality in his impressive work on tectonics. From a different perspective, Anthony Vidler stresses the uncanny space behind the mask in the expense of the tectonic.[35] Finally, this author's favorite Semperian line:

> only by complete technical perfection, by judicious and proper treatment of the material according to its properties, and by taking these properties into consideration and creating form, can the material be forgotten, can the artistic creation be completely freed from it, can even a simple landscape painting be raised to a high work of art.[36]

This statement of Semper is important because it moves beyond the romantic view of form as exclusive to the nature of material while, at the same time, it stops short of further intensifying, pushing the nihilism of modernity to its extreme, the destruction of the received tradition. Semper moves in between border lines separating theatricality from theatricalization, to deny material through the embellishment of material itself.

Semper's discussion of theatricality is also an aspect of his theorization of architecture as a cosmic art analogous to dance and music. Indeed the delight experienced in dance and music has no imitative basis. These arts pursue similar laws of structure and ornamentation implied in the Greek word *Kosmos*, meaning the simultaneous presence of order and ornament. As I have discussed elsewhere, "Music and dance differ from imitative arts in that a distinction between what is essential to them and what is excessive is almost impossible."[37] For Nietzsche "the cosmic symbolism of music resists any adequate treatment by language, for the simple reason that music, in referring to primordial contradiction and pain, symbolizes a sphere which is both earlier than appearance and beyond it." This statement from *The Birth of Tragedy* alludes to the Greek artistic mind and a Dionysian desire to express nature symbolically. Emphasizing the significance of polychromy for Greek architecture, Semper saw monumental architecture as beyond a decorated shed or an iconographic representation of its language. For him, architecture is an active part of an ensemble similar to the primitive sense of communal gathering for dance and choreography. Stressing the principle of dressing, such a setting would, at the end, become a stage-set in itself, a theatrical montage indeed. In addition to painting, Semper reminds us,

> We should not forget the metal ornaments, gilding, tapestry-like draperies, baldachins, curtains, and movable implements. From the beginning the monuments were designed with all these things in mind, even for the surroundings—the crowds of people, priests, and the processions. The monuments were the scaffolding intended to bring together these elements on a common stage. The brilliance that fills the imagination when trying to visualize those times makes the imitations that people have since fancied and imposed on us seem pale and stiff.[38]

Semper's vision of architecture is a symbolic form experienced in association with other cultural products. Indeed architecture is the crust of the life-world, framing, almost like the horseshoe shape of a stage, the totality of the everyday life experience; even those most remote archaic ones that are presumably washed out from the present objective world.

FROM THEATRICALITY TO SPECTACLE

Now what would be the consequences of such an experience in the realm of contemporary architecture? And what would be the index of the totality in the present high-tech modern capitalism? What kind of shared collective experience is left to us after the loss of aura? In response to these questions it is appropriate to recall Walter Benjamin's discourse on experience. According to Benjamin, the ritualistic value of the work of art is embedded in two things: first, that prior to the mechanical reproduction of art, the symbolism of art was understood indirectly, and second, that in order to communicate with this symbolism, one has to enter into the work itself. Mechanization and the introduction of mechanical reproduction into the world of cultural artifacts has dissolved the aura and adorned the work of art with different qualities. In a photographic or filmic reproduction of a painting or an event, the final work breaks the crust of its symbolic function by the very possibility of being ex-hibited and appropriated beyond its original context. The work also attains some qualities that are pumped into it by technology, thus repressing its cult value. Benjamin describes the new horizon opened by technologies of reproduction in terms of "optical unconscious" by which "a space informed by human consciousness gives way to a space informed by the unconscious."[39] Redemption of the work of art from its aura, therefore, generates a world of phantasmagoria, the spectacle, which in the present context of commodification of the life-world should be considered neither a mere technological effect nor, as Guy Debord reminds us, "something added to the real world—not a decorative element, so to speak. On the contrary it is the very heart of society's real unreality."[40] Once this is established, it is essential to explore the developmental tendencies of culture of spectacle for rethinking the idea of theatricality.

Studying the impact of the nihilism of modernity, Benjamin was skeptical of the restoration of any collective experience of the kind exercised through religion and language in pre-modern cultures. Knowing the fact that disintegration of every possible totality is essential for the project of modernity, one is left, according to Benjamin, with the choice of maintaining either an active affirmative, or a passive reactive position: "One takes the destruction as an opportunity to establish a new configuration of experience, the other intensifies the destruction."[41] To put his ideas in the context of current problems in architectural theories, one could justify the neo-avant-garde's exploitation of the formal implications of digital techniques for two reasons. First, the theatricalization of architecture might be seen as a radical move for those who see technology as the only index of totalization. This point of view considers technology determinant for social and cultural evolution, a position promoted by early modernist architects. Theirs was to cultivate the seeds of collectivity embedded in *technology* for socio-political ends. We might argue that the politics of the collective is indeed the missing point in the present turn to technology. Second, theatricalization takes for granted the perceptual experience of telecommunication technologies and cuts all ties that might connect architecture to the beholder. The result is an abstract form whose discrete charm competes with the fetishism of commodities.

Exploring the origin of the fetish, William Pietz reminds us that the word fetish derives from the Latin *facticius*, meaning "artificial in the sense of materially altered by human efforts in order to deceive" as opposed to genuine. The world "facticious" has also been used to connote the "unnatural fabrication of appearance, of the signifiers of exchange value, without the substance or use value that the appearance promised."[42] Reflecting on Karl Marx's idea of commodity fetishism, Jacques Derrida locates the "mystical character" of the commodity form in

> some theatrical intrigue: mechanical ruse (mekbane) or mistaking a person, repetition upon the perverse intervention of a prompter. ... There is a mirror, and the commodity form is also this mirror, but since all of a sudden it no longer plays its role, since it does not reflect back the expected image, those who are looking for themselves can no longer find themselves in it.[43]

Like commodities, abstract forms are invested with excess; the disappearance of tradition generates an architecture that is anonymous and unfamiliar to the beholder's collective memory. The lack is today occupied and energized by the image-making forces of telecommunication technologies, which endow architecture with gesture. It is the excess invested in the totality of the culture of spectacle that makes architecture today less remote from the everyday life experience of the beholder. In late capitalism, everything is "designed" and all products, including architecture look "cool!"[44]

Abstraction and anonymity are aesthetic implications of architecture's entanglement with the drive of commodification. There is also a degree of abstraction and anonymity in theatricality as far as the tectonic exceeds the material and technical exigencies of construction. Theatricality might be associated with what was alleged to be Courbet's "superficial realism," that is to say, the aspect that caused Courbet's realism to be seen as superficial is also suggestive of the fact that theatricality does not deny construction, but alludes to the latter's "structural-symbolic" expression. The differences also have to do with the fact that unlike the pictorial realm of painting, the beholder's relation to architecture is rather indirect. One does not design a building while having in mind the place of the beholder. Rather, in the manner of stage-set design, one conceives architecture as a back-stage, in front and around of which the life-world unravels.[45] The intention is not to present a passive picture of architecture but to underline the active role architecture plays in the construction of the condition of life, the project of architecture.

Exploring Benjamin's concept of experience, Howard Caygill suggests, "Architecture provides the main site for the interaction of technology and the human, a negotiation conducted in terms of touch and use. It is both a condition and an object of experience, the speculative site for the emergence of the 'technological *physics*.'"[46] Through use and touch and perhaps in spite of theatricality architecture has the capacity to absorb our attention and then direct us to a larger totality.[47] The idea is not to require a one-to-one correspondence between form and context, but to envision architecture that is more than either construction or a familiar sign. Excess questions foundations, setting the work in the "mirror-play of the world."[48] Obviously, in differentiating theatricality from theatricalization (gestural expression), emphasis is put on the "thing" character of architecture while undermining its pictorial appeal. The thingness of architecture necessitates a turning from pictorial considerations of the place of the beholder to his or her experience with architecture.

Beyond the fashionable appeal of the neo-avant-garde position, we are left with the choice of accepting the nihilism of technology, not because of its apparent radicalism, but because architectural tradition can survive only by being galvanized through new modalities opened in the dialectics of seeing and making. Furthermore, most architects believe that construction and the relationship of architecture to nature transcends the problematic duality between the subject and the object. How architecture relates to nature, to the forces of gravity, landscape, light and wind, is the bedrock of a shared collective experience as far as architecture's project is concerned. An affirmative approach to the nihilism of technology necessitates the recollection of the tactile sensibilities and tectonic solutions of architecture's ontological rapport with nature, recoding these received traditions in the light of the latest technological innovations. According to Benjamin,

> The past carries with it a temporal index by which it is referred to redemption.
> There is a secret agreement between past generations and the present one. Our
> coming was expected on earth. Like every generation that precedes us, we have
> been endowed with a weak Messianic power to which the past has a claim. This
> claim cannot be settled cheaply. Historical materialists are aware of that.[49]

Interestingly enough, in a prolegomenon to his theory of style Semper speculated that "These phenomena of artistic decline and the mysterious, phoenix-like birth of new artistic life arising from the process of its destruction are all the more significant to us, because we are probably in the midst of a similar crisis ... "[50] Here Semper sounds Benjaminian. However, a phoenix-like architecture similar to the work of surrealism has the potential to release in a snapshot what Benjamin referred to as "involuntary memories of an auratic" experience. In historicizing the "latest new" in the context of memories of an archaic past, architecture has the opportunity to counter excess. Architecture is construction plus something else. The implied surplus speaks for a joint articulating of the dialectics of tactile and tectonic solutions, juxtaposing a dormant past with the present technological experiences. In this context theatricality does not suggest formal playfulness: it vindicates the formative themes of architecture that are interwoven with the socio-political, cultural, and technological developments of the first decade of the new millennium. Appropriation of architecture in the vastness of culture is indeed at the heart of Semper's discourse on theatricality.

The "spatiality" implied in Semper's discourse on theatricality underpins the present discussion of space and theatricality in the context of the spectacle of late-capitalism. Equally important is the fact that, although virtual reality is a significant aspect of the present technological experience, it is not necessarily the only one that should be grafted onto architecture. Both theatricality and "spatiality" as such have been at work in various facets of the early experience of modernity, and more so in cinematography and montage. Previously I have discussed the idea of montage as a mode of construction appropriate to an architecture that accommodates the project of modernity.[51] Here I would like to suggest that what Semper, Wagner, and Nietzsche saw in the Greek theater is true of film, itself an ensemble of music, art, technology, and "the crowds of people." Pursued closely, montage, from its fragmentary stage setting to the art of cutting and sewing, frames a sense of theatricality equal to Semper's zeal for the "masking of reality."

My occasional return to film and its analogy to architecture also have to do with the fact that, in terms of reaching out and communicating with the masses, and the ties that every cultural product has made with capital and the marketplace, film is the only industry that comes close to architecture.[52] Still, as with architecture, the art of filmmaking has been transformed by the constant innovations taking place in the world of technology. The introduction of sound, color, widescreen, and lately digital techniques have opened up new horizons in the filmic experience and yet montage has remained essential for the art of filmmaking. This is also true for architecture. The entire history of architecture can be construed in the purview of changes that have transformed the concept of construction from *techné* to technique, and from the tectonic to montage.[53] As in film, so in architecture, montage can be utilized to evoke sensation and feelings appropriate to the purpose of a constructed space. This potentiality of montage is exploited in the best schools of architecture in the two dimensionality of digital technique. Perhaps, if ever the forces of gravity and thus nature are overcome, then, virtual reality might be translated into architecture in its full capacity. Until the time that such a dream-day is realized, we are better off dwelling on the concept of montage and articulating the tectonic of lightness and an experience of spatiality that are prevalent in the various production activities of today's culture.

Finally, Semper's and Bötticher's ideas should not be taken as dogmas. Faced with the historical eclecticism of his time, Bötticher suggested that one should neither take tradition for granted nor discard it totally. Beyond these two extremes he drew two conclusions that are worth citing here: "First, we must for the time being hold on to what has been directly handed down to us …. Second, it follows that we must not make use of tradition for its own sake." And he continues, we should "decide what part of tradition merely belongs to the past, was valid only then, and therefore must be rejected and what part contains eternal truth, is valid for all future generations, and therefore must be accepted and retained by us."[54] "Eternal truth?" Perhaps this is too strong an idea for these days. However, Bötticher's critical position on tradition is even more valid today. As mentioned previously, the forces of gravity and the importance of landscape are proper benchmarks to make a site (sight?), or a spectacle, exhibit an architectonic event, the experience of which would induce "disorientation," to recall

Heidegger, and open a different window onto the life-world. This is not a far-fetched theoretical demand. The following chapters are written to show two things: first, that present architectural practice is full of projects and buildings that affirm, to different degrees, the importance of montage, and theatricality, if not theatricalization. Second, in addition to the recent hasty association between Semper's remarks on dressing and the structural forms generated by digital technique, Semper's discourse on the four elements of architecture and his idea of theatricality are of interest today when techniques central to the culture of spectacle pervade most regions of our global village, and the same techniques have the potential to make architects re-think the principle of dressing.

The difficulty facing architecture today is how to use digital techniques and yet resist the prevailing culture of spectacle. How to extend, for example, Mies van der Rohe's skilful handling of the tectonic rapport between filling and frame in the National Gallery, Berlin, where the glass enclosure does not reinforce the frame. In Mies's aspiration to monumental effect, the frame rather seems to the eye to be completely rigid *in itself* while the glass enclosure is recessed. Emphasizing the antithesis between filling and the frame, Semper argues that, "the filling should never reinforce the frame, which in structural terms is *not even present*. The frame should seem to the eye to be completely rigid *in itself*, and the filling should be recessed, either *actually*, *apparently* (by means of color), or ideally by both means at once."[55] Therefore, in criticizing theatricalization in neo-avant-garde architecture, this book also intends to demonstrate the importance of the thematic of the disciplinary history of architecture (the culture of building) for the architecture of theatricality.

NOTES

1   Gilles Deleuze, *The Fold: Leibniz and the Baroque* (Minneapolis, MN: The University of Minnesota Press, 1993), especially the chapters "The Fold," and "What is Baroque?" For Deleuze's notion of "point of inflection," see also Bernard Cache, *Earth Moves* (Cambridge, MA: The MIT Press, 1995).

2   Gevork Hartoonian, *Ontology of Construction* (Cambridge: Cambridge University Press, 1994), 78.

3   Gilles Deleuze and Félix Guattari, *Kafka: Toward a Minor Literature* (Minneapolis, MN: University of Minnesota Press, 1986), 16–27.

4   Hal Foster, *Design and Crime* (London: Verso, 2004), 11.

5   Hal Foster, "Image Building," *Artforum* (October 2004).

6   Charles Bernstein, "Artifice of Absorption," in *Poetics* (Cambridge, MA: Harvard University Press, 1992), 9–90.

7   Charles Bernstein, "Artifice of Absorption," 1992, 29.

8   Charles Bernstein, "On Theatricality," in *Content's Dream: Essays 1975–1987* (Los Angeles, CA: Sun and Light Press, 1986), 205.

9   Maurice Merleau-Ponty, *The Visible and the Invisible* (Evanston, IL: Northwestern University Press, 1968), especially the chapter on "The Intertwining—The Chaism," 135.

10   Bernstein, "Artifice of Absorption," 1992, 86.

11   Michael Fried, *Courbet's Realism* (Chicago, IL: University of Chicago Press, 1990), 17. For a detailed discussion of Denis Diderot's ideas on theatricality see Fried, *Absorption and Theatricality: Painting and Beholder in the Age of Diderot* (Berkeley, CA: University of California Press, 1988).

12   Michael Fried, *Courbet's Realism*, 1990, 224.

13   On this subject see Kenneth E. Silver, *Esprit de Corps* (Princeton, NJ: Princeton University Press, 1989), 299–361.

14   Michael Fried, *Courbet's Realism*, 1990, 45.

15   Michael Fried, *Art and Objecthood* (Chicago, IL: University of Chicago Press, 1998), 153. The article was originally published in *Artforum*, July 1976.

16   Michael Fried, "Three Beginnings," in *Why Photography Matters as Art as Never Before* (New Haven, CT: Yale University Press, 2008), 5–36.

17   N. Baume, "It's Still Fun to Have Architecture: An Interview with E. Diller and R. Scofolio," in Baume, ed., *Supervision* (Boston: Institute of Contemporary Art, 2006), 118.

18   Hal Foster, "Architecture-Eye," *Artforum*, (February 2007): 248.

19   Gottfried Semper, *The Four Elements of Architecture* (Cambridge: Cambridge University Press, 1989), 144.

20   H.F. Mallgrave, *Gottfried Semper: Architect of the Nineteenth Century* (New Haven, CT: Yale University Press, 1996), 232.

21   Carl Gottlieb Wilhelm Bötticher, "The Principles of the Hellenic and Germanic Ways of Building with Regard to Their Application to Our Present Way of Building," in trans. Wolfgang Herrmann, *In What Style Should We Build?* (Santa Monica, CA: The Getty Center for the History of Art and Humanities, 1992), 147–68, 163.

22   Gottfried Semper, "Style in the Technical and Tectonic Arts," in *The Four Elements of Architecture*, 1989, 252.

23   Gottfried Semper, *Style in the Technical and Tectonic Arts; or Practical Aesthetics*, trans. H. Mallgrave and Michael Robinson (Santa Monica, CA: Texts and Documents, The Getty Research Institute, 2004), 760.

24   In addition to this author's contribution to the subject in *Ontology of Construction* (1994), the current turn to Semper comes full circle in Kenneth Frampton's *Studies in Tectonic Culture* (Cambridge, MA: The MIT Press, 1995), followed by *ANY*, 14 (1995).

25   H.F. Mallgrave, *Gottfried Semper*, 1996, 9.

26   Barry Bergdoll, *Karl Friedrich Schinkel: An Architecture for Prussia* (New York: Rizzoli, 1994), 28.

27   Barry Bergdoll, *Karl Friedrich Schinkel*, 1994, 14.

28   H.F. Mallgrave, *Gottfried Semper*, 1996, 87. See also Mitchell Schwarzer, "Freedom and Tectonics," in *German Architectural Theory and the Search for Modern Identity* (Cambridge: Cambridge University Press, 1995), 167–214.

29   Mitchell Schwarzer, "Freedom and Tectonics," 1995, 173.

30   Kurt W. Forster, "'Only Things that Stir the Imagination': Schinkel as a Scenographer," in John Zukowsky, ed., *Karl Friedrich Schinkel: The Drama of Architecture* (Chicago, IL: The Art Institute of Chicago, 1994), 18–35, 18.

31   Gottfried Semper, *The Four Elements*, 1989, 35.

32   Tilmann Buddensieg, "*Architecture as an Empty Form: Nietzsche and the Art of Building*,"
      in Alexandre Kostka and Irving Wohlfarth, eds, *Nietzsche and "An Architecture of Our
      Minds"* (Los Angeles, CA: The Getty Research Institute for the History of Art and the
      Humanities, 1999), 270.

33   Gottfried Semper, *The Four Elements*, 1989, 257.

34   Gottfried Semper, *The Four Elements*, 1989, 257.

35   Anthony Vidler, "The Mask and the Labyrinth: Nietzsche and the (Uncanny) Space of
      Decadence," in Alexandre Kostka and Irving Wohlfarth, eds, *Nietzsche*, 1999, 53–63.

36   Gottfried Semper, *The Four Elements*, 1989, 258.

37   Gevork Hartoonian, *Ontology of Construction*, 1994, 88.

38   H.F. Mallgrave, *Gottfried Semper*, 1996, 59.

39   Walter Benjamin, "The Work of Art in the Age of Mechanical Reproduction," in Hannah
      Arendt, ed., *Illuminations* (New York: Schocken Books, 1969), 217–52.

40   Guy Debord, *The Society of Spectacle* (New York: Zone Books, 1994), 13. For a thorough
      elaboration of the concept of phantasmagoria, see Susan Buck-Morss, *The Dialectics of
      Seeing* (Cambridge, MA: The MIT Press, 1989), 78–109.

41   Howard Caygill, *Walter Benjamin: The Color of Experience* (New York: Routledge, 1998),
      32. For Benjamin's reflection on experience, see his "The Storyteller," and "On Some
      Motifs in Baudelaire," both in Hannah Arendt, ed., *Illuminations*, 1969. Benjamin's
      work is critical for Massimo Caccari's discourse on modern architecture. See Caccari,
      Architecture and Nihilism: On the Philosophy of Modern Architecture (New Haven, CT: Yale
      University Press, 1993).

42   William Pietz, "The Problem of the Fetish, II," *Res* 13 (spring 1987): 23–45, 25.

43   Jacques Derrida, *Specters of Marx* (New York: Routledge, 1994), 155.

44   Reminding his reader of the distinction Adolf Loos and K. Kraus made between an urn
      and a chamber pot, Hal Foster correctly argues for architectural strategies that might
      resist the contemporary urge for total design, and "provide culture with running-room"
      (Foster, *Design and Crime*, 2004, 25).

45   Here I am benefiting from Michael Fried's discussion of Denis Diderot's differentiation
      between the place of audience in the construction of a dramatic tableau and the
      theatricality evident in Rococo art. See Fried, *Absorption*, 1988, 93. According to
      Diderot, "had it been understood that, even though a dramatic work is made to be
      represented, it is necessary that author and actor forget the beholder, and that all
      interest be concentrated upon the personages …" (Fried, *Courbet's Realism*, 1990, 94).

46   Howard Caygill, *Walter Benjamin*, 1998, 116.

47   See Gianni Vattimo's discourse on the interplay between locality and region in *The End
      of Modernity* (Baltimore, MD: Johns Hopkins University Press, 1988), 83.

48   Martin Heidegger "The Thing," in *Poetry, Language, Thought* (New York: Harper and Row,
      1971), 161–84. Gianni Vattimo presents an intriguing analogy between Heidegger's
      idea of *Stoss* and Walter Benjamin's discourse on shock. See Heidegger's "The
      Origin of the Work of Art," and Benjamin's "The Work of Art in the Age of Mechanical
      Reproduction." Written around 1935, both essays benefit from Georg Simmel's
      discourse on the human life in metropolis. According to Vattimo, both Benjamin and
      Heidegger highlighted the importance of art as a work disorienting the beholder, and

unbounding his/her expected sensations and habits. See Vattimo, "Art and Oscillation," in *The Transparent Society* (Baltimore, MD: Johns Hopkins University Press, 1992), 45–61. Also see Howard Caygill "Benjamin, Heidegger and the Destruction of Tradition," and Andrew Benjamin "Time and Task: Benjamin and Heidegger Showing the Present," both essays in Andrew Benjamin and Peter Osborne, eds, *Walter Benjamin's Philosophy* (New York: Routledge, 1994), 1–31, and 216–50 respectively.

49   Walter Benjamin, "Theses on the Philosophy of History," in Hannah Arendt, ed., *Illuminations*, 1969, 254.

50   Gottfried Semper, *Style*, 2004, 71.

51   Gevork Hartoonian, *Ontology of Construction*, 1994.

52   Interestingly enough, Michael Kahn, who has edited Steven Spielberg's films, suggests that, "The director is like the architect—it's his or her vision—and the editor is the builder, ... with Steven, it's like building a beautiful house" (quoted by Bernard Weineraub, "Hollywood's Kindest Cuts," *The New York Times* [August 20, 1998]: E1).

53   Here I am benefiting from Vittorio Gregotti's review of my *Ontology of Construction* published in *Casabella* 618 (December 1994): 2–4. The subject is further elaborated in Gregotti's recent book, *Architecture, Means and Ends* (Chicago, IL: University of Chicago Press, 2010).

54   Carl Gottlieb Wilhelm Bötticher, "In What Style Should We Build?," in trans. Wolfgang Herrmann, *In What Style Should We Build?*, 1992, 161.

55   Here I am paraphrasing Gottfried Semper in *Style*, 2004, 627–8.

3

Peter Eisenman: In Search of Degree Zero Architecture

Whether one agrees or disagrees with what he has built and written, the fact remains that Peter Eisenman has secured a significant position in contemporary architecture. His work has opened and left behind many formal and theoretical territories. From his engagement with the New York Five Architects, to his recent projects, Eisenman has relentlessly and uncompromisingly pursued the tradition of modern formalism. With its huge investment in intellectualism his work, ironically, does not touch on the basic premises of the project of the historical avant-garde. Instead of challenging institutions or wanting to integrate architecture with the life-world, Eisenman cultivates the progressive fruits of humanism; a discourse initially formulated by Andrea Palladio, then given a radical twist by the work of Piranesi,[1] and later institutionalized in the neoplasticism of the De Stijl group and the elementarist constructivism of the early twentieth-century avant-garde movements. His occasional turn to the topological aspects of the earth-work, though, is promising. In projects such as Cannaregio (1978), Aronoff Center (1996), and Memorial to Murdered Jews (2005), he sets up a rapport between the body and the object that is attributed to the minimalism of the 1970s. If this is a plausible theoretical window to look into Eisenman's work, then one should also consider two other vectors of his work. First, like Roland Barthes in *Writing Degree Zero* (1968), Eisenman has launched a radical challenge to architecture as an institution, denying it any purpose yet subjecting it to the thematic of the very process of such a denial. Dialectically, and this is the second vector, he has left himself with no choice but to indulge in architectural history to the point that he is an excellent teacher for those who want to pursue architecture's disciplinary history from a formalistic point of view. There is a price to be paid for all this: Eisenman's intellectual vigor has forced critics to see and analyze his architecture primarily from the point of view of themes and concepts on which he has written or lectured. In this encounter, the least that can be expected from his work is a demonstration of the developmental process of postmodern "theory," an interdisciplinary approach to cultural discourse without which a fair assessment of Eisenman's work would be difficult, if not impossible. That said, we should also notice another turn in Eisenman:

the velocity unleashed by electronic technology has nullified any theory that does not confirm the logic of this technique. This much is clear from Eisenman's "silence" during the last couple of years, whereas before this, his writings disclosed not only the state of his own architectural praxis, but also presented a concise formulation of the ongoing problematic of contemporary architecture. The architectonic implication of the suggested "closure" will be discussed in the final chapter of this volume. What needs to be said here is that a sense of periodization is central to any critical assessment of Eisenman's work.

An argument can be made for recognizing three departures in Eisenman's career. First, the early experimental years (it is not useful to mark the exact date of these periods since one stage overlaps the next) that culminated in what is called the Five Architects, during which time Le Corbusier's legacy was examined primarily from a formalistic point of view. At this initial stage, Eisenman's theoretical work was concerned with the post-war rapprochements on the thematic of humanist discourse since the Renaissance. We are reminded of Rudolf Wittkower's *Architectural Principles in the Age of Humanism* (1949), where architecture's symbolism is discussed in the light of the convergence that took place between religious and scientific ideologies. Starting with an interdisciplinary interpretation of culture, Wittkower "broadened the base of criticism and interpretation by bringing text into foreground, attempting to reconstruct the intentions of Renaissance architects from their treatises and drawings."[2] Interestingly enough Wittkower's aspiration had already been given a radical twist by Colin Rowe in the "Mathematics of Ideal Villas," first published in 1947 in the British journal *Architectural Review*, where, drawing lessons from cubism, the author makes analogies between Le Corbusier's Villa Stein in Garches and Palladio's Villa Malcontena. Influenced by Rowe, Eisenman recodes these traditions, first through Noam Chomsky's discourse on "deep structure," and later through Jacques Derrida's deconstruction theory.

In the second instance, attention should be given to the role Eisenman played in reinterpreting the received ideas of modernism in conjunction with themes borrowed from philosophy and literary criticism. This is evident from Rowe's assessment of the limits experienced by architects after the failure of the historical avant-garde. For Rowe, the emergence of "form" in the work of the New York Five Architects should be seen as the residue of a modernism that has exhausted itself.[3] Addressing semiotic issues, particularly the Saussurean split between the signifier and the signified, Eisenman articulated a disenchanted white abstract architecture, the silence of which recalls the impossibility of continuing the project of the historical avant-garde. This much is also clear from his fascination and yet intelligent criticism of Aldo Rossi's work, the content of which speaks for what might be called "the down of mourning."[4] And yet the austere, sad appearance of House II expresses nothing short of the exhaustion of the formalistic energies of both the Dom-ino frame, and the legacy of neoplasticism (Figure 3.1).

The best of Eisenman's work in this period discloses a struggle between two structures whose logos will first be shaken in House X (where a two dimensional L-shape form is extracted from squares and cubes), and then the entire formal structure of the cube taken apart in Fin d'Ou T Hou S of 1985. In these projects,

3.1   Peter Eisenman, House II, 1969–70. Photograph Courtesy of Peter Eisenman Architects, New York City

Eisenman purposely dismissed the fact that the Dom-ino frame was a construction system designed initially to facilitate the convergence between the art of building and modern techniques. He is, aware of the inevitability of the impact of construction and its implications for the façade's relation to the plan in any building. This much is clear from his analysis of Giuseppe Terragni's architecture: discussing the textual relationship between the corner and the façade in the Casa Giuliani-Frigerio, Rowe's contribution is recognized in the distinction he makes between the idea of façade and the idea of elevation, and the implied shift from the modernist engagement with the plan to that of the faced.[5] While the elevation was traditionally conceived as the plane separating the inside from the outside, or presenting the vertical datum of the planimetric organization, the idea of frontality introduces an autonomous surface, which since Renaissance architecture, according to Eisenman, has been manipulated to express symbolic and functional meanings. In addition, the plan is understood in a sequence of movements, the experience of which is a perception, whereas the faced "can be both actually perceived and conceptually understood."[6]

In "Houses of Cards" (1987), the idea of façade is presented as an abstract surface with no referential point, except that it conveys meanings initiated by its own textuality. This was indeed a design strategy to give a radical twist to Rowe's emphasis on the façade and to recode the traditional understanding of the façade/plan relationship. From now on the façade is related to its own plan. In Eisenman's words:

> The façade has a different conceptual basis from the plan, section, and volume. In one sense, it can be seen as a vertical plan or section that constitutes the outermost surface of a volume. While it is analogous to plan and section in this way, unlike these other two documented cuts, the façade has an actual quality by virtue of the fact that it can be physically perceived calling for a different type of reading. In fact, the façade can be seen as a flattened three-dimensional entity with its own plan and section. With conceptual equivalence to the two-dimensional plan and section.[7]

It might be suggested that at this stage, Eisenman's projects were informed by the historicity of the departure of the architecture of the eighteenth century from the hegemony of the classical language of architecture. This, we can argue, was another facet of Wittkower's influential text mentioned earlier. In the concluding section of his book, Wittkower suggested that, by the emergence of theories of the sublime and the picturesque, during the second half of the eighteenth century, there occurred a shift from "the object and the laws by which it was formed to the observer and his individual apperception. At this moment the classical tradition, and the confidence in the universality of proportions, lost its unique authority."[8] Regardless of how long the suggested rupture lasted, Eisenman approaches that historical moment as the *primal scene* from which one should extract a different re-interpretation of the very nature of that *event*. Employing contemporary philosophical discourses, the central task Eisenman took upon himself at this stage of his career was to recode the metaphysics of origin, progress, and history.[9] We might also see in Eisenman's relentless attempt to secure the autonomy of architecture, the anxieties motivated by the project of modernity in which "everything solid melts into the air," to recall Marshall Berman (1985). Interestingly enough, it was the idea of breaking down the box through which the site came to Eisenman's attention first, but also in follow up to Cannaregio, in Fin d'Ou T Hou S (1985), and then in the Wexner Center for the Visual Arts, Ohio State University (1983–89). As will be discussed shortly, the physical and historical properties of the site of this latter project did indeed save Eisenman from drifting away from history, and thus we see the inauguration of a different reasoning for his indulgence of the arbitrary game of fragmentation and formal playfulness.

To give an order, even a chaotic order, to the classical canon of architecture, Eisenman had to pick up the idea of "spine," which in conjunction with a given site would generate two important themes and enable him to put behind him the early experimental houses. Two projects, the Frankfurt Biocenter, BDR (1987),[10] and the Wexner Center, were conceived with an eye on program, the exigencies of the site, and the theoretical break from semiotics. From now on Eisenman would take advantage of the formal promises traced in Jacques Derrida's writings which in due time would be energized by incorporating computer programming into the process of design. The second departure in Eisenman's work also testifies to a vigorous intellectual conviction, though of a different nature; the metaphysics of architecture that he had intended to deconstruct earlier are now recognized as deeply rooted in the logos of humanism. The logos of the Cartesian grid implied in the Dom-ino frame, the deep structure of which had ignited the years of the Five Architects, now had to be revisited and muscled around. While site and program still remained important, Eisenman's work in the second period would "fold" and unfold the right angle so dear to Le Corbusier, theorizing the result in terms of what is called "weak form."[11] During this period, the early geometric forms, the cage of reason, are sliced into layers with no significant "purpose" except to brush the body of architecture with fictive texts

3.2   Eisenman Architects, Columbus Convention Center, Columbus, Ohio, 1990–93. Photograph by author

to the point that architecture becomes nothing short of a textual ensemble. This operation unfolded the possibility of a different strategy; the most recent projects of Eisenman are centered on diagram;[12] an abstract drawing motivated by the exigencies of the site or program but charged with layers of woven fabric-like tissues waiting to be "translated" into architectural forms. What remains significant in Eisenman's discourse on "diagram" is a turn to the disciplinary history of architecture, albeit perceived from a formalistic point of view. Differentiating his ideas from those critics who strictly discuss diagram in terms of Gilles Deleuze, Eisenman defined diagram in relationship to what he calls architecture's interiority, underlining "three conditions unique to architecture: (1) architecture's compliance with the metaphysics of presence; (2) the

3.3   Eisenman Architects, Aronoff Center for the Arts, University of Cincinnati, Ohio, 1988–96. Photograph by author

already motivated condition of the sign in architecture, and (3) the necessary relationship of architecture to a desiring subject."[13]

A few blocks away from the Wexner Center on the Campus of the University of Cincinnati, Eisenman built two buildings that were a prelude to a fresh beginning. Borrowing from Yve-Alain Bois and Rosalind Krauss's useful reading of Georges Bataille's concept of "formless," Eisenman intended to question the "legitimacy of the formal decisions made" in the name of function or the content of an object.[14] In the Columbus Convention Center (Figure 3.2) and in the Aronoff Center for Design and Art, total dematerialization and further intensification of the aesthetic of abstraction are called forth (Figure 3.3). Here Eisenman articulates an architecture that in more ways than one is formed and informed by "interiority," and a spine whose horizontal elongation alludes to the deconstruction of the cave as one possible origin for architecture discussed by historians. He presents a subtle convergence between *cave* and "interiority," which, according to him, "has nothing to do with the inside or the inhabitable space of a building but rather of a condition of being within. However, as is the case with the grotesque, interiority deals with two factors; the unseen and the hollowed-out."[15] Another characteristic of these two projects is their allusive "attachment" to something else, suggesting that the "weak form" cannot stand on its own except when is it turned into prosthesis. According to Silvia Kolbowski, the design of the Aronoff Center "leans" closely to the existing building, and the "conceptual models used to generate the *parti*—the overlapping, torquing, shifting, and stepping of series of forms and motifs, some of which are modified by open-ended logarithmic functions."[16] Leaning meticulously against an old structure, the new addition stretches its own body along with the topography of the site. The design of the Wexner Center, instead, dwells on the ghost of a bygone tower and the skeletal trace of a historic path (Figure 3.4). And yet, in the absence of any historical trace in the deserted site of the Columbus Center, the building had to mimic the twisting forms of the adjacent highway visible from the top floors of the hotel next to the project. Does the implied "absence," the trace of factual and fictive topography in these projects, resonate Eisenman's surgical approach to the once-upon-a-time dependency of architecture on nature? Or is it an allusion to a concept of beauty that is informed by geometry and the human body? If these speculations have merit, then we should ask another question: What other aspects of architecture are still to be tested in the laboratory of deconstruction theory? This is a dilemma,

3.4   Eisenman Architects, Wexner Center for the Visual Arts and Fine Arts Library, Ohio
State University, Columbus, 1983–89. Exterior view of tower. Photograph by author

indeed, which according to Kenneth Frampton, stems from Eisenman's "contradictory desire to both dissolve the essentially Humanistic body of architecture and yet to still remain capable of bringing its shadow into being." Frampton continues,

> It is surely significant that this dilemma seems to be capable of a
> convincing outcome where, as in the Biocentrum project, the thematic of
> the work is nature herself and where the lost authority of secularization
> is seemingly restored through the presence of an irreducible demiurge,
> even if this presence is acknowledged as a perennially re-constituted of
> the human brain ….[17]

The suggested dilemma is perhaps the only continuous thread running through Eisenman's work to date.

In one of his essays Eisenman presents a convincing argument for the continuity of architectural "tropes" generated since the Renaissance. Examining the dialogue between void and solid in Renaissance architecture, Eisenman prepares the ground to test his newest strategy, the "interstitial." The idea of the interstitial is, according to him, "different from and at the same time subverts Bramante's interstitial." He continues, "The process of the interstitial does not begin from either a container or a contained, even though all architecture is in some way traditionally legitimated by its function as container. This is not to say that there is no container or contained, only that these terms are no longer used to legitimate the work."[18] The article then enumerates the "design methodology" used in the Bibliothèque L'Institute Université, Geneva. The term "design methodology" recalls Christopher Alexander's attempt in the 1960s to introduce scientific and mathematical paradigms into the design process. He was concerned with addressing a broader theoretical spectrum of the post-war America when architects had either to channel design decision-making based on historicism, or else, to utilize problem-solving methods and techniques, which had passed their test in American military industries and were now available to be used in other production activities. This was indeed part of the new positivism that Alexander and others found useful, especially when design involved decision-making that concerned environmental and regional issues.[19] The idea of borrowing from other disciplines was indeed welcomed by neo-avant-gardes whose departure from both classicism and high-modernism had left them with no choice but to see architecture through windows opened by philosophy and literary criticism; a theoretical blockage, which, according to Fredric Jameson, highlights a different dilemma—the simultaneous return of the figurative and abstract aesthetics of modernism.[20]

Having established the three periods crucial to understanding Eisenman's architecture, it is now possible to propose three theoretical problematics that run through his oeuvre, each informed by theories of structuralism and post-structuralism with which he had a rapport since the 1960s. First, the dichotomy between the historicity of architecture and the autonomous nature of architectural ideas: no matter how hard one pushes for architecture's autonomy, the thematic of the disciplinary history of architecture should be considered central for any re-interpretation of architecture. Second, the critic's, i.e., Eisenman's, reading of the problematic of the institution of architecture is ideological through and through. To put it simply, how could Eisenman shake the foundations of architecture without grafting his own ideas onto the textuality of architecture? Manfredo Tafuri, for one, claimed that in writing Terragni, "Eisenman redesigns him; the free present is a further theoretical manifesto sustaining his architecture without a homeland, liberated beyond space and time. Eisenman too is a master of the art of *simulation*."[21] Third, to walk the tightrope that Eisenman travels, we have no choice but to approach his work through the dual protagonists of the architect and author. Problematic as this might seem, one should, nevertheless, accept the fact that Eisenman is one of the few contemporary architects to have made an effort to attend to, develop, and transform the discursive modalities of his own project more frequently than his critics could keep up with. Added to this observation is the historicity of Eisenman's project, the challenge he wants to launch against the institution of architecture.

Whereas the historical avant-garde's drive for formal autonomy and abstraction was situated by late nineteenth-century historicism, Eisenman's discourse on autonomy is motivated by, first, the recognition of the interiority of architecture, that which is architectural in architecture, a point of view that, paradoxically, is motivated by Eisenman's reading of deconstruction theory. If Derrida intended to underline the uncertainty central to any theoretical narrative, the project's transformation into architecture had no choice, at least in Eisenman's hand, but to give a new twist to the split between sign and signifier that structuralism had already established. What this means is that Eisenman embarked on a project whose main goal was to deconstruct the logos of formalism. To do that, he had to update *form* in the purview of the latest available theoretical development. Second, seen against postmodern eclecticism, the interiority Eisenman sought for architecture had no choice but to entertain the idea of *play* introduced into architecture by Robert Venturi's discourse on "both-and."[22] To create distance from the by then exorcised functionalism meant for architecture to engage in the game of assemblage for two related reasons: first, to confirm architecture's "learning from Las Vegas." Second, in the neo-avant-garde's attempt to secure itself from pop-culture, the art of building had no choice but to opt for a level of abstraction compatible with that of the aesthetic of commodity fetishism. Since the 1990s, formal playfulness, theatricalization, was the only terrain left in which the form could sustain its telos of radicalism.

To present a convincing argument for the suggested doubling involved in the theatricalization permeating Eisenman's architecture, the discussion should center on the diagrammatic vision of site where the introjections of the grid and the spine take place. To this end, the rest of this chapter will analyze two of Eisenman's important projects, and will note the architect's inclination for surface-topography, a subject that will be picked up in the final chapter.

THE ASHES OF THE GRID

Consider the Wexner Center, where a figurative tower and an abstract grid structure represent the metaphorical demise of both classicism and modernism (Figure 3.5). The dream-image quality of the tower, and the robust look of the scaffold recall the traces of the fortress and the path that once existed on the site. In addition to their location, every feature of these two structures is embellished to allude to the aesthetic of ruin: the brick veneer of the tower *appears* as much a fake as the synthetic stucco covering the hollowed parts of the tower. The tactile quality assigned to the entrance façade also endorses the idea of ruin, which, ironically, pays lip service to the classical idea of frontality. What this entails, in Eisenman's words, is that "representation insists on a completion that it cannot identify as absolute ... therefore it [representation] is always ruined in advance."[23] Furthermore, the juxtaposition between the picturesque qualities of the main façade and the

3.5   Eisenman
Architects, Wexner
Center, 1983–89.
Exterior view of
grid. Photograph
by author

abstract scaffold is a reminder of the postmodernist idea of "both-and" noted earlier. More interesting, is the main façade and its potential for association with those eighteenth-century drawings where the everlasting life of nature is depicted next to a ruined structure. Eisenman's masquerade of the main façade adheres to the aesthetics of fossil, rendering the stone stonier, as is the case in G. Battista Piranesi's *Carceri*. In the Wexner Center, the scaffold suggests the eternity of the Cartesian grid, though conceived to simulate ruin. The body of the building is indeed rotten!

And yet running on the north–south axis, the empty and naked body of the scaffold eludes the death of the corpus of humanism. With its dominant position, the scaffold endorses the enduring qualities of the aesthetic of abstraction. Interestingly enough, the tower and the grid represent the two major compositional elements central to early modernist fascination with formalism. In the Wexner Center, the line and the point define and confine the placement of other parts of the complex: the entrance is placed next to the tower but perpendicular to the scaffold. The library is placed underground on the east side of the site with no direct access to natural light; a design strategy implemented perhaps to prevent formal confrontation between the library's presumed massive volume and that of the scaffold. To assign the latter a dominant position in the overall composition of the complex, the entire body of the building is sliced into many layers, each following diverse axes, and a grid system that is motivated by the initial diagrammatic analysis of the site. Here theatricalization is sustained by the diagrammatic energies of the two elements of point and line. In retrospect, one might argue that it is the abstraction of the site and its permutation to a surface plane that will later sneak into Eisenman's architectural language, forcing the banishment of the line and point from his future projects.

In the Wexner Center, however, Eisenman's design economy departs from his previous experimental work, and scales down the vertical and volumetric demand of the right-angle dictated not only by the geometry of form, but also by the tectonic dialogue between the elements of load and support. The architectonic intentions of the scaling down are visible in every section drawing of Eisenman's latest projects. In these drawings a truncated and contorted cladding suppresses the tectonic of load and support. The strategy aims at a theatricalization of architecture whose tropes are sometimes carried into the interior space too. Next to the entrance, inside and above the stair leading to the main exhibition area of the Wexner Center, a suspended column stops short of touching the ground (Figure 3.6). To dramatize the theatrical scene further, the bottom of the suspended column is dropped a few inches below the imaginary plane of intersection where other columns and beams meet each other. Is this an accidental misfit between the structural grid system and the location of the stair that stands perhaps where it should be? Or is this a cardboard column painted the same color to resemble other structural members of the grid? Such a theatrical stage-set recalls the technique of shock utilized by the dadaists and surrealists,

3.6 Eisenman Architects, Wexner Center, 1983–89. Interior stairs. Photograph by author

a strategy that will be abandoned soon when "surface" emerges as the sole element, initiating a different reading of what is called the interiority of architecture.

The presented analysis of Eisenman's project should first be qualified at the theoretical level, and then revisited in conjunction with selected projects designed by Carlo Scarpa and Alvaro Siza, to mention just two architects whose work shares motifs central to the Wexner Center. The intention is to historicize the tropes contingent to contemporary architecture, and to demonstrate the architectonic implication of the difference between the tectonic of theatricality and theatricalization.

By way of introduction, it is necessary to reiterate the well-known story that the dadaists' and surrealists' use of shock techniques was in response to the compulsive situation inaugurated by the metropolis. Theirs was also conceived as an attack on the bourgeois idea of autonomy of art, and the modernist trust in technology. Not only have those techniques exhausted their formal effectiveness, the very enduring foundation of the historical avant-garde is rather questionable today. According to Peter Burger, "a further difficulty inheres in the aesthetics of shock, and that is the impossibility to make permanent this kind of effect. As a result of repetition, it changes fundamentally: there is such a thing as expected shock."[24] If the first occurrence of the concept of shock was contingent to the Europe of 1916,

3.7   Eisenman
Robertson
Architects, Fire
Station, Brooklyn,
New York, 1985.
Photograph
courtesy of
Peter Eisenman
Architects, New
York City

its re-use at the turn of the century can be called the "return of the repressed," a phenomenon which ironically fits in the cultural spectacle of late capitalism, where the return of the same in *difference* is the major ordering principle of everyday life. In welcoming all kinds of "returns," capitalism endorses the idea of the end of history as one manifestation of the globalization of its political and cultural structures.

Taking Hegel's idea of repetition, Slavoj Žižek has this to say about the changing symbolic status of an event in modernity: "When it erupts for the first time it is experienced as a contingent trauma, as an intrusion of a certain non-symbolized Real; only through repetition is this event recognized in its symbolic necessity—it finds its place in the symbolic network; it is realized in the symbolic order."[25] Still, criticizing Burger's historicization of the avant-garde, Hal Foster discusses the theory of avant-garde from the viewpoint of a Freudian reading of "repetition."[26] Associating Peter Burger's position with a dogmatic understanding of historicism, and following Fredric Jameson's discourse on periodization, Michael Hays suggests replacing the notion of neo-avant-garde with the "late avant-garde," wherein the term late speaks "of intransigence and survival beyond which one can go; of a moment in a larger trajectory beyond which one cannot go; of technique accumulated to the point of bleak rumination; of productive negativity."[27] If convinced by these positions, then we need to ask what symbolic order does the suggested return of avant-garde techniques in Eisenman's architecture aim to sustain? Eisenman's entire oeuvre demonstrates an attempt to question the symbolic content of architecture. In post-modernity, however, the re-use of modernist techniques simply facilitates architecture's entry to the "symbolic order" that is unfolding under late capitalism. This is another way of suggesting that the theatricalization permeating neo-avant-garde work places architecture at the heart of the culture of spectacle. There remains, in Eisenman's work, a conscious attempt on his part to avoid the tectonic of a trabeated construction system embedded in the orthogonal grid, which is central to the ontology of construction.

3.8   Carlo Scarpa, Banca Popolare di Verona, Italy, 1973. Photograph by author

To make these theoretical remarks more relevant to the problematic of contemporary architecture, it is necessary to recall the tectonic rapport between the columnar system, the wall, and the roof in Mies van der Rohe's Barcelona Pavilion; Mies's recoding of the classical understanding of the relationship between column and beam in the National Gallery in Berlin; and finally, his rethinking of the tectonic of these elements in the Crown Hall, ITT Campus.[28] In the third project, the tectonic of an exposed steel truss and column would become, interestingly enough, a point of departure for Eisenman to rehearse Theo Van Doesburg's aesthetics of the diagonal in the Brooklyn Fire Station (Figure 3.7). The play between the orthogonal and the diagonal is another trope by which Eisenman has chosen to liberate architecture from the encumbrance of the tectonic of column-and-

3.9   Carlo Scarpa, Olivetti Shop, Venice, Italy, 1957–58. Photograph by author

beam. Eisenman's investment in abstraction has pushed architecture into a realm of theatricalization, the aesthetic gravitation of which remains equally seductive as that of the fetishism of commodities.

The recourse to Mies is not meant to cap the tectonic possibilities of the column and beam, experienced throughout modern architecture. A case can be made for a perception of theatricality that is centered on the tectonic, and yet the work might address the motifs noted in the Wexner Center. Carlo Scarpa's entire work, for one, braces together the purposefulness of a chosen structural system and its theatrical articulation, to the point that the final product "appears" an artifice. In numerous buildings, including the Banca Popolare di Verona (Figure 3.8), and the Museo di Castelvecchio, Scarpa's treatment of column and beam reconciles the nineteenth-

3.10 Carlo Scarpa, the Brion Cemetery, Italy, 1967–78. View of the pavilion and "proppylaea." Photograph by author

3.11 Alvaro Siza, Museum of Santiago de Compostela, Spain, 1988–96. Exterior view. Photograph courtesy of Harry Margalit

century structural rationalists' vision with the theatrical embellishment of material and form. In the Olivetti shop (Figure 3.9), for instance,[29] the joint connecting the column to the beam, or the wall to the ceiling, operates as a disjoint. It gives these architectonic elements a chance for self-expression beyond the dictates of the forces of gravity or function. The vision of seeing and making that permeates Scarpa's work provides the stone of the interior stair with the chance to stretch itself further; to look lighter, and to dance in a space whose theatrical gesture, ironically, does emphasize the tactility of stone and steel. If the theatrical ambiance of this shop alludes to the consumer world of commodities, the broken body of the column in the Brion Cemetery (Figure 3.10) recalls the eternity of death and ruination. Here theatricality speaks for the dialogue between making and fabrication; between the materiality of steel and its denial through tectonic embellishment: the steel column has to be cut first, then tied together meticulously and, finally, pierced into a pond to imply a second cutting as detected in the column's reflected image in the water. Here the broken column anticipates its broken image in the water.

Dedication to material, purpose, and the tectonic of theatricality, noted in Scarpa, is also at work in Alvaro Siza's architecture. To shorten this detour from Eisenman's work, and to demonstrate how other contemporary architects entertain ideas such as fragmentation and theatricality, we shall discuss one particular work of Siza. In the Museum of Contemporary Art in Santiago de Compostela (Figure 3.11), the tectonic of load and support is articulated through the dialogue between cutting and connecting. Like other projects of Siza, the building is designed to accommodate the exigencies of the site. The triangular shape of the site splits the body of the building into two wings to converge at the southern edge. The composition underlines the location of the portico and the main entrance, both placed on the opposite end. To dramatize the implied hinge, the northern face of the wing that shelters the ramp and the stairs at the entrance is cut from its base and then connected by two short steel columns. The strategy of cutting, at first glance, recalls Mies's Concrete House (1923) where a continuous ribbon-like fenestration challenges the expected tectonic convention embedded in a masonry construction system. Siza's tectonic articulation is rather modest. It recalls the nineteenth century's dialogue between the culture of stone and steel, and the centrality of the idea of necessity for the tectonic. In this project, the cut makes an opening to bring light into the stair, and to stress the position of the main entrance. There is an ambiguity in Siza's tectonic imagination worth addressing. An opening flanked by two columns and a beam above is essential for the image of the gate permeating the architecture of antiquity. The image was given a new twist by the nineteenth-century American architect, Frank Furness, who would reduce the columns standing next to the main entrance to a decorative element. In Santiago,

3.12   Alvaro Siza, Museum of Santiago de Compostela, Spain, 1988–96.
Entrance porch. Photograph courtesy of Harry Margalit

3.13 Eisenman
Architects,
Aronoff Center,
Ohio, 1988–96.
Main entrance.
Photograph
by author

Siza recodes such an image without falling into the pitfall of simulation or repetition. The two short steel columns in this project disconnect the blank granite wall of a two-story volume from its base, creating a tectonic form whose theatricality alludes to the hinge on the other end (Figure 3.12).

THE SPINE OF THE GATE

Interestingly enough, the ghost of the Greek image of the gate haunts the Aronoff Center for Design and Art. Here the two concrete columns, standing in front of the main entrance, raise a volume that is grafted into the space between the new addition and the existing building (Figure 3.13). To dislocate the tectonic vision discussed in Scarpa and Siza's buildings, Eisenman's design discloses an image of the relationship between load and support that is nurtured by concepts developed in other disciplines. The second difference between Eisenman and Scarpa or, for that matter, Siza, has to do with the fact that for Eisenman space and its expressive quality is instrumental for the theatricality of the final form. Space, as such, has the least importance in the architecture of Siza and Scarpa: it is experienced through the tectonic of the constructed form and the tactility of material employed.

These critical observations are borne out on entering the Ohio Convention Center, where a large exhibition hall and the meeting rooms flank the spine of the building. The planimetric organization employed here is typical of Eisenman's public projects developed in the early 1990s. What is involved here is the play at work between the structural frame system and the volume that envelops various meeting rooms: these volumes are perceived to demonstrate their autonomy from the space marked by the structural grid. According to Eisenman "while there are actual columns in a regular pattern, the space is not conceptually gridded."[30] In the Ohio Convention Center, the spatial disjunction between internal spatial volumes and the structural grid is dynamited by what might be considered the volumetric extension of a plane marking the loading ducts located at the edges of the exhibition hall (Figures 3.14 and 3.15). The formal effect of this diagrammatic interjection is carried through the spine, ending at the face of the street façade. This formal play gives rise to two readings: first, the composition attempts to deconstruct the classical vision of part/whole relations, in general, and Louis Kahn's idea of served/service spaces in particular. In Kahn, the dialogue between these two spaces sustains the formal logic of a chosen type. Eisenman, instead, intends

3.14   Eisenman Architects, Columbus Convention Center, Columbus, Ohio, 1990–93. Photograph by author

3.15   Eisenman Architects, Columbus Convention Center, Columbus, Ohio, 1990–93. Photograph by author

3.16   Eisenman
Architects,
Columbus
Convention Center,
Columbus, Ohio,
1990–93. Aerial
view. Photograph
by author

to deconstruct typological order. Second, seen from the bird's-eye view, the mass of the Convention Center looks to be made out of many volumetric layers (Möbius strips?) each extending along spatial traces of a hypothetical moving truck (Figure 3.16). The design strategy makes the building simulate the undulating forms of the adjacent highway. It also divides and scales down the main street façade; the latter looks like a row of terraced houses stacked next to each other, perhaps to subdue the expected civic dimension of the complex (Figure 3.17).

The cladding of the street façade is colorful synthetic stucco, various layers of which are inscribed by a hypothetical axis. The best that can be made of these fractured surfaces is by way of association with the disjunction noted earlier between the interior volumes and the structural grid. Furthermore, the façade is a reminder of the ruined look of the tower of the Wexner Center. Here too the "face" of the building looks pale, soft, and bodiless. What design incentive might initiate the choice of color and the virtual look of this façade? Is the prevailing colorfulness and the virtual look of this project a reaction to the aesthetics of the white architecture of the so-called International Style, and the Five Architects? Or is it perceived in reference to the nineteenth-century debate on the polychromic origin of Greek architecture? If the latter guess is farfetched, the fact remains that Eisenman's work tends to internalize the aesthetic of artificiality, a strategy used to undermine the thingness of architecture in the first place, and to neglect the role of tectonics in the spatial experience of a building.

This much is clear from one's first encounter with the Aronoff Center where a whipped-cream-like coated surface covers the interior spine, a space that operates like a "time machine." Eisenman's intensive use of artificial light next to the daylight pouring from skylights negates any expected unity between time and space. Here the morphic effect, the fact that the spectator's vector of sight and body is constantly challenged by asymmetrical and undulating walls, and the grid of the ceiling provide

3.17   Eisenman
Architects,
Columbus
Convention
Center, Columbus,
Ohio, 1990–93.
Street elevation.
Photograph
by author

a cinematographic experience of the kind Auguste Choisy and Sergei Eisenstein attributed to the Acropolis.[31] From point of entry to the other end of the spine, where an exit door opens onto the vista of the city, one is positioned within the spatial permutation of a series of ascents and turns, each framing a partial image of the spine, the totality of which remains out of reach. A *promenade architecturale*? Yes, though different from the one at work in the Villa Savoye, for example. In the latter, the courtyard located on the main floor of the building balances the ascent to the roof and out into the open space. Le Corbusier's vision of space might be associated with what Eisenman characterizes as the classical and mechanistic sense of spatial organization.[32] In the Villa Savoye, however, most architectonic decisions, including the "free-façade," are made in order to externalize the interior volume of the building. This spatial experience is facilitated by the idea of the *promenade architecturale*.

The vision at work in the Aronoff Center operates towards different ends. Here, one's feeling is informed by the virtual quality of the space that is wrapped in layers of partition, the surfaces of which are exploited to endorse the singularity of the spine at the expense of other spaces. This much is clear from the corridor that leads to the design studios where a bare and almost depressing atmosphere reminds one of the *excess* invested in the spine. It also demonstrates the architect's intention to deconstruct the formal logic of served/service spaces, a typology that sees the design return, haunting in a disfigured composition that is ordered by the adjacent existing building and the topography of the site. Having experienced the excess inscribed into the spine, the access to the open air at the other end of what might be called a Möbius strip, kindles a kind of redemptive feeling discussed by Gaston Bachelard.[33] Nevertheless, the importance given to the spine in this project evolved, as suggested earlier, out of the architect's conscious decision to underline the bodily experimentation of space in the topological rapport established between the earth-work (the terraced levels of the spine) and the roofing. To these two horizontal planes we should add the vertical plane of the existing building. As such the dialectics of moving and looking into the "interior" of architecture is the closest Eisenman comes to Richard Serra's turn to the field.[34]

Throughout his career, Eisenman has taken every opportunity to question the culture of building, themes internal to the disciplinary history of architecture. In an interview he claims,

> that architecture participates in what I call the continual unfolding of existence, that architecture, like any other discipline, has the capacity to do that, and that there is what I would consider to be a disciplinary specificity to architecture, so that even though the deconstructionists say that everything is one, and there's an intertextuality, and that there is no subject, I believe there is a subject, I believe there is a disciplinary specificity to all disciplines and what I believe one is looking to do—in addition to anything else—is find what that disciplinary specificity is in architecture.[35]

Even though his design strategies aim at the abstract articulation of dualities such as column/wall, structure/space, and void/solid, his main intention remains centered on denying those oppositions any substantial role in the tectonic articulation of architecture. Only the deconstruction of the metaphysical content of these dualities and its formal results are considered worthy of attention, and this to him is enough of a strategy to inform the content of "critical" practice. Eisenman claims that, "Form in architecture is all we have. So formalism in architecture is different from formalism in language, in painting, in literature, because formalism in language is only one means of communication; in architecture it is the only means."[36] His critical eye does not fall on the ideological content of the problematic rapport between technology and architecture. Interestingly enough, Eisenman's writing never addresses the question of technology and its implications for architecture, particularly the historical transgression from *technė* to the tectonic, and montage.[37] The concept of making and the way it is woven into the ideological domain, at least in late capitalism, has no place in his theoretical work either. Instead of addressing the relationship between technology and ideology, Eisenman is, seemingly, more interested in discussing the loss of architecture's power in the amelioration of social ills.

Consider Eisenman's following observation: "Since the mid-eighteenth century, architecture has been sustained by ideological politics. With the demise of ideology we ask what role architecture plays in international capital. Can plastic architecture still ameliorate social problems, or is only an architecture of infrastructure viable?" And he continues, the "ideology of form that once resided in the plastic is seen as irrelevant."[38] Obviously, the major objective and subjective thinking essential to the formation of the modernist vision of architecture is inaccessible today. Gone also is the position that would consider technology a critical force in moving the new-born industrial society away from the physical and aesthetic remnants of the old regime. It is even arguable that the trust the Werkbund and the Bauhaus placed on technology was aimed at distancing architecture from historicism. Nevertheless, Eisenman's claim for the "demise of ideology" dismisses the criticality of the process of technification of architecture,[39] a subject that might be considered of critical importance in his own turn to formalism.

That the postwar situation was informed by a different understanding of technology might be detected in Mies's statement, dated 1928:

> Technology follows its own laws and is not man-related. Economy becomes self-serving and calls forth new needs. Autonomous tendencies in all these forces assert themselves. Their meaning seems to be the attainment of a specific phase of development. But they assume a threatening predominance. Unchecked, they thunder along. Man is swept along as if in a whirlwind. Each individual attempts to brace himself singularly against these forces. We stand at a turning point.[40]

In retrospect, what is significant in Mies's claim is a concept of technology that is independent of the modernist's social vision of architecture, but that also anticipates the present situation when technology is "visibly" functioning as an ideological force. This is not to deny the fact that today there is no broad concession among architects, artists, and thinkers about the redemptive power of technology. Nevertheless, since Mies, and following theories advanced by Walter Benjamin and Martin Heidegger, we must consider if modernism's strive for formal autonomy was not itself centered on the ideology of technology, and the latter's drive to conquer architecture, among other cultural products, and finally, to what extent such a project, i.e., the technification of architecture, is facilitated by the advent of electronic techniques.

That there is no reason today to discuss socialist, democratic, and even fascist architecture is obvious. What should be noted, however, is that everyday life does not unravel in a vacuum of political and economic decision-making, even though the present globalization of capital and information technologies attempts to insure the possibility of overriding every perceivable ideological obstacle, even those motivated by politics of late capitalism. Interestingly enough, Eisenman says about politics and architecture: "… I think architecture is a form of politics. I believe that architecture does make political statements. There is no doubt. I mean, I was just in Naples recently, and three of the great buildings that I saw in Naples, in the most beautiful shape, were built by Mussolini. But that doesn't mean I agree with Mussolini's politics." And later in the same interview he adds: "… my work basically says that while I may have my own personal political leanings, or I may have affinities to conservative politics, when it comes to architecture, ultimately its politics is autonomy."[41] Modern institutions and corporations, similar to the pre-modern-day palaces and churches, exercise certain pressure on architecture, albeit discretely, through what Žižek calls "ideological fantasy;" this is not to mask a given reality, but a way of offering "the social reality itself as an escape from some traumatic real kernel."[42] Whether the kernel of contemporary trauma in architecture can be attributed to Mies's deterritorialization of the language of modern architecture, or to the failure of the project of the historical avant-garde;[43] the loss has raised several critical issues as far as the crisis of architecture is concerned. Globalization of capital and the infusion of telecommunication technologies into every aspect of the life-world should be considered critical for the permeation of "ideological fantasy," and its contribution in pushing architecture into the bedrock of spectacle nurtured by the politics of late capitalism.

Along with other neo-avant-garde architects, Eisenman has made an attempt to transgress the *Zeitgeist* disregard of the latter's dialogical rapport with technology. He is, nevertheless, concerned about the possibility of "critical" architecture, which might avoid the formalism formulated by Rowe and the historicity attributed to Manfredo Tafuri's discourse. What "critical" means to Eisenman has to do with a project, at work in various forms since the fourteenth century, the primary task of which is to sustain the continuity of architecture's autonomy, using both theoretical and technical potentialities of a given *Zeitgeist.*[44] However, he is correct in insisting on the importance of technology for opening new perceptual horizons and affecting artistic production processes;[45] he also strikes a major chord in warning young architects about the two-dimensional and diagrammatic function of drawings produced by computer, and the fact that those drawings are far removed from the realm of architecture. He, as do other architects, checks those diagrams constantly against architectural tropes.[46] What Eisenman dismisses in his rather promising remarks is the essence of technology, which according to Heidegger, is not technological.[47] Unnoticed in Eisenman and other neo-avant-garde architects in their unreserved fascination with what computer programming can do for architecture is the backward gaze of Walter Benjamin's angel. Reminding his reader of Adolf Loos's search for *place,* Massimo Cacciari observes:

> The "freedom" of the avant-garde and the hubris of its criticism shatters the
> delicate balance of the figure of the Angel and dissipates the feeble messianic
> strength that it announces to us. On the other hand, the avant-garde decrees
> the "once upon a time," and reduces things to "eternal images"—on the other, it
> turns its gaze on the future and, like a future teller, looks for "what lies hidden in
> the womb." For the Angel, on the other hand, the ephemeral of the present senses
> that of the past, and its future lies in the moment, which is origin. And in any case,
> how could the Angel destroy all presuppositions, if the very happiness for which
> he yearns is itself presupposed?[48]

What is involved here is: the "freedom" experienced in mediatic technologies denies the intelligibility of the dissonance existing between techno-scientific space and how such a dissonance can be the subject matter of what Cacciari calls a "game of a combination of places."[49] The denial also involves the tectonic, how to make a virtue out of material without losing sight of the dialogical relationship between the ephemeral and the permanent.

Even though the prospect of winning over the digital seems dim today, the fact remains that in late capitalism, technology is infused into the cultural, and plays a dramatic role in framing the contemporary way of seeing and making. And yet technology does more. Discussing Heidegger, Leo Marx recalls György Lukács and Karl Marx's idea of reification, arguing that, similar to commodities, technology exerts some power over us to the point that social relations are "mysteriously endowed with an objective, even autonomous character."[50] Here the idea of autonomy alludes to something more than the eighteenth-century separation of mechanical arts from the fine arts, and the subsequent autonomy of architecture from the pre-modern political and cultural institutions. Leo Marx's discussion of

autonomy speaks for the ways commodities "appear" independent from their use-value, and thus sublimate the object within the aesthetic of fetishism. Up-rooted from "Real," to use Žižek's word, telecommunication technologies enforce the aesthetic of theatricalization; seductive and autonomous forms floating in a field empty of purpose and material, waiting to be rendered as form. It is in this context that Eisenman's critical practice is channeled into a formalistic game, thus yielding to the aesthetic of commodity fetishism. His most recent works, however, are appealing, beautiful, and cool![51] These projects also celebrate the spectacle and the virtual victory of ideology. Eisenman's architecture also recalls what *écriture* meant to Roland Barthes,[52] the "morality of form," the zone of freedom where personal signature connotes nothing but the thirst for identity.

3.18   Eisenman Architects, City of Culture of Galicia, Santiago de Compostela, Spain, 1999– ongoing. Digital diagram. Image courtesy of Eisenman Architects, New York City

It remains to be seen in what direction the tropes emerging in Eisenman's most recent work, the Cultural Center at Santiago de Compostela, Barcelona, Spain, will lead (Figure 3.18). For one, *technique* is used in this project to recall the most archaic, the merging of architecture into the landscape more vigorously than the subject was treated in his previous work. What is involved in Eisenman's turn to the surface topography is the possibility of a more radical departure from tropes central to humanist architecture, the singularity of geometry, the idea of frontality, and the anthropomorphism that he had wished to deconstruct in his early experimental work.

NOTES

1   See the analogies Luca Galofaro makes between Peter Eisenman's design in the Aronoff Center and Piranesi. Galofaro, "A Starting Point," in *Digital Eisenman* (Basel: Birkhauser, 1999).

2   James S. Ackerman, "Architectural Principles in the Age of Humanism," *Harvard Design Magazine* (fall 1988): 64.

3   Colin Rowe, "Introduction," in *Five Architects* (New York: Wittenborn, 1972), 3–7.

4   On this subject see Gevork Hartoonian, *Modernity and Its Other* (College Station, TX: A&M Texas University, 1997).

5   Peter Eisenman, *Giuseppe Terragni: Transformations, Decompositions, Critique* (New York: Monacelli Press, 2003), 33. For Gevork Hartoonian's review of Eisenman's book see *Architectural Theory Review*, 8:2 (2003): 232–6.

6   Peter Eisenman, *Giuseppe Terragni*, 2003, 115.

7   Peter Eisenman, *Giuseppe Terragni*, 2003, 34.

8   Here I am benefiting from James Ackerman's review of Wittkower's book. See Ackerman, "Architectural Principles in the Age of Humanism," 1988, 65.

9   I am thinking of Peter Eisenman's "The End of Classical: The End of the Beginning; the End of the End," *Perspecta* 21 (summer 1984): 154–72.

10   This project is discussed in Gevork Hartoonian, *Modernity and Its Other*, 1997.

11   The idea of "weak-form" was not only driven by J. Derrida's writing, but also Gianni Vattimo's discourse on "weak-thought." For Vattimo, see *The End of Modernity* (Baltimore, MD: Johns Hopkins University Press, 1988).

12   Peter Eisenman, "Diagram: An Original Scene of Writing," in *Diagram Diaries* (New York: Universe Publishing, 1999), 26–43.

13   Peter Eisenman, "Diagram: An Original Scene of Writing," 1999, 30.

14   Peter Eisenman, "Zones of Undecidability: The Interstitial Figure," in Cynthia Davidson, ed., *Anybody* (New York: Anyone Corporation, 1997), 240–47. For Yve-Alain Bois and Rosalind E. Krauss see *Formless: A User's Guide* (New York: Zone Books, 1997).

15   Peter Eisenman, "En Terror Firma: In Trails of Grotextes," in Artie Graafland, ed., *Peter Eisenman: Recent Projects* (Amsterdam: Sun, 1989), 23.

16   Silvia Kolbowski, "Fringe Benefits," in *Eleven Authors in Search of a Building* (New York: Monacelli Press, 1996), 234.

17   Kenneth Frampton, "Eisenman Revisited: Running Interference," in Artie Graafland, ed., *Peter Eisenman*, 1989, 47–62, 60.

18   Peter Eisenman, "Zones of Undecidability," 1997, 32.

19   Christopher Alexander, *Notes on the Synthesis Form* (Cambridge, MA: Harvard University Press, 1964).

20   Fredric Jameson, "'End of Art' or 'End of History,'" in *The Cultural Turn* (New York: Verso, 1998), 73–92.

21   Peter Eisenman, *Giuseppe Terragni*, 2003, 292.

22   Robert Venturi, "Contradictory Levels: The Phenomenon of 'Both-And' in Architecture,"
      in *Complexity and Contradiction in Architecture* (New York: The Modern Museum of Art,
      1966), 30–45. See also my reading of the idea of "both-and" in Gevork Hartoonian,
      Modernity and Its Other, 1977.

23   Quoted in Andrew Benjamin, *Architectural Philosophy* (London: The Athlone Press,
      2000), 182.

24   Peter Burger, *Theory of the Avant-garde* (Minneapolis, MN: University of Minnesota
      Press, 1984), 80. For a discussion that concerns the differences between American
      avant-garde of the 1970s and the historical avant-garde see Andreas Huyssen,
      "The Search for Tradition: Avant-Garde and Post-modernism in the 1970s," *New
      German Critique* 22 (winter 1981): 23–40. For a critique of Burger see K. Michael Hays,
      Architecture's Desire (Cambridge, MA: The MIT Press, 2010). For Gevork Hartoonian's
      review of Hays's book see *Architectural Science Review*, 53:2 (2010): 276–7.

25   Slavoj Žižek, *The Sublime Object of Ideology* (New York: Verso, 1995), 61.

26   Hal Foster, "What is Neo about the Neo-Avant-Garde," *October* 70 (1994): 5–32.

27   K. Michael Hays, *Architecture's Desire*, 2010, 11.

28   For an extended discussion of these issues see, Gevork Hartoonian, *Ontology of
      Construction*, 1994, 68–80.

29   For a comprehensive discussion of the tectonic in Carlo Scarpa, see Kenneth Frampton,
      Studies in Tectonic Culture (Cambridge, MA: The MIT Press, 1995), 299–334.

30   Peter Eisenman, "A Conversation with Peter Eisenman," *El Croquis* 83 (1997): 6–20.

31   I am thinking along the lines of Yve Alain Bois' introduction to "Sergei M. Eisenstein:
      Montage and Architecture," *Assemblage* 10 (December 1987): 111–31. See also Yve
      Alain Bois, "A Picturesque Stroll around Clara-Clara," *October* 29 (summer 1984):
      33–62, where the author explores the play of "parallax" in Richard Serra's work with
      concluding remarks on Le Corbusier's Villa Savoye and the notion of *promenade
      architecturale*.

32   Peter Eisenman, "Vision Unfolding: Architecture in the Age of Electronic Media," in Luca
      Galofaro, *Digital Eisenman*, 1999, 87. The title of the essay recalls Walter Benjamin's
      famous essay "The Work of Art in the Age of Mechanical Reproduction." Reflecting on
      the historicity of mechanistic vision inscribed in perspective, Eisenman attempts to
      discuss the architectonic implications of the fold for a different vision of architecture's
      interior space. On contemporary discourse on vision and visuality, and its implication
      for Le Corbusier's *promenade architecturale*, see Gevork Hartoonian, "The Limelight of
      the House Machine," *The Journal of Architecture* 6, 1 (spring 2001): 53–80.

33   Gaston Bachelard, *The Poetics of Space* (Boston, MA: Beacon Press, 1969).

34   Here I am benefiting from Hal Foster, *The Art-Architecture Complex* (London: Verso,
      2011), 134–65.

35   Quoted in an interview with Robert Lock, July 27, 2004.

36   Peter Eisenman, "Interview with Peter Eisenman," *Zodiac* 15 (March/August 1996):
      105–15, 107.

37   See this author's discussion in the introduction to Gevork Hartoonian, *Ontology of
      Construction*, 1994.

38   Peter Eisenman, "Eleven Points on Knowledge and Wisdom," in Cynthia Davidson, ed.,
      AnyWise (Cambridge, MA: The MIT Press, 1996), 49–51.

39   I have discussed this subject in "Critical Practice," *Architectural Theory Review* 7, 1 (2002): 1–14.

40   Quoted in Fritz Neumeyer, *The Artless Word* (Cambridge, MA: The MIT Press, 1991), 207. According to Neumeyer, Mies van der Rohe was influenced by Romano Guardini who saw "human existential conditions in dialectical opposition between 'dynamic and static,' 'duration and flux,' and 'position and change'" (Neumeyer, 1991, 196–236).

41   Interview with Robert Lock, 2004.

42   Slavoj Žižek, *The Sublime*, 1995, 45.

43   On this subject see Gevork Hartoonian, *Modernity and Its Other*, 1997.

44   See Peter Eisenman's introductory remarks in, *Eisenman Inside Out* (New Haven, CT: Yale University Press, 2004), xi.

45   Peter Eisenman, "Vision Unfolding," 1999, 84–9.

46   Peter Eisenman, "Processes of the Interstitial," *El Croquis* 83 (1997): 21–35, 29.

47   See Martin Heidegger, "The Question Concerning Technology," in *The Question Concerning Technology and Other Essays* (New York: Harper, 1977), 3–35.

48   Massimo Cacciari, *Architecture and Nihilism: On the Philosophy of Modern Architecture* (New Haven, CT: Yale University Press, 1993), 149.

49   Massimo Cacciari, *Architecture and Nihilism*, 1993, 172.

50   Leo Marx, "Technology: The Emergence of a Hazardous Concept," *Social Research* 64, 3 (fall 1997): 965–88. While praising Martin Heidegger, Leo Marx insists on the socio-political aspect of technology rather than its metaphysical. He highlights the extent to which technology is infused with everyday life to the point that we are unable to define it and see its perils.

51   On Peter Eisenman's most recent work, see the final chapter in this volume.

52   Roland Barthes, *Writing Degree Zero* (New York: The Noonday Press, 1968).

4

Bernard Tschumi: Return of the Object

Peter Eisenman's search for autonomy of form involves recoding the tropes of humanist architecture. His deconstruction of architectural themes that have accumulated since the Renaissance uses a strategy derived from textual analysis, one that dispenses with the importance of the ontology of construction, the art of building. Indeed, a crusade against architecture is the thread running through neo-avant-garde architecture.[1] In contrast to Eisenman's "play" with the metaphysics of architectural discourse, Bernard Tschumi thinks of architecture as being in line with conceptual art. During the mid-1960s, the institutionalization of the modernist vision of art and architecture gave rise to deteriorating conditions which, according to Charles Harrison, launched a two-fold task: "the first requirement was to establish a critique of the aesthetics of Modernism. This entailed the development of appropriate art-theoretical and art-historical tools. The second requirement was to establish a critique of the politics of Modernism. This entailed the application of socio-economic forms of analysis."[2] This artistic development of the 1970s projects the object into the dialogue between art and language, the architectonic implication of which is to repress themes endemic in the modernist vision of the object. To do away with the conventions of approaching the work based on its sensual properties, its relationship between form and content, the conceptual in architecture concerns the process and the object. Here the object is "both the form and the meaning simultaneously."[3] To this end, the conceptual in architecture involves the synthetic dimension of form; the relationship between various elements that informs the structure of its form. Conceptual architecture, therefore, involves an *a priori* design intention that not only informs the design process, but also structures the final result, i.e., the object. Underlining this attitude is a return to the theme of nihilism whose devaluation of architecture aims at an object that is not formalistic, and yet—like Michel Foucault's reading of *Ceci n'est pas une pipe*[4]—seeks to shake the image of architecture held in the eye of the beholder. Tschumi's contribution to contemporary architecture has to do with his theoretical distance from the formalism of Colin Rowe, on the one hand, and the Eisenmanesque deconstruction of Rowe's formalism, on the other. As we noted in the previous chapter, Eisenman's return to tropes of humanism had to do with Rudolf Wittkower's book, *Architectural Principles of the Age of Humanism* (1949).[5] The book challenged George Scott's reading of Renaissance architecture, paving the way for a formalistic interpretation of architecture which will become significant for architectural theory.[6]

In Tschumi's work, *transgression* of the normative elements of architecture is achieved not by fragmentation or the technique of shock, but through the insertion of "event" into the space separating the object from its signification. Disjunction between architecture and its institutional hegemony involves emptying the object of its conventional connotative context, and reinterpreting a given program free from its formal contingencies. These two strategies suspend the axiom of "form follows function," and charge architecture with a sense of space that is pregnant with "event." In this development, the rehabilitation of earlier avant-garde work such as constructivism and situationist "terror" is utilized not for their original ends, but as a radical choice against postmodern historicism and the formalistic play practiced by some members of the New York Five Architects. Interestingly enough, Hugh D. Hudson Jr. has this to say about neo-avant-garde use of languages that are associable with the Russian constructivists:

> The Western architects carried revolutionary Soviet architecture home not in
> its genuine revolutionary form—as a series of social problems centered on
> the question of how to organize human activity within and around the built
> environment in such a manner as to transform human interaction from capitalist
> competition to socialist cooperation—but rather as merely another style of
> art, as a collection of glass rectangles within which corporate chiefs could sit
> comfortably while watching the urban poor on the streets below.[7]

The specificity of Tschumi's architecture, however, has to do, I claim here, with a sense of objectivity where matter-of-factness compromises the historicity of the *Neue Sachlichkeit* with the theatricalization that prevails in the present culture of spectacle. What this means is that instead of demystifying "return" by strategies that emphasize the process of design, Tschumi attempts to recode the idea of objectivity in the purview of tactile and spatial sensibilities that are central to the concept of return.

The critical nature of Tschumi's work presupposes a theoretical paradigm different from modernism. What needs to be looked at here are the architectonic implications of a major theoretical shift, from the tradition in which the critic or the historian would mediate between a work and its signification to a postmodernist situation where the architect sets the theoretical premises of any criticism addressing his or her work.[8] Thematic dualities such as theory/practice, form/content, and subject/object are rethought within the limits of architecture's disciplinary history, and in the theoretical space opened by themes developed in other disciplines.

The spatial opening I am alluding to has its own historicity. In the nineteenth century, modernization had already expanded architects' horizons of sight and construction. Among other reactions to this historical opening, Gottfried Semper's position is different; he mapped architecture in the vicissitudes of industries that at a glance have the least to do with the art of building. His writings on style and the origin of architecture embody a sense of spatiality that should be read as part of a larger process of recoding the mental and physical space of modernity. One might suggest that postmodernity means, in the first place, an expansion of the disjunctive spatiality (at work since the early years of modernization) beyond economic and technical domains to include the cultural. Not only has this last development distanced us from the ethos of modern architecture, but more importantly, it has drastically transformed the present everyday life to the point where the totality nestled at the heart of Semper's discourse on theatricality is no longer sustainable.[9]

And yet, what differentiates the present cultural discourse from modernism should also be addressed. Among many other developments, the 1966 publication of Robert Venturi's *Complexity and Contradiction in Architecture* initiated a different approach to modern architecture.[10] During those years, modern architecture was checked and reexamined by extraordinary paradigms—most notably, literary paradigms such as semiotics and structuralism. Communication theories and phenomenology also mapped the crisis of architecture differently.[11] The New York Five, for example, approached architecture as more than a mechanistic interpretation of the relationship between form and function, presenting it as a conceptual phenomenon devoid of "purpose." Theirs was deeply motivated by formalistic issues that had been at work since the De Stijl group and the Russian constructivists. Eisenman was among those who first charged architecture with theories of semiology, and then straitjacketed it with Jacques Derrida's deconstruction theory. On the other side of the Atlantic, influenced by the student uprisings of the 1960s and the work of Archigram, Tschumi framed architecture in the light of concepts such as "disjunction" and "event,"[12] embedded in cinematic experience. This much is clear from his critical reflections on postmodernism: "This perverted form of history borrowed from semiotics the ability to read layers of interpretation, but reduced architecture to a system of surface signs, at the expense of the reciprocal, indifferent or even conflictive relationship of spaces and events."[13] However, in differentiating Tschumi's work from the Five and other postmodernists, the fact remains that the architecture of the post-1960s was touched by the idea of the "death of author," and its implications for "design" is worth examining.[14]

To question the role of the author does not mean literary "death," or the banishment of meaning in architecture. The idea of the death of the subject rather speaks for the end of the "grand narrative"—a subject dear to the project of the Enlightenment—whose absence in postmodern discourse has opened a space where "theory" undermines the limits enforced by history and disciplinary considerations. This move from history to theory has given architects the chance to resume a different rapport with their subject matter. Tschumi's meditations on the Hegelian supplement and the death of architecture, Michael Hays writes,

> are less motivated by the end-of-art debates, already well rehearsed if not over by 1975, than by a different dawning awareness of the particular historical fatedness of architecture itself—of a specific cultural production, perhaps the most deeply social of all, now inevitably suffering its own unique, historically determined recontainment, reterritorialization, implosion after more than two centuries of opening, transgression and revolt.[15]

This development has made the task of the architecture critic difficult. Instead of

> *analyzing the concrete formal and compositional aspects of a work, the critic*
> *now has to develop a meta-narrative in order to disclose the architect's operative*
> *mode of thinking. From now on, architecture will be the formal result of one*
> *analytical procedure among many other possible ones by which an architect can*
> *deconstruct the metaphysics of architecture.*[16]

Reading Tschumi's work, Sylvia Lavin makes the following observation:

> *Two developments that may appear to move in opposite directions have together*
> *left contemporary architecture in a kind of discursive black hole: the tendency*
> *to pursue theoretical issues within an increasingly distant historical context, a*
> *development initiated by Manfredo Tafuri; and the total instrumentalization of*
> *theory as operative design method.*[17]

Therefore, neither the tropes of this or that style, nor the formal articulation of a given function, not even the symbolic or semiotic representation of an idea—none of these invigorate the realm of design today. The nullification of history and themes evolved through architectural practice, at least during the 1980s, has shifted architects' attention either to interdisciplinary discourse or to the tropes that were marginal for modernists. One implication of this unfolding is that "through careful efforts, one can disclose the repressed contents of a work and gain access to a new interpretation."[18] If this is suggestive of an *object* whose actual realization necessitates the banishment of the architect's (author's) design aptitudes, then, Tschumi is right to claim:

> *To achieve architecture without resorting to design is an ambition often in the*
> *minds of those who go through the incredible effort of putting together buildings.*
> *Behind this objective is the desire to achieve the obvious clarity of the inevitable,*
> *a structure in which the concept becomes architecture itself. In this approach,*
> *there is no need to design "new" abstract shapes or historically grounded*
> *forms, whether modern, vernacular, or Victorian, according to one's ideological*
> *allegiance; here the idea or concept would result in all the architectural, spatial,*
> *or urbanistic effects one could dream of without reliance on proportions, style,*
> *or aesthetics. Instead of designing seductive shapes or forms, one would posit an*
> *axiom or principle from which everything would derive.*[19]

Nevertheless, the axiom dearest to Tschumi is "programming," if understood not as an end in itself, but a departing point for an architecture of disjunction. Louis Martin, for one, traces Tschumi's early fascination with the concept of "paradigm" as defined by Thomas Kuhn. According to Martin, Tschumi "replaced the word 'science' of the original text [*The Structure of Scientific Revolutions*] with the word "architecture" in his own" without mentioning Kuhn's book as the main reference. In Tschumi's defense, Martin goes further, suggesting that since Kuhn's original idea "in the field of science" had been "integrated into architecture" by Tschumi's text, and since this grafted paragraph had been appropriated into Tschumi's architecture, therefore, "Tschumi's text remained autonomous." Hence the equation—architecture is science—has existed since the beginning of Tschumi's formative years. The idea of "axiom" in relation to architecture reads like the replacement of scientific truth with epistemology in the post-Kuhnian age, both of which are efforts to re-examine, break away, and somehow still carry on the project of modernity.[20] Reinterpreting a given program, Tschumi's architecture is concerned with the fabrication of space, the body's motion in space, and the space-time-program axiom.[21] Through *reprogramming* (deconstruction), Tschumi turns these rather abstract themes into concrete and site-specific "building elements." The body, space, and event unravel a peculiar sense of objectivity, the architectonic implications of which I intend to explore in several of Tschumi's projects.

THE GARDEN OF FOLLIES

On April 8, 1982, the late François Mitterrand announced an international competition for a "21st-century Park" to be located at the heart of a working-class district near Paris. In December of the same year, Tschumi, then a 37-year-old artist/architect and instructor at the Cooper Union, won the first prize out of 472 entries from 37 different nationalities.[22] The Parc de la Villette, "the largest discontinuous building in the world," was Tschumi's first built project and according to him, the first building worthy of the name "architecture of disjunction."[23]

An earlier competition had been announced on January 22, 1976, during the presidency of Valéry Giscard d'Estaing, that involved planning a 55-hectare park, la Villette. Different concepts of urban park, time, and program mark the differences between these two competitions. During the 1970s, the heyday of postmodern architecture and urbanism, the city was still treated as a monument whose image was shaped by the fine composition of many fractured urban parts. Such a romanticized urban typology was best depicted in the Krier brothers' projects, where the design aimed at patching up the fragmented metropolis. For them, the collective memory of the past and its representation was seen as a major factor in enforcing any order. This was a logical reaction, for some architects, against the brutal urban renewal projects that mowed down miles of existing urban fabrics only to replace them with an instant pop-up version of commercial landscape. Whether an aestheticized planning filled with Arcadian civility and bourgeois elegance could reconcile the broken promise of utopian modernism was the right question to ask in the light of the postmodernist approach to the city. The irony, at least in the case of the la Villette competition, was that a lush urban park packed with bulging vegetation, picturesque pathways, and meadows running through the network of canals and parkways was also the vision of the French state officials.

The program for the 1976 competition called for a general plan to create a park and to patch up built-up areas, and to keep the main focus on filling an "open space"—the land released after eviction and demolition—with the French state's vision of a park. It is rather telling to examine the entry projects for the 1976 competition (published in *Architectural Design Profile 15*) as an illustration of how much things would change in just six years. However, for the 1976 competition, Tschumi submitted a Baroque plan, emphasizing fortification along the northeastern border of la Villette and a bar

4.1   Bernard Tschumi, Parc de la Villette competition entry, 1976. Image courtesy of Bernard Tschumi Architects, New York City

of low-rise courtyard houses hugging the curved periphery of Paris (Figure 4.1). In the introduction to his submission, titled "Le Jardin de Don Juan,"[24] Tschumi portrays the modern architect as a Don Juan who would sell his/her formal solution with seductive metaphors. Tschumi traces this line of thinking in the urban vision of Marc-Antoine Laugier, Le Notre, and even Le Corbusier, to demonstrate how since the eighteenth century architects have tried to mask the fact that the city has become a battlefield for order and disorder, chaos and regularity, rationality and sensuality.

Tschumi reminds us of Laugier's conviction that "one must look at a town as a forest," and that "he who knows how to design a park could conceive a plan for a city."[25] This analogy, or assemblage of garden with the city, attains its modernist vision in Le Corbusier's *Urbanisme*, where the alleged idea of "mask" combines variety with uniformity in detail.[26] Against these historical references, Tschumi recounts the eagerness of architects in planning a visionary landscape that would give rise to a mutual exclusion between existing conditions and its potential interpretations. To avoid this dilemma, Tschumi renounces representation and makes analogies between representation and mask. According to him, although a mask might enhance the material quality of the appearance, "by its very presence, it says that, in the background, there is something else."[27] This allusion to "appearance," or rather the "disappearance" of all other possibilities, allows the "Don Juan architect" to indulge in "games of interior reflection and fulfillment of hidden desires."[28] Pointing to the seductive power of the mask, Tschumi rejects utopian solutions based on utility and reason, arguing that these solutions exclude sensuality and eroticism. Pursuing excess in pleasure rather than seeking pleasure in excess, he sees the ultimate pleasure of architecture in "that impossible moment when an architectural act, brought to excess, reveals both the traces of reason and the immediate experience of space."[29] Contextualizing this aspect of Tschumi's work, Michael Hays sees a historical connection between the 1970s quest for autonomy and the contemporary tendency for the "production of effect."[30] This much is clear from postmodernists' criticism of the modernist general tendency for formal homogeneity, and the justification of the postmodernist juxtaposition of different languages as a rhetorical source. Polarization of "effect" achieved a critical dimension outside the discipline of architecture, most importantly in Roland Barthes' *The Pleasure of the Text* (1973). To break away from structuralism's binary system, Barthes highlighted the split between the text (object) and its reading (writer/reader subject). He wrote that only a subtle subversion, a "third term," can escape the structural paradigm linking the apparent forms with the contested potentialities. In literature this "third term" is pleasure, as argued by Barthes: "The text of pleasure is not necessarily the text that recounts pleasures ... The pleasure of representation is not attached to its object ... one could say that the site of textual pleasure is not the relation of mimic and model (imitative relation) but solely that of dupe and mimic (relation of desire, of production)."[31] Barthes' book was inspirational for Tschumi's search for pleasure in architecture. According to Hays, Tschumi's discourse on event offers "a possible third term between the contradiction of autonomy and negation: it is both autonomy and negation and, indeed, should reveal the productivity of the contradiction even as it dissolves the contradiction."[32] Thus the actualization of pleasure demands manipulation of the space that rests between "mask" and the building.

Tschumi's proposal for the 1976 competition entry was a hybrid of Piranesi's Il Campo Marzio dell'antica Rome, Parc Monceau de Carmontelle, and Parc de Versailles. The design strategy posits architecture as a language game that is not in search of meaning, but maps a site where conflict overcomes order, where concept collides with the movement of the body in space. However, in 1976, even after the successful transposition of Barthesian "pleasure" and its "subtle subversion"— eroticism—into "Le Jardin de Don Juan," the pleasure of the "mask" still could not find its full expression. It is in Le Fresnoy, as we will see shortly, that Tschumi finally conceives architecture as a place for the production and dissemination of artwork though blended with didactic taste.[33]

The International Competition of 1982 called for a new model of urban park appropriate to the coming century. Surrounded by railways and highways, the 55 hectares of the Parc de la Villette is marked by two perpendicular waterways: the Ourcq Canal to the east of Paris, running into the suburbs, and the St. Denis Canal, which extends from one loop of the Seine to the other. The circulation of the Parc is a composite of an orthogonal system expressing pedestrian movement, and several seemingly random curvilinear routes called "Thematic Gardens Paths." The first root connects the two Paris gates (east–west) to subway stations (north– south), forming a cross along two canals with direct access to the most frequent activities. The thematic garden path links various parts of the park to form a circuit. These lines are given architectonic expression by a north–west 5-meter-wide covered structure with an express lane for mass movement at park level. And south–west a 5-meter-wide bridge structure provides two levels of walkway, which slice the park into two zones at the lower level, and reconnect visually at the higher level for a broader vista. The straight lines are for speedy movement with maximum protection, the curvilinear routes are for pleasure with maximum varieties. The ribbons of the thematic garden paths allude to William Kent's picturesque layout and are joined by different surfaces which are infused with assorted thematic gardens. These surfaces (planes?) are the receivers and containers of the regularity of a grid and the flux of the movements; they provide horizontal spaces for play, games, markets, mass entertainment, etc. In the shapes of circle, triangle, square, and free curve, these surfaces are each determined programmatically: grass for prairie, stabilized surfaces for light athletics, and so forth.

Instead of emphasizing the urban greenery, the 1982 competition aimed at turning an edge condition—both geographically and ethnically—into a center of activity, creating parallel networks where "[m]etropolitan unity disintegrates into plurality and peripheries," as described by the initiator of the program, François Barré. There were intense and often quarrelsome debates throughout the process over whether to combine wilderness and geometry or to secure a man-made landscape; to guarantee the stability of a natural setting, or to reinstate a system of values, and finally, how to extend the spirit of science and technology into the next millennium.

Mitterrand desired a complex and imaginative ensemble that would incorporate the City of Music and the National Museum of Science and Technology, and

Industry into the future park to compose a "little city" within the city of Paris. Thus a new type of space had to be invented and Tschumi's entry provided the best solution for several reasons: it recognized the need to de-structure and de-center programmatic needs; it dispersed the sheer scale of the required facilities; it treated the periphery as urban landscape rather than a boundary separating the cultural from the natural; and most importantly, it planted the "follies" as constantly evolving spaces to allow superimposition or juxtaposition between function, form, and event. We read in Tschumi's proposal:

4.2   Eisenman Architects, Cannaregio Project, 1978. Plan. Image courtesy of Peter Eisenman Architects, New York City

> We aim neither to change styles while retaining a traditional content, nor to fit the proposed program into a conventional mould, whether neo-classical, neo-romantic or neo-modernist. Rather, our project is motivated by the most constructive principle within the legitimate "history" of architecture, by which new programmatic developments and inspirations result in new typologies. Our ambition is to create a new model in which program form, and ideology all play integral roles.[34]

Superimposing an abstract system of geometry—point, line, and plane—over the existing condition, Tschumi envisioned a "degree zero" situation that would soften the binary conflict between program and site, and would mediate between concept, program, and all given constraints. His proposal combines a network of paths that are punctuated by freestanding structures. The composition recalls the grid system Peter Eisenman employed in the Cannaregio project (1978) (Figure 4.2). Eisenman wanted to expose the "constraining" or "framing" power of geometry on architecture. Articulating the void left by modernism and the rationality epitomized in Le Corbusier's Venice Hospital project (planned for the same site), Eisenman plots Le Corbusier's grid throughout the site. A series of square holes punctuates the intersections of the grid where the ground is excavated to expose the virgin earth as a *tabula rasa*. These square holes were occupied by several pink—(or Venetian red)—objects that according to Eisenman "contained nothing upon close examination": they only contaminated the squares.[35] Inserting "theory" into the process of conceptualization and design, both Tschumi and Eisenman expose and thus displace the doctrine of modernity. However, the differences between these two architects' strategies should be underlined.

Expanding the horizon of abstraction beyond the scope of modern architecture, Eisenman framed the ontology of architecture within a chain of empty signs. His re-writing of the avant-garde doctrine introduced a severe architecture that could collapse under its own weight. Tschumi, instead, dispensed with the metaphysics of a form-giving process and instead registered the architectonic expression of the body-in-motion, and event-space within and beyond the limits of architecture. According to him, both the formalism and regionalism of the 1970s dismiss "the multiplicity of heterogeneous discourses, the constant interaction between movement, sensual experience, and conceptual acrobatics that refuse the parallel

4.3   Bernard Tschumi, Parc de la Villette, 1982. Photograph courtesy of Bernard Tschumi Architects, New York City

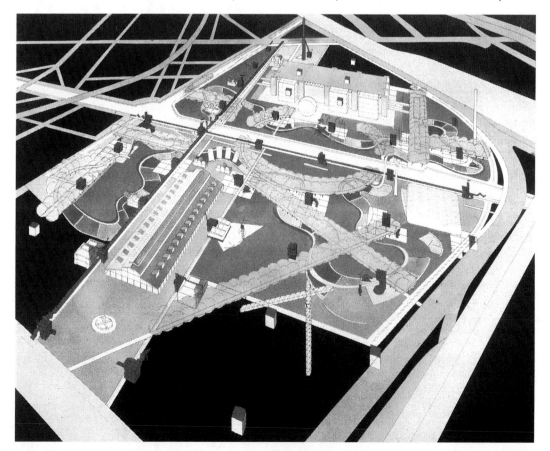

with the visual arts."[36] Tschumi's statement speaks for architecture's tendency to internalize ideas and concepts that are extraneous to the discipline. If the power of architecture resides in its limits, then one could claim that Tschumi activates the energy resting in the zone between architecture and its limits of signification.[37] In Parc de la Villette (Figure 4.3), the abstract system of point-line-plane shields the site beyond the exigencies of the context, yet this network is thickened and given its formal body through time-event-space to use terms suggestive of the conceptual and physical traces of the body-in-space.

The red "follies" punctuate the entire site at 120-meter intervals, as the point-grid coordinate system. Each of these $10 \times 10 \times 10$-meter cubes offers a variation upon one theme, a neutral space waiting to be programmed and transformed. Constructed with reinforced concrete and clad in red-enameled aluminum panels, the de-materialized follies become the instant forming collage or pastiche of signs that makes room for the event to take place. And yet, in the transgression of the classical and modern canons, the follies fall somewhere between the two realms of architectural and machine objects. Tschumi's machines are not alien objects: they are disintegrated and incomplete cubes, each offering a different solution to the problem of function and structure. Tschumi maps these objects in a structure of points, grids, and planes.

Tschumi's project combines Paul Klee's ideas of composition with Le Corbusier's vision of the city. But where Le Corbusier's Plan Vosion would undermine the cultural values of the *status quo*, Tschumi maps la Villette as a possibility already present in modern architecture. This esteem for the "Other" of the same favors *difference* rather than dirtying one's hands with the invention of new forms. Echoing Mies, Tschumi wrote, "I am not interested in form. I attack the system of meaning. I am for the idea of structure and syntax, but no meaning."[38] One cannot dismiss the presence of Wassily Kandinsky's *Point and Line to Plane* (1926) in Tschumi's strategy of system of event-movement-space. It is also impossible to avoid detecting the Russian constructivist's ghost in the red follies spotting the Parc. No matter how hard the avant-garde struggles to get away with history, the latter comes back to "mask" the maker's original "sin"—an act of intervention—as evidenced by the frequent "return of the repressed." Tschumi's appropriation of Iakov Chernikhov's drawing for *The Construction of Architectural and Machine Forms* (1931) is a telling tale in modernists' utilization of the idea of found object; itself a symptom among many of the other "returns" endemic to postmodern conditions.

However, once history is suspended, the process of disjunction reduces the object to an empty shell in need of new life. The red-painted metal cladding of the follies is indeed a transparent mask; it hides as much as it reveals, in terms of both the form's underlying structure, as well as the form's dormant history, i.e., constructivist objects (Figure 4.4). The excess (theatricality?) here breaks the limits forced by the dialogue between structure and ornament. Here ornament stretches its body to infuse into the thin layer of the red cladding. Thus the body of architecture is immunized and the red paint ossifies the historical avant-garde's political intentions. There is a price to be paid for any transgression: the playful constructs of the Russian constructivists spoke for the pleasure sought in changing

4.4   Bernard Tschumi, Parc de la Villette, Folly. Photograph by J.M. Monthiers,
courtesy of Bernard Tschumi Architects, New York City

the mode of production; in Parc de la Villette, the pleasure has shifted from the antinomies of the production system to the discrete realm of consumption.[39] The body is charged with erotic sensations as one wanders around, within, and moves up or down the follies. Gone also is the collective body, whose education and emancipation from the toil of labor was the goal of at least some circles of the Russian constructivists. Their failure has made room for the current neo-avant-garde to pursue a hedonistic notion of pleasure that ends in the theatricalization of space—a step heading directly into the fetishism of commodities.

LE FRESNOY: MASKING THE ROOF (1992–98)

Bernard Tschumi won the competition for Le Fresnoy in February 1992 (Figure 4.5). The proposed program by the National Studio for Contemporary Arts in Tourcoing fitted perfectly with Tschumi's major theoretical concerns. Quite apart from the interdisciplinary nature of Le Fresnoy, the chosen site was an immense popular entertainment complex in operation from 1905 to the early 1970s. Among the existing buildings, a thousand-seat cinema and a huge roller-skating rink with a metal-frame roof dominated the site. These empty shells, ruins if you wish, provided an ideal site for Tschumi to test his early ideas in a context totally different from Villette.

Dwelling on the experience of cinematography, *The Manhattan Transcripts* presents "architecture of disjunction" in a diagram superimposing the gridiron blocks of Manhattan over the plane of Central Park. In this process, "the geometrical and rectangular blocks of the Manhattan grid begin to interpenetrate, to superimpose themselves on the organic contours of Central Park, before transforming into something radically different."[40] The concept recalls a previous exercise, a montage of the Rietveld-Schröder House, in Utrecht, the Netherlands, with Palladio's Villa

4.5   Bernard Tschumi, Le Fresnoy National Contemporary Arts, Tourcoing, France, 1991–97. Photograph by author

4.6   Bernard
Tschumi, Le
Fresnoy National
Contemporary
Arts, 1991–97.
Plan drawing.
Image courtesy of
Bernard Tschumi
Architects, New
York City

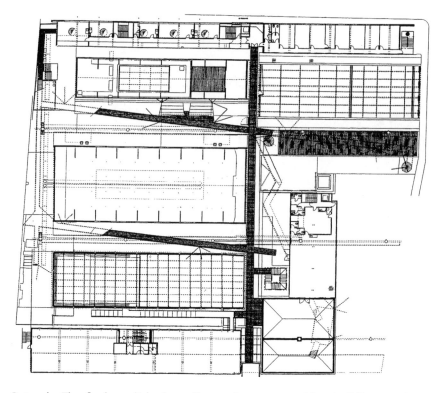

Rotonda. The final result had no direct references to either buildings, and yet looking closely, the formal traces of both villas in the final composition cannot be dismissed. This early exercise is the underpinning strategy in Le Fresnoy: Tschumi charges the existing buildings with a different life, and grafts new institutional and technical "bodies" onto objects that already have been dismembered from their previous organism.

4.7   Bernard
Tschumi, Le
Fresnoy National
Contemporary
Arts, 1991–97.
Photograph by
Peter Mauss,
courtesy of
Bernard Tschumi
Architects, New
York City

Tschumi's solution is straightforward but complex: He inserts two new volumes (perpendicular to each other) into the empty lot of the existing L-shaped buildings (Figure 4.6). The kernel of Tschumi's concept involves a roof-plane that hovers over the entire complex. His proposal recalls Mies van der Rohe's two photomontages: the Chicago Convention Center designed in 1953, and the Concert Hall of 1942. In the latter, the freestanding figure of the roof is dramatized by the invisibility of the structural supports. Standing under the roof of Mies's Concert Hall, a person could experience an in-between space that floats within and around the horizontal

and vertical planes. Nevertheless, Tschumi's concept of roof is different; it operates like a mask with visible connections to the body beneath. Looking at the presentation drawings as well as experiencing the actual building, one cannot but think of the roof as a mask covering an upward looking face (Figure 4.7). The surface of this mask is shaped, cut out, and framed in response to the actual needs of the

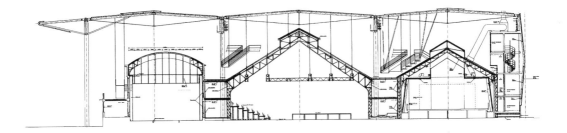

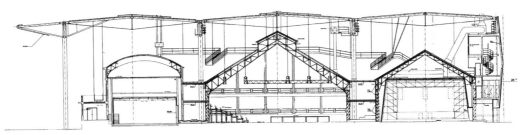

body beneath. Tschumi's operative approach does not stop here: he deconstructs the very idea of mask itself. It is in this project, 15 years after "Le Jardin de Don Juan," that Tschumi, I believe, has finally achieved the architectonic equivalent of a Barthesian "third term"—pleasure without a cause.

The surface of the mask-like roof is devoid of any representational or symbolic effects. Moreover, contrary to the conventional idea of mask, Tschumi radicalizes the space resting between the mask and what is masked. This in-between space, whose floor is the roof of the existing building, its ceiling compromising the surface that covers the entire complex, is the site of the "event." The space also houses the media technologies needed to energize the existing ruins. It also provides room for stairs and catwalks that operate almost like the infrastructure of an urban landscape. These "service" elements are suspended from the roof, stretching up and down and around the existing buildings without touching them. Looking at the section drawings of this building (Figure 4.8), one is reminded of the metal fire-escape stairs that hang from the solid masonry walls of Manhattan's townhouses; it is also a reminder of the sense of placeless space envisioned in Piranesi's *Carceri*.

Through disjunction, Tschumi embellishes and elevates a marginal space to the level of an ornament. In his words, "This extraordinary space derived from the concept appears as a 'gift' or 'supplement:' a space where anything might happen, a place of experimentation; a place located on the margins. This in-between space quickly became a fundamental condition of the project."[41] The space between mask and the face becomes the site of accidental events and bodily pleasure.[42] It also charges architecture with qualities beyond its conventional limits. Here "begins the articulation between the space of senses and the space of society, the dances and gestures that combine the representation of space and the space of representation."[43]

4.8   Bernard Tschumi, Le Fresnoy National Contemporary Arts, 1991–97. Section drawing. Image courtesy of Bernard Tschumi Architects, New York City

4.9   Louis Kahn, Richards Medical Laboratories, Philadelphia, 1957–60. Photograph by author

In the report on the Le Fresnoy project, Tschumi designates László Moholy-Nagy and Frederick John Kiesler as the precursors for his ideas of space, event, and the body. However, with regard to his intention to transform a marginal element into "supplement," I would like to introduce another precedent that is mostly deleted from the index of the neo-avant-garde circles. Tschumi's rumination on in-between space and its architectonic implications at Le Fresnoy could be associated with Louis Kahn's discourse on served/service spaces.[44] Consider Kahn's Alfred Newton Richards Medical Research Building, on the campus of the University of Pennsylvania, completed in 1965. Here, multiple staircases and service ducts are grouped and turned into major tectonic figures. Furthermore, the building's concrete structure, partly cladded and partly revealed in the façade of research rooms, houses the conduit of technical services whose tectonic articulation at the entrance porch deconstructs the conventional distinction between structure and ornament (Figure 4.9).

Tschumi's reversal of this tradition ends in a concept of roof that shelters a heterogeneous body unfolding a different dialogue between structure and ornament. For Kahn, the tectonic is the site for articulating structure ornamentally; Tschumi's strategy aims at converting one's attention from the tectonic to space. It is true that "event" cannot take place in the absence of architecture, however, in subduing the power of architecture's representational dimension, Tschumi radicalizes the pleasure experienced in event. "[A]rchitecture seems to survive in its 'erotic' capacity only when it negates itself, … in other words, it is not a matter of destruction or 'avant-garde' subversion, but of transgression."[45] Obviously the "erotic capacity" of architecture is embedded in a space whose architectonic elements, I believe, are denied any significance, and yet this space provides an enclosure (mask?) for rationally organized programmatic needs.

Thus in spite of Tschumi's intellectual capacity to subvert the literal idea of excess, his work posits a sense of "objecthood" absent in the work of most of his deconstructivist colleagues. There is no room in Tschumi's work for formalistic playfulness, nor does he wrap architecture's structure with folds. "The challenge is to try to find the poetry in the excessive rationality," Tschumi claims, and he continues, "I always say that the excess of rationality is irrational."[46] In spite and perhaps because of this strategy, in Le Fresnoy, the roof, an important tectonic element, stands above and over everything, including the event triggered by it (Figure 4.10).

4.10   Bernard Tschumi, Le Fresnoy National Contemporary Arts, 1991–97. Photograph by author

A CONTEXTUAL RENDEZVOUS: THE LERNER STUDENT CENTRE

In a lecture delivered to the Graduate School of Architecture at Columbia University in 1998, Tschumi presented three projects that are framed by an existing context. Besides Le Fresnoy, both the competition entry for the MoMA's expansion and the Lerner Center demonstrate architecture's problematic relationship with institutions and the linguistic forces of the context. Focusing on the Lerner Center raises the question that if it is true that there is a sense of nihilism in Tschumi's discourse, then in what ways does his architecture differ from the early modern architects' appropriation of the same theme. And secondly, in spite or perhaps because of this difference, what is the architectonic dimension of the objectivity implied in the Lerner Center? (Figure 4.11.)

4.11   Bernard Tschumi, Alfred Lerner Hall Student Center, Columbia University, New York, 1994–99. Photograph by author

Tschumi has correctly suggested that a matrix of two languages, the city of New York and the campus of Columbia University, inform the Lerner Center building. Thus the final project accommodates the civic language of the architecture of Broadway (Figure 4.12), and keeps in tact the morphology of the campus designed by McKim Mead and White. The façade on the Broadway side makes room for a rusticated base and a wall clad in brick the surface of which is punctuated in harmony with the general features of the architecture of Broadway. One noticeable peculiarity of this building, among others of Tschumi's

4.12   Bernard Tschumi, Alfred Lerner Hall Student Center, Columbia University, New York, 1994–99. View from Broadway. Photograph by author

4.13   Bernard Tschumi, Alfred Lerner Hall Student Center, Columbia University, New York, 1994–99. Photograph by author

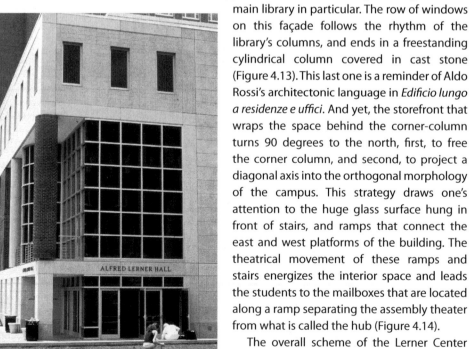

works built to date, is a sensible juxtaposition of different materials, though mostly embellished beyond conventional detailing. Thus the rustic base at the street side ends with a cornice made out of glass-block, to mimic the cast-stone cornice of the adjacent building.

The campus side also enjoys a mixture of different languages whose overall composition creates a sensible rapport with the surrounding buildings and the main library in particular. The row of windows on this façade follows the rhythm of the library's columns, and ends in a freestanding cylindrical column covered in cast stone (Figure 4.13). This last one is a reminder of Aldo Rossi's architectonic language in *Edificio lungo a residenze e uffici*. And yet, the storefront that wraps the space behind the corner-column turns 90 degrees to the north, first, to free the corner column, and second, to project a diagonal axis into the orthogonal morphology of the campus. This strategy draws one's attention to the huge glass surface hung in front of stairs, and ramps that connect the east and west platforms of the building. The theatrical movement of these ramps and stairs energizes the interior space and leads the students to the mailboxes that are located along a ramp separating the assembly theater from what is called the hub (Figure 4.14).

The overall scheme of the Lerner Center is informed by program; it combines administrative, leisure, and student activities. These requirements create, according to the architect, "a dynamic hub that acts as a major social space." The result is a U-shaped plan whose parallel arms are kept apart by what is described as a "black box theater," with a mansard-like roof that mimics the traditional skyline of New York City. The copper roof and the linguistic diversity employed both in the campus face and the civic face ironically recall Adolf Loos's design strategy in the Goldman and Salatsch Building, Michaelerplatz. The association is not far-fetched if we recall Loos's nihilism; he denied architecture's capacity to carry any symbolic representation except in monuments and tombs. In the Lerner Center, as in the Looshaus, a montage of different languages recodes the theme of nihilism. While Loos's strategy was directed at modernists of the Bauhaus and the secessionists of Vienna, Tschumi, instead, uses the gravitational forces of institutional languages to turn the glass façade into a theatrical stage-set.

4.14 Bernard Tschumi, Alfred Lerner Hall Student Center, Columbia University, New York, 1994–99. Interior view. Photograph by author

This move definitely departs from Loos's negative thought: to save the protean claim of the past from the modernists' zeal for the new. Loos was also obsessed, according to Massimo Cacciari, "with renouncing language that claims to be liberated from all presuppositions and to serve as text in itself. He sees in it the diabolical gesture of those who abandon the past, who do not recognize the right that it has over us, and hence persist in desiring its overthrow." Juxtaposing Loos's thought with Walter Benjamin's "angel of history," Cacciari suggests that, "the freedom of avant-garde and the hubris of its criticism shatter the delicate balance of the figure of the Angel and dissipate the feeble messianic strength that it announces to us." Cacciari continues:

> On the one hand, the avant-garde decrees the "once upon a time," and reduces things to "eternal images"—on the other, it turns its gaze to the future and, like a fortune teller, looks for "what lies hidden in its womb." For the Angel, on the other hand, the ephemeral of the present senses that of the past, and its future lies in the moment, which is origin. And in any case, how could the Angel destroy all presuppositions, if the very happiness for which he yearns is itself presupposed?[47]

However, a closer study shows that, despite his different take on "nihilism" and his departure from the Loosian rearguard position, Tschumi's strategy has special merit.

The tactile quality invested in the interior space of the Lerner Center alludes to a discourse of space/time that broadens the gap between this building and the Looshaus. Where Loos would choose interior materials to raise the sensation

4.15   Bernard Tschumi, Alfred Lerner Hall Student Center, Columbia University, New York, 1994–99. Interior view. Photograph by author

of *heimliche*, and to resist the silence of Metropolis, Tschumi reverses Loos's strategy by internalizing "bourgeois emptiness" (see below) into an architectural idiom. Cladding concrete slabs with wood or stone, and covering ramps and stairs with glass, Tschumi creates a "cool" ambiance whose tactile qualities are further stressed by the exposed concrete beams, perforated metal sheets, and a space-frame structure that hooks the stairs together and supports the front glass (Figure 4.15). The *unheimliche* sensation of this public space is balanced by the sheer pleasure of the body in ascending and descending the ramps and stairs, and more importantly, in the excitement experienced upon anticipation of an "event" as one approaches the mailboxes. Nevertheless, the hub, housing the public stairs and ramps, is a genetic space: it is an atrium rotated 90 degrees to expose its face not to the sky but to the campus and through a large glass surface. The space is also mundane in terms of its "raw" use of steel, glass, stone, and concrete. These materials are entertained to create a haptic sensation peculiar to the twentieth century's industrial buildings of the SoHo area, if not the tactile sensibilities invested in the best subway stations of New York City.

These historical allusions could be extended further: in the Lerner building, a montage of different materials and languages recall the dialogue between stone and steel employed in the best buildings of late nineteenth-century Europe. These historical structures, mostly wrapped in classical or Gothic garment, house exposed steel structures in the interior. This analogy is assured by the kind of detail Tschumi employs to connect (or to hang) the stairs at the center of the hub with the adjacent concrete beams (Figure 4.16). Here a three-dimensional space frame mimics an upheld image of a hand to recall details depicted in Viollet-le-Duc's visionary drawing for a "concert hall," where a finger-shaped steel member leads the forces of gravity from the roof to masonry wall. It also recalls Alvar Aalto's wooden truss in the Säynätsalo Town Hall building, just to mention a more contemporary precedent. These historical associations endorse the import of the theme of renunciation in Tschumi's work. And yet, what makes his architecture different from the image-oriented world of postmodern architecture is that these historical allusions are ironically channeled through another return: the return of the idea of new objectivity prevalent in early 1920s architecture.

To discuss the presence of objectivity in Tschumi's work involves examining Ernst Bloch's "Building in Empty Spaces." In this short essay, Bloch criticizes the *Neue*

Sachlichkeit and characterizes the abstract non-ornamental surface of such architecture as "bourgeois nothingness."[48] For Bloch, the new sobriety, even through generous use of glass, cannot hide its emptiness. Bloch presents a conclusion that foreshadows the neo-avant-garde aspiration for an aesthetic of abstraction that is motivated by the recent marriage between electronic technologies and architecture:

> *Today's technology, which is itself still so abstract, does lead out of the hollow space, even as it is fashioned as an aesthetic one, as an artistic substitute. Rather this hollow space penetrates the so-called art of engineering (Ingenieurskunst) as much as the latter increases the hollowness by its own emptiness. The only significant thing in all this is the direction of departure of these phenomena generated by themselves, i.e. the house as a ship.*[49]

4.16   Bernard Tschumi, Alfred Lerner Hall Student Center, Columbia University, New York, 1994–99. Interior view. Photograph by author

Bloch's statement provides a conceptual tool to charge Tschumi's architecture with critical importance: in the Lerner Center, engineering and technology elevates a functional "box" into a theatrical stage-set; not to allude to "the house as a ship," but to call attention to the status of object in a culture dominated by the fetishism of commodities. Tschumi's architecture meets with the phantasmagoria of the commodity world through the remnant of an image of objectivity that is peculiar to the architecture of *Neue Sachlichkeit*. The latter's matter-of-factness is in part a remnant of the realist architecture of the first decade of the last century which stayed faithful to the claim of the past without rejecting modernization.[50] In realist architecture there is an ideological pretense for reality and the necessity for its artistic presentation that sneaked into the abstract forms of *Neue Sachlichkeit*. In this transmission, the traces of the past were hygienically purged to equate the final product to the exigencies of the production line.

Tschumi's architecture recollects this historical moment of objecthood but, at the same time, his architecture internalizes a different level of the aesthetic of abstraction that marks the transformation of culture from modernism to postmodernism. Here I am benefiting from Fredric Jameson's insightful distinction between realism, modernism, and postmodernism.[51] Reading Giovanni Arrighi's book *The Long Twentieth Century*, Jameson reassesses postmodern culture in terms of the complexity of abstraction involved in a situation when capital has become global.

Today, what is called postmodernity articulates the symptomatology of yet another stage of abstraction, qualitatively and structurally distinct from previous ones, which I have drawn on Arrighi to characterize as our own moment of finance capitalism: the finance capital moment of globalized society, the abstraction brought with it through cybernetic technology ....[52]

For Jameson, artifacts associated with these three periods of artistic production differ from each other according to the level of abstraction that separates one period from the other. Accordingly,

The ideological and social precondition of realism—its naïve belief in a stable social reality, for example—are now themselves unmasked, demystified, and discredited; and modernist forms—generated by the very same pressure of reification—take their place. And, in this narrative, the suppression of modernism by the postmodern is, predictably enough, read in the same way as a further intensification of the forces of reification, which has utterly unexpected and dialectical results for the now hegemonic modernism itself.[53]

4.17   Bernard Tschumi, Alfred Lerner Hall Student Center, Columbia University, New York, 1994–99. Photograph by author

Thus from now on, detached from the exigencies of labor, tools, and regional limitations, money becomes capital—an abstract floating entity—moving from one region to another, and expanding its horizon while leaving behind many "empty lots," i.e., bourgeois nothingness. In the context of this historical development, every cultural product is charged not only with the cool fetishistic attraction of commodities, but also with the floating and hyperactive world of images

that are generated by telecommunication technologies. Postmodern architecture appropriates this aesthetic moment of abstraction in both neo-avant-garde and historicist idioms. However, the peculiarity of Tschumi's architecture rests in the way it appropriates theatricality not through images but by structuring free-floating images (architectural languages?) through a perception of objectivity that is encoded in the architecture of *Neue Sachlichkeit*.

There is another facet to the Lerner building that I like to associate with Bloch's article cited earlier. Facing the linguistic power of the architecture of the campus and Broadway, Tschumi deserves credit for inserting the architectonic site of pleasure in the empty lot separating the Lerner Center from the existing building to its north side. The lesson one might learn from his strategy is rather ironic: in a metropolis like New York City where "bourgeois nothingness" is spread wall to wall, the empty lot, a degree zero state of signification, provides

the only site where an architect could leave his/her mark on the city. At the same time, such a mark cannot escape its own historical limitations: most early avant-gardes could not secure architecture from the aesthetic impact of abstraction and the images set in motion by the technologies of modernization (Figure 4.17).

Likewise, the neo-avant-gardes have no choice but to entertain the current level of abstraction expressed in the aesthetic of commodity fetishism. The huge glass wall crowning the hub of the Lerner Center presents a stage-set that recalls one moment of the 1920's avant-garde fascination with theatrical stages, but also the current esteem for the theatricalization of architecture. This reading is convincing when one approaches the Lerner Center from the monumental stairs of the Law School building (Figure 4.18). The freestanding corner column subverts the classical symmetry of the campus in a "weak" mood, and yet accentuates a diagonal axis. The implied diagonal perceived from the campus-side is felt strongly in every turn of the body's movement from one ramp to the next stair or *vice versa*. Here Tschumi has generated a well-proportioned "interior" space that transgresses the bourgeois emptiness for theatrical ends.

Taking two strategic steps, the "architecture of disjunction" takes pleasure in the separation of architecture from its collective function. Obviously, the current emphasis on autonomy of form limits architecture's critical engagement with what might be called "construction of the condition of life": a socio-political network compromising production, communication, and the very act of place making.[54] Devoid of any political function, architecture is directed towards defying its own boundaries. In addition, the modernist zeal for temporality (fashion?)

4.18   Bernard Tschumi, Alfred Lerner Hall Student Center, Columbia University, New York, 1994–99. Photograph by author

dispenses with the culture of building; a move enforced by the prevailing capitalist ideology, the ultimate goal of which is to drag architecture further into the orbit of commodification. This move, ironically, and perhaps because of the neo-avant-garde reluctance to resist ideology, embellishes architecture not in the realm of tectonics, but in the continuation of the aesthetic at work in the culture of spectacle. In this mutation, excess ceases responding to the dialogue between structure and ornament; it rather ends in the embellishment of the object by cashing in on forms from the historical past, if not from other resources.

This observation could be taken as a general denominator of an avant-garde architecture that is touched by post-structuralist theories. If this is the case, then one could suggest that two thematic changes inform the present architecture. First, suspending architectural tropes such as style, ornament, monument, and the tectonic, the neo-avant-garde architects entertain the formal heritage of modern architecture as a found object empty of any historical connotations. Second, the post-structuralist emphasis on the autonomy of the text has opened a horizon of intellectual work in which "theory" transcends disciplinary boundaries. While this last development has underlined cultural issues concerned with gender and ethnic diversity, its reception in architecture has been rather mixed.[55] Nevertheless, the neo-avant-garde sees an interdisciplinary approach as a means to overcome the long-lived attachment of architecture to power and institutions. Ironically, Le Fresnoy—an inter-disciplinary artistic institution by inception—turns out to be the best site for Tschumi to practice the architecture of disjunction. This is also the case with the Parc de la Villette, and the Lerner Center, where institutional ties are cut by metamorphosing architecture to "mask."

Tschumi's stress on the deconstruction of program has been successful in shifting design away from metaphysical issues, and thus, differentiating his own architecture from other neo-avant-garde projects. An interest in the deconstruction of program sets the stage for a spatiality whose pleasure is experienced by the body's movement along ramps, stairs, and even escalators. Moreover, his hesitation to indulge in the invention of new forms, programmed through computer technologies, and the suggested objectivity, insulates his architecture against the dominion of image. Interestingly enough, there is a dichotomy in Tschumi's search for pleasure in architecture and the objectivity, which ironically exists in the aesthetic of *Neue Sachlichkeit* and in Gottfried Semper's discourse on theatricality. In Tschumi's work as well as in the new objectivity of the 1920s, pleasure is sought in a form whose material and technique is charged with excess. The abstract forms of the *Neue Sachlichkeit* were enchanting not only because of the banishment of ornamentation, but also because the object looked surreal and unfamiliar. The same is true for the idea of theatricality: even though the discourse of tectonic is centered on "necessity," the implied sense of objectivity in Semper's theory is not framed by material or technique but the way the matter draws attention to construction artistically. What this means is that in the tectonic technique is embellished metaphorically.

Of interest here is one of Tschumi's recent projects, Zenith de Rouen in France (Figures 4.19 and 4.20). Designed to house various public events, the final form compromises a rectangular exhibition space and a concert hall whose half-circular

4.19   Bernard Tschumi, Zenith de Rouen. Photograph by Peter Mauss,
courtesy of Bernard Tschumi Architects, New York City

4.20   Bernard Tschumi, Zenith de Rouen. Interior view. Photograph by author

envelope is in sharp contrast to the former's horizontal posture. Here, every aspect of these two main volumes of the complex is embellished to convey tectonic metaphors. Framed out of a trabeated structure and clad in steel and glass, the lightness and aesthetic delicacy of the exhibition volume contrasts with the heavy and robust concrete-cast volume of the concert hall. More interesting are the ways all kinds of difference in this project are articulated tectonically, including those originating in structural and mechanical needs, as well as those initiated by the transgression of program. Thus, according to the architect, "acoustical concerns led to a complete double-envelope surrounding the concert hall."[56] On the other hand, the space separating the concrete-stepped seating and the inner skin of the exterior are doubled by the form of a broken torus of insulated corrugated metal that envelopes the entire complex. Columns and stairs, creating an ambience of event, mark the space that fills the void between the concert hall and the exterior envelope. Similar to the Lerner building, the entire project in Rouen is seemingly conceived to underline the theatrical nature of a public event. Theatricality is experienced in the crowd's movement in the interior space, and is inscribed in the corrugated exterior enclosure; it looks like a fabric hung from three masts. In addition to the tension cables holding part of the roof system, the vertical extension of the masts, visible from distance, recall the primordial tectonics of tent and festive structures. Also noteworthy is the tectonic rapport between the envelope and the roof, a motif dismissed in contemporary architects' obsession with "surface," a subject explored on many occasions throughout this book.

The Zenith project is of significance for two additional reasons: first, the theatricality attributed to this project confirms the following theoretical observation central to the tectonic: that, architecture is not a direct product of construction, and yet the physical material of the building, the core-form, puts architecture in the track of technological transformations and scientific innovations. The same might be said about the art-form, the only venue by which architecture is charged with aesthetic sensibilities that are, interestingly enough, informed by perceptual horizons offered by the world of technology, and tactile and spatial sensibilities deeply rooted in the disciplinary history of architecture. Therefore, while the core-form assures architecture's rapport with the changes taking place in the *structure* of construction, the art-form remains the sole domain where the architect might choose to imbue the core-form with those aspects of the culture of building that might side-track the formal and aesthetic consequences of commodification essential to the cultural production of late capitalism, and yet avoid dismissing the latest technological developments. This observation can be taken to underline the influence of Russian constructivists in the work of Kenneth Frampton, Bernard Tschumi, Rem Koolhaas, and Zaha Hadid, and highlight these architects' difference from others who equally were influential for the formulation of architectural discourse of the 1980s.[57] In the Zenith de Rouen, dialogue between the constructed form and the clothing is dramatized not just by the materiality of concrete, steel, or glass, but the way one material is clad by another. This building enjoys a sense of "nothingness," if not the Miesian almost nothing, seemingly unraveling the tectonic of Tschumi's idea of empty space pregnant with event.

Second, the *parti* entertained in most of Tschumi's projects subscribe to a concept of contextualism that is radically different from the postmodern semiological concern, and the present rush towards digital imagery. Holding the space behind, the envelope of the Zenith de Rouen attains a sense of autonomy (objectivity?) capable of conceptualizing the context. Located in the district of Rouen outside Paris, the tectonic figuration of the envelope of the concert hall alludes to vernacular sensibilities of the kind legible not only in the early last century's industrial structures, but also in the early villas of Le Corbusier, and a few early good works of Mario Botta, as noted by Frampton. And yet, unlike these two architects, Tschumi does not exploit the separation of enclosure from structure for stylistic or aesthetic ends; Tschumi's articulation of the envelope in the Lerner Center, for example, aims at decontextualizing the classical vocabulary of the campus architecture. Again, what this means has to do with the objectivity implied in Tschumi's work, the materiality of which is embedded in the tectonic of cladding and the frame, if only to invigorate a different experience of the context. Not only

4.21   Bernard Tschumi, Athletic Center, University of Cincinnati, Ohio, 2001–06. Image courtesy of Bernard Tschumi Architects, New York City

is this much clear from most of the projects discussed in this chapter, but it is also the case with the Athletic Center, University of Cincinnati, Ohio (Figure 4.21). In this project, the design concept evokes the metaphor of the organic implied in Semper's concern: how to give life to dead material. Reflecting on the materiality of stone and stereotomy, Semper suggested that, in tectonic construction "different parts has resulted" not from "a structural mechanical formal expression," but from "very different kind of activity. Artistically enlivened, supporting elements become organicism … "[58] In the Athletic Center, the form and fenestration of the envelope recall motifs central to a twining structural fence, the main structural elements of which merge with the columns below. The tectonic and aesthetic articulation of the body animates the creature-like head of the building, as if looking towards the adjacent stadium. In return, the animated form of the building, considered either as a freestanding infill or a contextual freeform, evokes its context, even though the attention remains focused on the building itself.

The idea of objectivity as discussed throughout this chapter positions Tschumi's architecture beyond the crossroad of modern and postmodern debate. His work neither internalizes the zeitgeist of the present digital age of reproductivity, nor aims at introducing a new style, as was the case with the *Neue Shachlichkeit* movement. At another level of consideration, projects such as Zenith de Rouen and Vacheron-Constantin in Geneva, Switzerland (2004) are exceptional for introducing urban architecture into a context that are marginalized according to the logic of town and country division. And this in consideration of the fact that in late capitalism still the tendency is for the densification of old metropolitan centers where capital investment is rewarded and backed by the prevailing culture of spectacle.

NOTES

1   Georges Bataille, for one, articulated the theoretical premises of the idea of questioning the institutional power of architecture. See Denis Hollier, *Against Architecture* (Cambridge, MA: The MIT Press, 1989).

2   Charles Harrison, "Conceptual Art and Critical Judgment," in Christian Schlatter, ed., *Conceptual Art, Conceptual Forms* (Paris: Galerie de poche, 1990).

3   Peter Eisenman, "Notes Towards a Conceptual Architecture: Towards a Definition," in Eisenman, *Eisenman Inside Out* (New Haven, CT: Yale University Press, 2004), 14. The essay was first published in *Design Quarterly*, 1971.

4   Reading René Magritte's painting, Michel Foucault points to two important developments that have taken place in Western painting. The first reveals the separation between "plastic representation and linguistic reference," and the second, the long reliance of painting on resemblance as a communicative means. See Foucault, *This Is not a Pipe* (Berkeley, CA: University of California Press), 1983.

5   The historicity of Wittkower is discussed in Alina Payne, "Rudlof Wittkower and Architectural Principles in the Age of Modernism," *Journal of the Society of Architectural Historians* 53, 3 (September 1994): 322–42.

6   For Colin Rowe, see his *The Mathematics of the Ideal Villas and Other Essays* (Cambridge, MA: The MIT Press, 1976).

7   Hugh Hudson, *Blueprints and Blood: The Stalinization of Soviet Architecture* (Princeton, NJ: Princeton University Press, 1994), 14. For this author's reading of the contemporary turn to historical forms, see Gevork Hartoonian, *Modernity and Its Other* (College Station, TX: A&M Texas University, 1997).

8   On this subject see Mark Jarzombeck, "The Disciplinary Dislocations of (Architectural) History," *Journal of the Society of Architectural Historians* 58, 3 (September 1999): 488–93.

9   On this subject see Chapter 2 in this volume.

10   See Kate Nesbitt, ed., *Theorizing a New Agenda for Architecture Theory, 1965–1995* (New York: Princeton Architectural Press, 1996), 16–71.

11   For a collection of essays discussing the possibility of "meaning" for architecture beyond modernism, see Charles Jencks and George Baird, eds, *Meaning in Architecture* (New York: George Braziller, 1970). The book presents various views addressing issues such as semiology and architecture; the importance of the public and private dimensions of architecture; and finally what was called "use" and typological study in architecture. For a critical evaluation of architecture of the recent past see, Michael Hays and Carol Burns, eds, *Thinking the Present: Recent American Architecture* (New York: Princeton Architectural Press, 1990).

12   For the notion of event, see Gilles Deleuze, "What Is an Event," in *The Fold: Leibniz and the Baroque* (Minneapolis, MN: University of Minnesota Press, 1993), 76–82. For Deleuze, the conditions for an event to unfold are "produced in a chaos, in a chaotic multiplicity, but only under conditions that a sort of screen intervenes."

13   Bernard Tschumi, *The Discourse of Event*, a catalogue for an architectural exhibition held at the Architectural Association, London, 1979, 6.

14   The idea of the death of the author is implied in most philosophical and literary texts written during the second half of this century. The term was first coined by Michel Foucault in *Language, Counter-Memory, Practice* (Ithaca, NY: Cornell University Press, 1972). Also see Fredric Jameson, "Periodizing the 60s," in Sohnya Sayer and Andres Stephanson, eds, *The 60s without Apology* (Minneapolis, MN: University of Minnesota Press, 1984).

15   K. Michael Hays, *Architecture's Desire: Reading the Late Avant-garde* (Cambridge, MA: The MIT Press, 2010), 139.

16   Gevork Hartoonian, *Modernity and Its Other, 1997, 37.*

17   Her suggested solution concerns "autocriticism," at work in Tschumi's reading of Le Fresnoy. See Sylvia Lavin, "Inter-Objective Criticism: Bernard Tschumi and Le Fresnoy," in Bernard Tschumi, *Le Fresnoy: Architecture In/Between* (New York: Monacelli Press, 1999), 175–6.

18   Kate Nesbitt, *Theorizing a New Agenda*, 1996, 150.

19   Bernard Tschumi, "Introduction," in *Le Fresnoy*, 1999, 9.

20   Louis Martin, "Transpositions: On the Intellectual Origins of Tschumi's Architectural Theory," *Assemblage* 11 (1990): 22–35.

21   For further elaboration of these themes, see Bernard Tschumi, *The Manhattan Transcripts* (London: The Academy Editions, 1981).

22   See Marianne Barzilay, *L'invention du Parc* (Paris: Graphite Editions, 1984). The entire book documents the 1982 competition.

23　A. Papadakis, C. Cook, and A. Benjamin, eds, *Deconstruction: Omnibus Volume* (New York: Rizzoli, 1989), 174–83.

24　Bernard Tschumi, *L'Architecture d'aujourd'hui*, 187 (October–November 1976): 82.

25　Marc-Antoine Laugier, *An Essay on Architecture (1753)* (Santa Monica, CA: Hennessey & Ingalls, 1977), 121–33.

26　See Le Corbusier, *The City of Tomorrow, Translation of Urbanisme* (1925) (New York: Dover Publications, 1987), 72–80.

27　Bernard Tschumi, *Architecture and Disjunction* (Cambridge, MA: The MIT Press, 1998), 91.

28　Bernard Tschumi, *L'Architecture d'aujourd'hui*, 1976, 83.

29　Bernard Tschumi, *L'Architecture d'aujourd'hui*, 1976, 89.

30　K. Michael Hays, "The Autonomy Effect," in Giovanni Damiani, ed., *Bernard Tschumi* (New York: Rizzoli, 2003), 7. Hays has further elaborated on his theoretical approach in *Architecture's Desire* (Cambridge, MA: The MIT Press, 2010). For this author's review of Hays's book (2010) see *Architectural Science Review* 53 (2010): 276–7.

31　Susan Sontag, ed., *A Barthes Reader* (New York: The Noonday Press, 1982), 404–13.

32　K. Michael Hays, "The Autonomy Effect," 2003, 10.

33　For Roland Barthes, textual pleasure is not something that the author plants into the text. The pleasure of text exists because of the possibility of reading, and hence re-writing it by the reader. Barthes goes further and establishes a metaphorical link between text and human body; "the text itself, a diagrammatic and not an imitative structure, can reveal itself in the form of a body, split into fetish objects, into erotic sites. All these movements attest to a figure of the text, necessary to the bliss of reading" (see S. Sontag, *A Barthes Reader*, 1982, 410).

34　Bernard Tschumi, "The Park: An Urban Park for the 21st Century," *Progressive Architecture* 66, 1 (1985): 90–93, originally published in *International Architect,* 1 (1983): 27–31.

35　Jean-Francois Bedard, ed., *Cities of Artificial Excavation: The Work of Peter Eisenman, 1978–1988* (New York: Rizzoli, 1994).

36　See the following note.

37　Bernard Tschumi, "Architecture and Limits, I, II & III," in Kate Nesbitt, ed., *Theorizing a New Agenda*, 1996, 152–67. All three essays were originally published in *Artforum* (December 1980), (March 1981), and (September 1981) respectively.

38　Peter Blundell Jones, "La Villette," *Architectural Review* (August 1989): 54–9.

39　I am alluding to Fredric Jameson's insightful criticism of Roland Barthes's shift from a political discourse detectable in the book titled *Mythologies*, to one where class issues are swept aside. If Barthes's *Writing Zero Degree* could escape what Jameson calls the "nightmare of history," his next work, *The Pleasure of the Text,* took rather a different direction. "It is now through reception rather than production that History may be suspended, and the social function of that fragmentary, punctual jouissance which can break through any text will then be more effective to achieve that freedom from all ideologies and all commitments (of the Left as much as of the Right) that the zero degree of literary signs had once seemed to promise" (Fredric Jameson, "Pleasure: A Political Issue," in *The Ideologies of Theory* [Minneapolis, MN: The University of Minnesota Press, 1989], vol. 2, 68).

40　Bernard Tschumi, *Le Fresnoy*, 1999, 36.

41   Bernard Tschumi, *Le Fresnoy*, 1999, 42.

42   Bernard Tschumi, *The Manhattan Transcripts*, 1981.

43   Bernard Tschumi, "Architecture and Limits II," in Kate Nesbitt, ed., *Theorizing a New Agenda*, 1996, 160.

44   Interestingly enough, in his reading of the roof at Le Fresnoy, Alain Guiheux recalls Louis Kahn's Great Synagogue of Jerusalem where "a space is closed by the simple proximity of thick dividing walls, …" (see Guiheux, "Critical Workshop," in Bernard Tschumi, *Le Fresnoy*, 1999, 89).

45   Bernard Tschumi, "Architecture and Transgression," *Opposition* 7 (winter 1976).

46   Bernard Tschumi, *GA Document Extra*, 10 (1997): 151.

47   Massimo Cacciari, "Loos and His Angel," in *Architecture and Nihilism: On the Philosophy of Modern Architecture* (New Haven, CT: Yale University Press, 1993), 149.

48   Ernst Bloch, "Building in Empty Spaces," in trans. J. Zipes and F. Mecklenburg, *The Utopian Function of Art and Literature* (Cambridge, MA: The MIT Press, 1988), 186–99.

49   Ernst Bloch, "Building in Empty Spaces," 1988, 190.

50   For a comprehensive study of the different facets of architecture of realism see H.F. Mallgrave, ed., *Otto Wagner* (Santa Monica, CA: The Getty Center for the History of Art and the Humanities, 1993), particularly part III, "The Changing Dialectics of Modernity." Also see Stanford Anderson's essay "Sachilchkeit and Modernity, or Realist Architecture," in Mallgrave, *Otto Wagner*, 1993, 323–63.

51   Fredric Jameson, "Culture and Financial Capital," *Critical Inquiry* 24, 1 (autumn 1997): 246–65.

52   Fredric Jameson, "Culture and Financial Capital," 1997, 252.

53   Fredric Jameson, "Culture and Financial Capital," 1997, 256.

54   On this subject see the final chapter in Gevork Hartoonian, *Ontology of Construction* (Cambridge: Cambridge University Press, 1994), 89.

55   The most interesting voice concerning this issue will be Mary McLeod's "Everyday and 'Other' Spaces," in Debra Coleman, Elizabeth Danze, and Carol Hendersson, eds, *Architecture and Feminism* (New York: Princeton University Press, 1996), 1–37.

56   Giovanni Damiani, *Bernard Tschumi* (London: Thames & Hudson, 2004), 124.

57   Gevork Hartoonian, "An Architecture of Limits," in Harriet Edquist and Helene Frichot, eds, *Limits; SAHANZ04*, vol. 1 (Melbourne, 2004), 214–20.

58   See Gottfried Semper, *Style in the Technical and Tectonic Arts; or Practical Aesthetics*, trans. H.F. Mallgrave and Michael Robinson (Santa Monica, CA: The Getty Center, 2004), 728. On the significance of the "organic" for the tectonic discourse see the final chapter in this volume.

5

Rem Koolhaas: Exuberant Object of Delight

The previous chapter, on Bernard Tschumi, is now followed by chapters on Rem Koolhaas and Zaha Hadid respectively. The decision for this sequencing is to draw attention to the extent to which the work of Russian constructivism colors the work of all three. If the reader agrees with this author's historicization of Mies van der Rohe in the broader consideration of the project of modernity,[1] then, it is plausible to posit the following: the Miesian exhaustion of the tectonic of steel and glass architecture left postmodernists with the choice of considering *history* as a backward move forward. Instead of re-thinking the closure Mies had established during his American tenure, or siding with those who turned to the simulation of historical forms, these three architects reworked various aspects of constructivism outside of the historicity of the project of the historical avant-garde. This is not to dismiss their disparities, but to highlight each of these mentioned architects' take on the concept of otherness. We are not concerned with the otherness of the vernacular as compared with classical architecture, or the otherness implied in pitting the low arts against the high arts. Instead, we have in mind Oswald Mathias Ungers' "cities within the city," a concept that Koolhaas was aware of through his collaboration with Ungers during the 1970s.[2]

Instead of plotting an ideal city, Ungers' strategy focused on reusing selected formal principles established by the heroic period of the early modern architecture movement. On the background of political and cultural dialogue between Germany and the Soviet Union, Ungers became pedagogically engaged in the megastructural urban interventions fusing "two fundamentally antithetical traditions: on the one hand, the Russian avant-garde thrust toward monumental and dynamic structural form; on the other, a fragmentary Piranesian poetic, appropriate to the devastated landscape of Berlin."[3] The idea was not to replicate forms codified by history, but to modify them for a different use and context. Drawing on the managerial policies of a large industrial complex, and the transformation of a big production compound into reasonably sized units, Koolhaas proposed that the future planning of Berlin should be "substantiated in the image of Berlin as a city-archipelago."[4] The historicity of Ungers' experimental work and its appropriation by Koolhaas say something about the state of the dialectics of theory and practice in modernity. In its drive to conquer every aspect of the life-world, modernization leaves behind residues, aspects of which in due time are re-assimilated into the system. This nightmarish view of one's relation with the past in modern times structures the tale of the neo-avant-garde architects' tendency to reactivate the inherited modernist formal and design strategies.

The implied temporal prioritization will be taken here to discuss a number of Koolhaas's projects, which, I believe, demonstrate the architect's close engagement with the state of architecture in late capitalism. Without wanting to refer to a particular point in time, the assumption is that at some point of his praxis, Koolhaas came to the realization that the commodification of the life world is total, and that architecture is on the verge of internalizing the aesthetic of spectacle. Beyond its implication for current visual culture, Hal Foster's discourse in "image building,"[5] is worth noting; he demonstrates, among other things, the operative mechanism that obscures the otherness of the part as it relates to a larger totality, a phenomenon not alien to the project of modernity. Therefore, if at one stage of Koolhaas's career, the notion of "hybridity"[6] emerged as a strategy addressing the aforementioned otherness, that strategy is forsaken in the latest production of the Office for Metropolitan Architecture (OMA).

Many critics have suggested that different sources influenced Koolhaas's work of the 1970s.[7] In addition to the Italian Superstudio, mention is made of Ivan Leonidov's and Salvador Dalí's takes on *l'Angelus*, a painting by Jean-François Millet (1858–59). To this list, one should add a few generic aspects of the work of Le Corbusier and Mies, each being used as the palimpsest for an architecture that still wants to retain its hold on the notion of otherness. What this means theoretically is that, like a few artists of the late 1970s,[8] Koolhaas tried to position his work within the utopian aspirations of the 1920s on the one hand, and the neo-avant-garde radicalism of the post-1960s student uprisings on the other. Still, starting from Robert Venturi's notion of "both/and," and without following the latter's formalistic or historicist implications, Koolhaas unabashedly felt comfortable with the encroachment of the commodity form on architecture's autonomy. There is a price to be paid for this. Unlike few artists/architects, he did not use these aforementioned remnants of history to resist the system. He was evidently satisfied with the ambiguity of the final design's attractiveness, the *look*, the aesthetic, the sublime beauty of the object.

The following brief reworking of selected projects presented in *Delirious New York* (1978) allows us to explore the ways in which the OMA re-approaches the contemporary crisis of architecture, and to examine its implications for the aesthetic of theatricalization. I would like to bring to the reader's attention a closure, or entrapment implied in the title and drawing of two projects, the *City of the Captive Globe* (1972) (Figure 5.1) and the *Exodus, or the Voluntary Prisoners of Architecture* (1971–72) (Figure 5.2). If in the latter delineation, the element of wall delivers the limits of a vision (totality?), the

5.1   OMA, *The City of the Captive Globe*, 1972. Image by Madelon Vriesendorp, courtesy of OMA

block is introduced as the *parti* to capture the same vision in the former project. In addition to this, both drawings are charged with excess and theatricality. This is evident from the tilted bird's-eye view presentation of both projects, and from the gestural position of walls injected into the two main walls of the second project. Even though the *City of the Captive Globe* was produced as part of the architect's study of Manhattan, it, nevertheless, alludes to the presence of something *out there* (the other), a phenomenon informing his discourse on architecture's relation to the city. One thinks of the *Berlin Wall* and the *block*, two strategies of subdivision and spatial domination, but also of the architectonic elements that have recurred throughout history on varying scales, be it a Palladian villa or the urban fabric of Manhattan.

5.2   OMA, *Exodus, or the Voluntary Prisoners of Architecture*, 1972. Image courtesy of OMA

As a student at the Architectural Association in London, Koolhaas studied the Berlin Wall both as an architectonic element of division, and as the formal that has the potentiality to express human drama in modernity. This Berlin, according to Fritz Neumeyer, "winds throughout the early projects of the Office of Metropolitan Architecture, whose history—how could it be otherwise in this city—started directly at the Berlin Wall."[9] However, deliberately absent in Koolhaas's vision of metropolitanism is that which in Le Corbusier's *Plan Voisin* made the slate clean for the emergence of a new and coherent vision of urbanism. And yet, the American architecture Koolhaas posited in the *Delirious New York*, Felicity Scott writes, "exemplified a direct relation to capitalist development insofar as it was devoid of the polemical discourse and political and utopian cast of the European avant-garde."[10] In the two delineations under consideration here the spectator does not see or know what is beyond the walls, or why only a segment of the city is captured. One can only conjecture that the utopia implied in Le Corbusier's vision of the city was no longer appealing to the architects of the 1970s, at least after Ungers' experimentation with Berlin as a Green Archipelago. Ungers' "city within the city," Pier Vittorio Aureli writes, "was not the creation of an idyllic village as opposed to the fragmentation of the city, but an attempt to reflect the splintering form of the city from within the architectural artifact."[11] This, however, does not mean that *totality* was extinct. The very fact of blocking part of a larger city in Koolhaas's two drawings suggests the presence of a non-visible totality, which soon after the demolition of the Berlin Wall, and the disappearance of the territorial delineation between the city and the countryside, would turn out to be the very real of one's everyday life experience in late capitalism: a totality without exterior, if you wish.[12] It is perhaps for the same reason that the concept of "otherness" gained currency in most critical investigations of architecture of the 1970s.[13]

Needless to say, the theatricality implied in *otherness* is, at least, in the *City of the Captive Globe* aestheticized, that is, it becomes spectacle on its own right. In the same drawing, selected buildings from the depository of modern architecture are put at the top of regular bases to connote the essentiality of the grid and block systems for the void experienced in Manhattan. For the OMA, Manhattanism is the "melting pot of 'isms,' a paradoxical source of Metropolitan unhappiness and anxiety; so the city can become a laboratory of the collective unconscious."[14] The aestheticization delivered by an object's detachment from an invisible totality is also at work in the *Voluntary Prisoners of Architecture* if compared with Ivan Leonidov's competition entry project for the Palace of Culture, Moscow, 1930.

The significance of theatricality for Russian constructivist architecture was discussed in Chapter 1. Here it is sufficient to note that the suggested otherness had no place in Leonidov's project. In Koolhaas's words, the best work Leonidov produced concerned institutions such as the Workers Club that was integral to the new communist culture.[15] Even though its breakdown was already working both from within and without, there was no reason for the Soviets of the 1920s to doubt the possibility of establishing a transparent rapport with the real, understood in the following terms: that history, conceived since the Enlightenment, has accomplished one of its major tasks, that is the realization of the first working-class revolution worldwide. Benjamin H.D. Buchloh writes, "in the context of the Soviet Productivists, the emergence of a new proletarian public sphere was formulated at every level as a historically possible and necessary shift that artistic practices could assist initiating."[16] This is clear from the delineated paintings and architectural forms of El Lissitzky and Kasimir Malevich who, unlike their European counterparts, used abstraction to highlight a space almost detached from the earth, as we know it. This is a useful theoretical scenario. Speaking theoretically, it avoids the formalistic interpretation of the abstract and placeless geometries that structure Leonidov's project, which, interestingly enough, recurs in various segments of the *Exodus* and instigates the aesthetic of the theatricalization and Manhattanism noted earlier.

WHATEVER IT TAKES!

Yes, whatever it takes is the motto of the OMA to sustain the strategic usefulness of otherness for the firm's early work. Where generic elements of Mies or Le Corbusier structure a number of early projects, others demonstrate the architect's conclusive departure from the concept of totality, which makes architecture's strategic detachment from urbanization meaningful. From the first group, the discussion will primarily concern the Kunsthal, Rotterdam (1992), and Educatorium, Utrecht (1997). Starting with the OMA's competition entry for the Très Grande Bibilothèque (TGB), Paris, and the Sea Terminal, Zeebrugge, both from 1989, this chapter will then present a close investigation of the Seattle Public Library (1999), Casa da Música, Porto (2008), and the Central Chinese Television (CCTV) Headquarters, Beijing, 2009.

If the two elements of piloti and horizontal window make Villa Dall'Ava (1991) look familiar, the association with Le Corbusier's early villas does not go further. Drawing from the introverted Roman houses, the design of this early project provides a secluded space surrounded by glass walls tinted with various colors.[17]

5.3   OMA, Maison à Bordeaux, France, 1998. General view. Photograph courtesy of OMA

With its theatrical third-floor figure looking over its territorial wall, the Maison à Bordeaux (1998), instead, captures the Miesian tectonics at work in Riehl House (1910) (Figure 5.3). That this project's imposing concrete volume should house the children's bedroom can only be guessed from its playful circular concrete openings. Still, the steel beam running above the roof of the house recalls the late Miesian pavilion type, the IIT School of Architecture, Chicago, where part of the building is buried underground. In Maison à Bordeaux and other projects from the same period, particular elements of Mies's and Le Corbusier's work are reactivated through what is called "paranoid-critical interpretation." Facing the anxiety caused by the assumption that all good and bad intentions have already taken place, including what is still unknown, Koolhaas's methodology calls for "conceptual recycling, the worn, consumed contents of the world," assuming that "ever-new generations of false facts and fabricated evidences can be generated simply through the act of interpretation."[18] Convinced that the architects of the 1920s had already reached and tested the limits of modern architecture, Koolhaas saw his task as reinterpreting the most common and advanced architectonic element of that experience using available contemporary building techniques and aesthetics. These historical references, however, are not literal. In most cases they look both ambiguous and familiar, something seen somewhere previously, but not so sure. Take for example the Dutch Embassy in Berlin (Figure 5.4) where the cut in the L-shaped volume of the complex recalls Mies's Tugendhat House, Brno (1930). Similar to the latter building, the "hole" in the OMA's project makes visual connection between the adjacent street and the building's internal podium, extending the view to the river on the opposite side.

Likewise, the Miesian use of exposed steel beams returns in the Kunsthal to be offset by the rooftop sculpture of a camel (Figure 5.5). Is this in reference to the TV

5.4   OMA, Dutch Embassy in Berlin, 2003. Exterior view. Photograph by author

antenna Robert Venturi mounted on the top of the Guild House (Philadelphia), or should it be taken as a commercial billboard? The latter analogy is convincing considering the fact that the building is sandwiched between a highway, Westzeedijk, and the museum's park. These two landscapes, one a major feature of urbanization, the other a remnant of the natural life of the past, are kept at a distance by an external ramp (Figure 5.6). The location of this element of circulation, and the entire project speak for architecture's mediating role in modernity's drive to absorb and recode the

5.5 OMA, Kunsthal, Netherlands, Rotterdam, 1992. View from the highway. Image by Philippe Ruault, courtesy of OMA

natural into the ongoing processes of urbanization. This reading is supported by the allegorical connection made between the wooden dressing of the ground floor columns of the restaurant and the park's woodland (Figure 5.7).

Otherwise a Miesian box, most of the projects discussed below exemplify OMA's three strategies: they seek to nullify the formal implications of the Dom-ino frame; to recode the notion of the open plan, intensifying the scope of circulation and subdivision of the internal volume; and finally, to charge the interior space with visual aesthetics mostly drawn from the use of various materials, and this in association with the aesthetic traditions of Dutch painting.

Consider the rectangular plan of the Kunsthal and its subdivision into three unequal segments by the road running perpendicular to the external ramp and parallel to the highway. Together the three areas of the plan house three halls and a lecture room. No architect visiting the building could fail to experience the

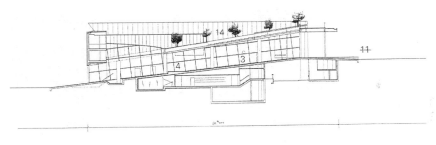

5.6 OMA, Kunsthal, Netherlands, Rotterdam, 1992. Section drawing. Image courtesy of OMA

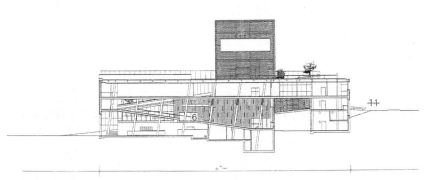

5.7   OMA, Kunsthal, Netherlands, Rotterdam, 1992. Image by Hans Werlemann, courtesy of OMA

full force of the principle of the *promenade architecturale*, and the role it plays in the theatricalization of one's spatial experience of the external ramp, interwoven into an internal ramp and the vertical volume of the elevator. To solidify the created spatial maze, the elevator's volume soars above the roof visible from the highway and the park, and this in reference to the roof garden placed on a steel ramp outside and parallel with the external ramp. These suggested spatial complexities are better understood through the section drawings of the complex. The spatial articulation of the Kunsthal works like a graft knotting together the two main halves of the plan.

A less frequently discussed dimension of Koolhaas's architecture is the use of diverse materials for dramatizing the spatial maze. Steel, wood, glass, synthetic materials, and exposed concrete (the sloped lecture theater modulated by a flanking curtain wall) are juxtaposed to generate a theatrical ambience. Kenneth Frampton comments thus on this design aspect: "the theatrical character of the internal space throughout, derives in large measure from the applications of decorative neon lighting, close to the surface of the principle ceiling." Artificially illuminated materiality, Frampton writes, "encounters a concept that is essentially graphic rendered as though it were a three dimensional form."[19] As such, the aesthetic of theatricalization is indeed a recurring theme in the most successful work Koolhaas has produced to date. The fact that most of these projects generate a theatrical ambience along ramps and stairs is suggestive of a dramatic shift in the idea of public space once identified by grandiose entry halls, podiums, and/or the classical orders used for the main entry façade. The shift speaks for an economy of selection where public gathering spaces have to be minimized. One prominent example of this can be found in the design of most contemporary train stations including that of the Euralille. Gone in this process, call it the privatization of public space, is the tectonic of detailing. In most instances, Koolhaas is not shy of showing how materials are simply connected to each other, using the least amount of detailing as if the assembled structure is "waiting to be undone, unscrewed."[20]

Of these observations mention should also be made of the main stair rising over the foyer of Congrexpo (1994) and the north ramp stairs of Educatorium (1997). Of particular interest is the radical transformation of the idea of free-plan and the frame structural system notable in the latter project, aspects of which were already examined in the Kunsthal. Here too, the main semi-rectangular floor plan of the Educatorium is divided into four parts: two for the auditoria and the other two, located above the main entry, for what are called examination rooms (Figure 5.8). A Kahnian distinction between served and service spaces, instead, structures the placement of corridors and the main stairs located at the edges of the volume. Entering the complex, a ramp leads the visitor to the cafeteria, which, as with the Kunsthal, occupies the entire floor level. With another ramp leading to the two

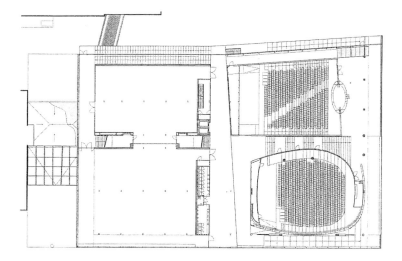

5.8   OMA,
Educatorium,
Netherlands,
Utrecht, 1997.
Floor plans. Image
courtesy of OMA

main auditoria, the arrangement of these two spaces within half of the rectangular plan recalls Le Corbusier's design for the Assembly and Secretariat in Chandigarh where, similar to a toy box, smaller containers are placed next to each other. This strategy of subdivision appealed to a Koolhaas who had already encountered the limits imposed by the *block*, a Manhattanesque strategy of subdivision.

Still, there is another generic element of Le Corbusier's architecture detectable in the Educatorium: that the side and main elevation of the building should follow the sectional profile of the building's interior space (Figure 5.9). In addition to the strategy of converting section into elevation, equally noteworthy is the twist given to the section of Le Corbusier's Villa at Carthage, Tunis (1928). Whilst this villa's sectional interlocking informs the two projects under consideration here, Koolhaas's innovative departure from modernism relates to the general tendency for stacking various floors on top of each other, a by-product of the frame-structure system. Lifting up the horizontal plane, as if "the surface is malleable and pliable," Koolhaas makes an effort to get away from the piloti effect where the floors are detached from the ground. Thus, the surface "becomes part of the vertical continuum."[21] Reworking through the Jussieu Libraries, Paris (1992–93), Peter Eisenman further suggests that this project of the OMA initiates a shift from the strategy of hybridity to that which informs projects such as the Seattle Public Library and the Casa da Música, Porto, both discussed in the following pages. The aforementioned sectional extension into the façade, nevertheless, allows Koolhaas to conceive void "as an inversion of *poché*, as a conceptual armature," Eisenman writes.[22] Consequently, the rigidity of the Dom-ino frame is sublimated, and the ground implied in the open-plan is transformed into ramps either as a vehicle of circulation or as slightly tilted floors for accommodating the seats of the auditorium. Echoing Eisenman, Roberto Gargiani observes, "the continuous paths cut into the prismatic volumes of Kunsthal and

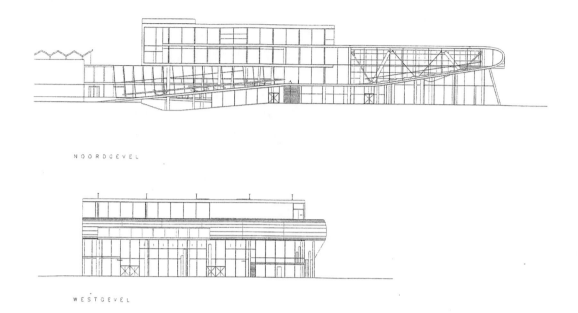

NOORDGEVEL

WESTGEVEL

5.9 OMA, Educatorium, Netherlands, Utrecht, 1997. Section/elevation drawing. Image courtesy of OMA

Deux Bibiliothèques Jussieu form the prelude to a new, more assertive symbolic and functional continuity that begins to appear in the work of OMA."[23] To these remarks, we should add the prevailing "look" that aims to become part of the aesthetic of a mass commodified culture, a phenomenon penetrating all cultural territories, including the OMA's project carried out in China, as we will see shortly. Yet, and somewhat ironically, what makes Koolhaas's work singular can be associated with the visual aesthetics advanced by the early Dutch avant-garde artists.

The breadth of this subject cannot be given complete justice here. The reader should, however, be reminded of two historical moments in Dutch visual culture. In the first place, mention should be made of the portrait paintings where, to follow the art historian Alois Riegl, the internal figurative composition seems pregnant with a sense of theatricality that draws the spectator's attention.[24] In Rembrandt's paintings, for example, an anamorphic use of perspective curtails the expected spatial distance between the subject (spectator) and the object (painting). In the *Syndics of the Clothmaker's Guild* (1662), the depicted figures are doing their best to reach out, and at the same time to invite the spectator to enter into the painterly scene imaginatively, thus closing the painting's spatial circle. In the second historical moment we are reminded of the visuality propagated by the De Stijl movement. Consider the Café l'Aubette in Strasbourg, designed by Theo van Doesburg in 1928, where the spatial experience is informed by the physical body of the building—that is, its form and geometry—and by the virtual space evoked by the colorful diagonal lines furnishing the café's horizontal and vertical surfaces.

Of these strategies of visual sublimation and their architectonic implications mention should be made of the corridor behind the two main auditoria of the Educatorium. The space is dramatized using non-linear and non-homogeneous materials. The continuous concrete curve covering the rear of the ramp and auditorium recall the earlier suggested analogy with Le Corbusier's villa. The volume is cut halfway by a projected rectangular glassed volume clad in wood on the inside. The ensemble pumps visual continuity between floor and ceiling. The same volume's profile, however, simulates the egg-shape projection room, located on the opposite side, as if it is extruded from the curved volume of the rear end. The spectacle experienced in this corridor is also at work in the auditorium's ovoid interior, the walls of which are either clad in wood or are panes of glass allowing visual access to the landscape.

If the recoding of the modernist idea of open-plan and frame structure is the strategy underpinning the projects discussed thus far, a radical turn to *totality* helps in grasping the OMA's understanding of *modernity* at the time when capital and information are distributed and consumed globally. In addition to the implied shift in Eisenman's formal interpretation of Koolhaas's architecture, the projects discussed in the following pages attempt to emulate what Marshal Berman has discussed in terms of "socialist realism," connoting a strategy by which one should make the best out of given circumstances. This is important not only in reference to the idea of "dirty realism" attributed to Koolhaas's design strategy,[25] but also in consideration of his sympathy with Russian constructivist architecture, and the global real (good and bad) permeating present everyday life. What this means can be phrased in the following words: if the common thread running through today's architecture is the internalization of the visual spectacle permeating the cultural products of late capitalism, then one way to dismiss the architectonics of theatricalization is to transfer the latter into architecture's internality. Fredric Jameson writes: "the individual construction can once again discover a vocation to enact the totality, albeit in an inversion of the modernist gesture."[26] We have seen earlier in these pages how this strategy works through Koolhaas's recoding of the open-plan, for example. What makes the next two projects different from the Kunsthal is the exaggeration of the aforementioned transference to the point that architecture now is turned into a container of such an operational recoding. Losing its modernist political agenda, the OMA's architecture now seeks to "explore this new freedom aggressively."[27] The shift has two consequences evident in the competition entries for the Zeebrugge Sea Terminal, Belgium, and the Très Grande Bibliothèque (TGB), France.

It is not too far-fetched to suggest that the transference of theatricality into the internality of architecture provides the architect with an opportunity to engage in a radical re-interpretation of program. In the present situation, when architecture is on the verge of the total absorption of spectacle, and when "institutions assess designs primarily in terms of their advertising and public-relations values," Hubert Damisch writes, it is to the credit of Koolhaas to "defend against all and sundry, the eminently 'modern' notion of the program, by opposing to the cult of signs and simulacra," the unconscious processes of metropolitan culture.[28] Furthermore, and paradoxically, most attempts aiming to withdraw the object from the present visual spectacle turn the work into an alien if not a surreal work, and this in consideration of the fact that no matter how the concept of *big* is rendered by the OMA, it was, nevertheless, already at work in the American shopping malls and in today's virtual space, the latter a boundless store of information and data. Interestingly enough, the aesthetic of theatricalization is delivered today either through display and seductive commodities (mall), or in the euphoria of surfing from one virtual space to another (media websites).

Consider the Très Grande Bibliothèque (TGB), Paris, where several repository blocks float within the library's internal volume. The voids keeping these blocks apart, both vertically and horizontally, are assigned to public spaces and information data. The volumetric organization can be associated with a series of Pablo Picasso's paintings where the nude bodies of several females float in an invisible container. The OMA's design is also a reminder of Alberto Giacometti's *Objets mobiles et muets* where disagreeable objects, symbolizing death and sex, are hung from the work's cage-like frame. The analogy to the body, however, delivers the radicalism at work in both vertical and horizontal sections of the TGB. Similar to the corporeality of the body, the volume of this project is composed of various independent organs. Similar to the scans taken from various sections of the body, the plans of the Bibliothèque vary from one level to another both in shape, in the composition of its aggregates, and in the assigned functions (Figure 5.10). According to the architect, "in this block, the major public spaces are defined as absences of building, voids carved out from the information solid."[29] The suggested organic analogy is not meant to return to the body as a perfect entity symbolizing the architecture of humanism. It, rather, recalls the Latin word *organicus* meaning both organic and mechanics, in connection with Jameson's observation that what is presupposed in Bibliothèque "is that ultimate rejoining and re-identification of the organic with the mechanical that Gilles Deleuze and Donna Haraway, each in his or her very different ways, theorize and celebrate; but within a category—that of totality—alien to either of them."[30] As noted earlier, the idea of totality delivered in this project presents the constellation of already known generic elements dear to modernism.

Even in its obvious references to Le Corbusier's Chandigarh, the design still does its best to dismantle the connection the French architect would make between the Dom-ino frame and its related planimetric organization. Having allocated most of the service areas to one side of the rectangular volume of the TGB, an attempt is made to minimize the spatial and functional bearing of the grid structural system. The strategy, however, does not deliver the full operation of the OMA's public projects where a deliberate effort is made to

5.10   OMA, Très Grande Bibliothèque, Paris, 1989. Plan drawing. Image courtesy of OMA

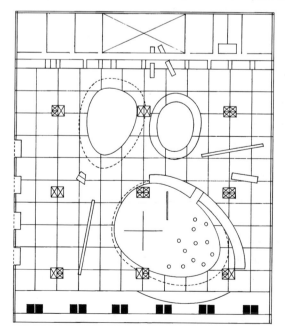

resolve the conflict between the freedom of the internal spatial enclosure and the limits imposed by the chosen columnar structural system. To this end, and taking advantage of Vierendeel beams first used in an early scheme of the Kunsthal,[31] the design of the TGB should be considered a reductive statement equating tectonics with the structural and at the expense of the representational. With the assistance of Cecil Balmond,[32] and having in mind Louis Kahn's use of concrete Vierendeel trusses in the laboratory section of the Salk Institute of Biological Studies,[33] freedom of internal spaces is secured by re-examining the structural potentialities of the element of wall. Dividing the plan into five parallel zones of 12.5 meters, the continuous vertical reinforced concrete walls allowed the architect to cut them freely into any shape or volume. In doing so, the spatial limits imposed by both the Dom-ino frame, and the space/structure integrity implied in Kahn's idea of *room* are avoided. The final structural system seems, however, developed in the hypothetical turn of the vertical stratification of the floors of the Dom-ino system through 90 degrees. Thus, a correspondence between section and plan is established wherein the space becomes column free! The theatricalization charged to the structural system of the TGB is balanced by the tectonic rapport established between the block of the service container and a series of X-shaped columns placed at the entry level (Figure 5.11).

Aspects of the above strategies for recoding a few architectonic elements of the early modernism are also evident in the Zeebrugge Sea Terminal. Take the balloon shape of the main space, which looks like a lighthouse, an appropriate analogy as far as the purpose of the contained space is concerned, a seaport terminal. Regardless of where the initial conceptual scheme originated, the final decision concerning the building's surface articulation highlights the essentiality of enclosure for architecture. The variety of surface punctuations, especially the triangular window-cuts of the office area, and the glazed dome are suggestive of the self-supportive nature of the project's enclosure. These tectonic considerations are convincing considering the autonomy of the internal space/structure economy. Like an electrical bulb, the main volume sits above a base, which comprises roads and ramps. Still similar to a balloon, the bottom surface is tucked into these infrastructural elements.

The final form, however, has its precedent in the architect's repertoire One Is reminded of what is called "Piranesian Space; delirious infrastructure," a drawing prepared for the Lille project, 1989. A spiral volume of various infrastructural means hovers, like a bundle of cloth, above a train station (TGV). It seems the intention was to connect the soaring hotel to the train station whose escalators run in different directions. This cartoon-like image, however, epitomizes the OMA's grand *project*, which is concerned with absorbing the urban into architecture, to recall Ungers again.[34] We are also reminded of another project of Koolhaas; the Serpentine Pavilion (2006), a spectacular ovoid-shaped inflatable canopy floating above the gallery's lawn. Made from translucent material, the canopy's articulation with the wall enclosure below is nothing but a radical twist to the tectonic conventions of the earth-work and the roof-work. The overall form of the Zeebrugge considered, attention should be given to the Globe Tower, a project that could not escape

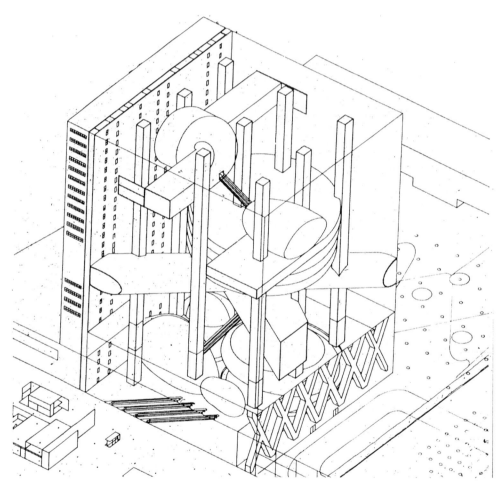

5.11   OMA, Très Grande Bibliothèque, Paris, 1989. Axonometric view. Drawing courtesy of OMA

the critical eye of the author of *Delirious New York*. Designed by Samuel Fried, the Globe Tower was intended to house various functional spaces including an aerial hippodrome, hotel, ballroom, and other facilities expected to entertain its 50,000 temporary residents. Similar to the OMA's Sea Terminal, the Globe Tower was designed to sit above various modes of transport, including a subway and railways, one branch of which runs into the sea like a pier for boats.[35]

Still, the surreal and floating shape of the Sea Terminal denies any conventional tectonic articulation of the earth-work. Jameson correctly observes that the form's floating "means a radical absence of ground as such."[36] And the architect suggests that the whole thing should be considered a junk space "sealed, held together not by structure, but by skin, like a bubble."[37] Thus we have the form's elusiveness and its dismissal of the tectonics of any import. This, however, does not mean that there is no tectonics at work in the project. I would go further and argue—and this in association with the work of neo-avant-garde architects discussed throughout this manuscript—that the tectonic is ontological to architecture regardless of the architect's theorization and intention to disengage from the subject. That the tectonic is the subconscious of architecture is one reason why architecture is not *architecture* if it does not have an enclosure, for instance. This is not to say that every articulation of enclosure, including the current shift to surface is conceived and embellished in reference to its constructed form, that which is behind the cladding. The tectonic discussed throughout this volume offers a strategy for critiquing contemporary architecture's shift to theatricalization. Having established this theoretical paradigm, it is also important to say that, similar to the obscure aesthetics of commodity fetishism, this particular project of the OMA is exemplary of architecture's tendency to become an object of beauty in its own right.

Finally, the last two projects of the OMA discussed above share a number of commonalities, including size, particular tactile sensibilities, and formal elusiveness. One might suggest that the sum total of these attributes generates an ethereal ambience of the kind evident in Leonidov's Dom Narkomtjazjprom, Moscow (1933). Similar to the latter, the simplicity and serenity of the OMA's projects adhere to a *totality* that in return allows the object to rise out of its context if only to suggest "a gradual unfolding of the future away from the past."[38] This is achieved by the imposition of a "nondifferential form," which in the context of the playfulness permeating contemporary architecture, "enables the differentiation of what goes on around it."[39] The above two projects also confront the crisis of contemporary architecture, and reproach modernism in a postmodern mode. The OMA's work refuses "the positive inquiry into semantics, the structural semiotics that have characterized so many attempts to develop 'true' language in recent years. Nor does it intend to anthropologize its production with a false mask of humanism." Anthony Vidler continues: the OMA does its best to "disrupt all previous 'natures."[40] Whereas the strategies surrealism pursued were mostly in criticism of modernism's general tendency towards the *Neue Sachlichkeit*, Koolhaas's built and unbuilt projects present an open field of experimentation for recoding a few basic formal solutions established by modernism. The OMA does this beyond the postmodernist idea of both/and rhetoric. In Felicity Scott's words, Koolhaas's work "is cast neither as assimilation nor as opposition to expanding capitalist forces but as a strategy of occupying the anachronistic interstices concurrently emerging amidst incompatible technological systems."[41] We have already noted in the previous chapter the strategic importance for Tschumi to reiterate what Ernst Bloch called the empty lot, a residue left behind by the production and consumption cycles of capitalism. Whatever this means theoretically today, it is to Koolhaas's credit to charge architecture with an image the very modern architectonic elements of which *look* out of time and place. In other words, his architecture contemplates the modernity of architecture as the archaic past of the present culture of spectacle, in recollection of Walter Benjamin's notion of dialectical images discussed in previous chapters.

TWISTING THE FRAME

From what was said about Koolhaas's strategic approach to the generic achievements of modernism, we can posit the following. In the early decades of the last century there was enough space within the totality of capitalism under construction for architecture to still keep a hold on its disciplinary history and yet present itself as the agent of social and political transformation. That space today has been overtaken by the culture of spectacle. If one agrees with this observation, then, it is possible to suggest that Eisenman's recent work, for example, takes topology as one possible theme for making an opening into the suggested ideological "closure." One is reminded of his design for Galicia, Spain, and the Memorial to the Murdered Jews of Europe, Berlin (2005). As we will see in the last chapter, the former project sought to avoid the "Bilbao effect," and at the same time to smooth the tectonic transition from the enclosure to the roof. In the second project, the uneven arrangement of stelae assumes the outline of a topological wave. There will be more on architecture's turn to topology in the next chapter when Zaha Hadid takes the stage. The following discussion, instead, underlines the OMA's different take on topology and surface-enclosure, the latter considered by many architects, including Greg Lynn, as the trademark of contemporaneity. Without touching on the complex subject of contemporaneity,[42] the intention here is to expand the scope of the following question: how can architects today pursue Semper's tectonic of theatricality without dismissing the technological and aesthetic aspects of contemporary culture?

The question concerns Koolhaas's design for the Seattle Central Library where the *envelope* is not treated as surface (Figure 5.12). Somewhat similar to a tent, the building's enclosure covers the void, the library's main public space, including internal volumes each housing different parts of the program. Instead of using idioms such as cladding, or dressing, the notion of envelope is used here to highlight the design's particular take on the tectonics. Consider this: the word cladding suggests covering or adding a layer of different material to an existing surface. Dressing, on the other hand, means covering a mass for a particular representational goal, abstract or otherwise. For cladding, one is reminded of Mediterranean architecture where white stucco is applied over a masonry

5.12   OMA, The Seattle Public Library, Seattle, Washington, 2004. Exterior view. Photograph by author

structure. For dressing, one thinks of Andrea Palladio's use of classical orders in the Basilica Vicenza (1549), where the architect intended to smooth and embellish the remnants of Gothic irregularities, for example. Therefore, instead of treating the cover either as an abstract surface, or for that matter a shell (Greg Lynn's blob shapes), or the pneumatic structures in fashion during the 1960s, Koolhaas's design tries to modify the modernist idea of skin and bone tectonics. One is reminded of Mies with the Seagram Building and Le Corbusier with the Unité d'Habitation, Marseilles. In both cases the element of clothing is conceived along the notion of "thickening the wall," albeit with two different tectonic intentions. In Le Corbusier's case the surface punctuations are decided in reference to the individual units. Mies, instead, articulated a surface dressing that is more in tune with the prevailing industrial materials and the idea of wrapping a singular volume.

In the Seattle Library, the tectonics of the Seagram Building is twisted in two distinct ways. On the one hand, the steel and glass envelope of the building works similarly to a braided cover. Interestingly enough, in Semper's theory of dressing, the technique of braiding is considered advantageous to that of weaving mainly because its elements do not "necessarily have to cross one another at right angle as required by weaving."[43] Koolhaas writes; "The skin performs almost every task that is not performed by the diagram. It gives the overall identity, structure, organizes earthquake resistance, performs as technical membrane—breathing in and out—and also creates the necessary lighting conditions."[44] On the other hand, the building's final form is similar to a hollow rectangular container twisted and pushed down, and then enveloped by a grid system combining panes and aluminum mullions. Many formal deflections of this conceptual container are articulated in response to the building's base (earth-work), a concrete box, the exterior profile of

5.13   OMA, The
Seattle Public
Library, Seattle,
Washington,
2004. Interior
view. Photograph
by author

which is edited in reference to the slope of the site and programmatic considerations such as the main entrance located on the ground floor.

It is interesting to note that the animated envelope of the building evokes different sentiments compared to the theatricalization permeating most digital architecture. The building is animated "not by anthropomorphic or physiognomic similarities … but by abstract energy relations created by juxtaposition of its volumes and surfaces, creating an almost magnetic decorum."[45] This quality of the work should be attributed to two things. In the first place, the original concept of the building's space and its envelope emulates the idea of a braided net that covers both the served and service spaces (Figure 5.13). Also, it can be attributed to the strategy of putting the administration area at the top of the book stacks (the spiral), a move that allows the architect to distribute the remaining spaces (various public reading areas and circulation) around, above, and below the service space. Contrary to most surface architecture, the building is not generated by the sole power of digital programming either; its form, pleat, textures, and structure are, rather, conceived according to the proposed program diagram, wherein three rectangular boxes are held apart by public spaces. Obviously, the design registers a tectonic thinking that departs from the core-form and art-form dichotomy. According to Balmond, "architecture and structure become part of each other in this project with external cascade and internal drift. The void itself becomes the shaping factor."[46] This is clear from the location of the building's concrete columns, few of which are vertical. However, according to the principal engineer of the project, "where columns are not vertical, they are sloped or skewed in the most direct way to support the transition between where a load is applied and where it is best resisted."[47] What is involved here concerns the architectonic consequence of Koolhaas's initial spatial concept, the void. It also concerns the envelope that in this particular case does not follow the given separation between the clothing and the mass, even though not much of the latter's conventional connotation is left intact.

Of further tectonic modifications at work in this project mention should be made of the conventional articulation of the earth-work and the frame-work, and tropes such as the veranda, which in a suggestive way is placed at the rear side of the building, even though the building does not go so far as to address the issue of frontality. The building's face, according to Ayad Rahmani, "has given way to a kind of interface … in which activities are inserted and hyper-energized."[48] Furthermore, the perceived spatial envelope recodes the traditional notion of ornament as an addition to the structure. In the Seattle Library, the interplay between various materials turns the envelope into a structural ornament in its own right. It is to the architect's credit to rethink the tectonic, transforming the material fabric of the building into fabrication.

Thus in the Seattle Library one sees Semper's theory of dressing in a different light. The design provides unmediated access to the essentiality of roofing and clothing in spite of architecture's inevitable entanglement with the present aesthetic culture of commodification. And yet, having Steven Holl's Chapel of St. Ignatius (see Chapter 8 of this volume) within walking distance, one cannot but ask what role does architecture play in the city? The subject will be taken up again in this volume. Here suffice it to say that, exploring various elements of tectonics, the *object* in these two different projects is turned into an anonymous urban figure. Neither building emulates the postmodern esteem for semiological communication, nor buys the current tendency for surface spectacle. Their difference is significant, however: whereas one can hardly apprehend the Seattle Library as civic architecture, Holl's project engages the thematic of the culture of building, such as the atmospheric use of natural and artificial light, water, typological and tectonic figurations associated with civic architecture, even though these tropes are reactivated beyond their conventional limits. Contrary to Holl's tendency for the civic, the Seattle Library is an urban provocateur! The disappearance of the line separating the element of wall from the roof in this project should be seen as a deliberate act of erasure of the façade, which has been known for a long time as the public face of civic architecture.

SCULPTED TECTONICS

Whilst geometry is central to the image-laden drawings produced by digital programming, there are a few contemporary architects who attempt to intermingle geometry with sculptural tectonics. Besides Hadid's architecture, which will be discussed in the next chapter, one is reminded of the OMA's Casa da Música in Porto, where, similar to Claude-Nicolas Ledoux's "the House of Agricultural Guards," the building looks as if it has been tossed like a stone into the landscape. The theatrical placement of this monolithic volume on its site is evident in the entry slab's protrusion as it steps down to the ground (Figure 5.14). Of further interest are the two major stereotomic cuts, which position the building parallel to the main axis of the city (Figure 5.15). The building's site, the park on the Rotunda de Boavista, is nevertheless transformed from a hinge between the old and the new Porto into "a positive encounter of two different models of the city."[49] This transformation is supported by additional cuts, which happen to follow the spatial organization of the building and are detectable in the longitudinal section (Figure 5.16). With two window openings at each end of the volume, the void created by the main auditorium provides visual connectivity between the suggested two parts of the city. And yet the building's section introduces another topographical layer to Porto's playful landscape.

Thus, the collective invested in this project complements its monumental gesture to reactivate a different notion of *res publica*. This is important not only in consideration of Alvaro Siza's sculptural tectonic of Fundacao

5.14   OMA, Casa da Música, Porto, 2005. General view. Photograph by author

5.15   OMA, Casa da Música, Porto, 2005. Aerial view. Photograph courtesy of OMA

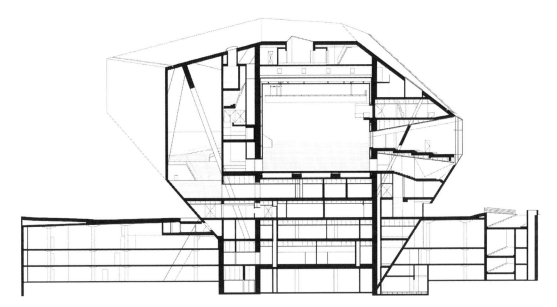

Ibere Camargo, Brazil, but also of the civic architecture delivered in the Miesian tectonics of column and roof, the Berlin National Gallery, the civic historicity of which is lost in the large scale projects of Renzo Piano, for one. Still, where both Frank Gehry's Disney Concert Hall (see Chapter 7) and Hans Scharoun's Berlin Philharmonic Concert Hall exemplify what I would call two moments of subjective creativity, the buildings of Siza and Koolhaas are theatrical notes in the otherwise aesthetic tranquility delivered by the large projects of Piano, the addition to the Art Institute of Chicago, and also by the architecture of digital expressionism. There are two issues involved here: that the idea of big discussed by Koolhaas should not be taken literally; and that, born of the womb of a hand-in-craft *métier*, architecture cannot bear the burden of large-scale programmatic needs unless it turns itself into a shelter, no matter how articulated its architectonics might be.

Of further interest in the projects of Siza and Koolhaas is the interior void, the public hearth. Whereas Siza's project bears some similarity to Frank Lloyd Wright's Guggenheim Museum, New York City, a different case should be made to discuss the OMA's building in Porto. The aim is not to place importance on the role civic architecture plays in the creation of public spaces, but on what does remain of the civic when the design of a house is magnified to accommodate a different program, as is the case with the Casa da Música.

Both with central churches and Gothic cathedrals, a non-architectural phenomenon dictated the geometrical organization of the plan and the volume. The humanist metaphysics of representation, the interplay between circle and square and/or the cross-shaped plans, were further transformed during the nineteenth century when new building types were in demand. Consider the Hal de Machine where the size and the geometry of the plan mainly follow the building's function. Of these typological transformations mention should also be made of a series of fine work produced during the early decades of the last century, one

5.16   OMA, Casa da Música, Porto, 2005. Longitudinal section drawing. Image courtesy of OMA

distinctive mark of which is the public void designed for different purposes. Along with numerous examples, one is reminded of Frank Lloyd Wright's Larkin Building, Buffalo (1904), where the columns extending to the glazed ceiling surround the building's rectangular central open space. In addition to the fact that this building anticipated the secularization of public space, what Frampton calls the vulnerability of the workplace to the "dictates of production"[50] should direct our attention to the Larkin building's planimetric organization. The volume rises out of a central rectangular void surrounded by service spaces and a structural system that integrates the two.

A similar case can be made for the Casa da Música, the final design of which emerged out of Koolhaas's design for a house called Y2K, Rotterdam (1999). Following the client's request, this unbuilt house comprises a central rectangular gathering space surrounded by various service spaces the overall form of which resembles a cut diamond. The suggested transformation in size, from small to big, necessitated a structural system different from the one sought for the house, and obviously different from the one used in the Larkin Building. It is to this tectonic shift that the technique of cut is introduced here to highlight its strategic role suspending the spectacular look permeating most digitally programmed architecture.

Without emulating the playful forms that align architecture with the present spectacle, the cuts implemented in the monolithic mass of the Casa da Música should be discussed in the context of "competing mediating disciplines, of rival forms of knowledge, to which architecture, with its occasional claim to autonomy, has long sought to belong."[51] Of these, mention should be made of the theatricality invested in the look of the building in relation to its structural system. Whereas the turn to the sculptural in the late work of Le Corbusier, and its consequential influence on brutalism, had to do with the materiality that more often than not was conceptualized in the image of a masonry construction system, no unitary structural system informs the Casa da Música. The main rectangular box of the concert hall, for example, has its own structure whose two long vertical sides are supported by what are called "wall columns."[52] This technique was first tested for Très Grande Bibliothèque, but in Porto the "wall columns" emerged out of a four-story crust structure.

Radically transformed in this project is the tectonics of earth-work and frame-work: not only is the top slab of the above-mentioned crust split and lifted to make an entry for the car-park underground, also transformed radically, is the expected distinction between the element of roofing and wrapping. The self-supported rectangular auditorium allows for a different articulation of the lateral enclosure, the extension of which is decided by the length of a smaller auditorium, on the one end, and the circulatory volume on the opposite. A further tectonic consequence of pushing the enclosure outward is the twist given to the Miesian column and wall rapport evident in the Barcelona Pavilion (1927).[53] Whereas the embellished partitions of the Pavilion are positioned to defy the visual consequences of its structural grid system, in the Casa da Música the columns are positioned so as to project both the internal volume and its external envelope. Similar to the tectonics of fortification, props are used in the main lobby either to keep apart the two adjacent walls, or to transfer part of the upper level weight to the slab below and through a slanted concrete column.

In the Casa da Música, the structural set-up is architectural. A *primitive* articulation of the tectonics of column and wall dominates the entry lobby, and this in contrast to the architect's strategic attention to material embellishment, be it of fabric, wood, corrugated glass, or ceramic. A few embellishments connote regional sensibilities, and others are highly image driven of the kind seen in the best work of the OMA. And yet, if transformation in size and typological modification are part of the OMA's strategic recoding of concepts such as the civic and monumentality, how should these issues be approached in China where urbanization is unfolding beyond the historicity of Europe and America of the mid-twentieth century?

BENDING THE TOWER

Modernization involves territorial transformation requiring architecture to play a constructive role. This is clear from early modernization history not only of Europe and America, but also of Japan and other countries, a few of which were late in entering this historical process. The common cord running through modernization can be called "creative destruction"—the cyclic demolition and rebuilding of the urban landscape—wherein the city dwellers had to confront the resulting environmental chaos, and to accept along with it the psychological consequences of urbanization.

The processes involved in the modernization of China are distinctly different from those for other latecomers. The suggested uniqueness has to do with a global situation that is informed by the emergence of international corporations, and the flow of media technologies across national borders. Yet, the aforementioned de-territorialization of landscape and population remains a major factor even today. This is evident from Jia Zhang Ke's clever film *Still Life* (2006), in which he presents a filmic analogy between destruction of the built form and the disintegration of working-class families in a Chinese province. Depicting aspects of Chinese modernization and its impact on the migration of labor, the film is reminiscent of some passages of Frederick Engels's observations in *The Condition of the Working Class in England in 1844* (1845). If the rise of the *Neue Sachlichkeit* movement was the major architectural consequence of early modernization taking place in Europe, the Chinese case demonstrates a monumental tendency towards showcasing architecture across the board. Architects from around the world (with a limited connotation applied to the term "architect") are invited to fill the landscape of China with works, few of which contribute any understanding of the political role architecture should play in late capitalism.

An exception to this rather unqualified generalization is the OMA's design for the Central Chinese Television (CCTV) Headquarters in Beijing (Figure 5.17). The idea here is to map Koolhaas's project within the historicity of the tall building and its two significant turning points—Louis Sullivan's Wainwright Building (1895), and Mies's Seagram Building (1958)—and to demonstrate the modifications involved in the typological development of the tall building.

Sullivan's text, "The Tall Office Building Artistically Considered," written in 1896, demands attention. Starting with the economic and technological imperatives of the time, Sullivan set himself the task of theorizing the tall building, according

5.17   OMA, The CCTV Headquarters, Beijing, 2002. Perspective drawing. Image courtesy of OMA

to a programmatic analysis centered on its essential verticality. Even today, it is important to note the way Sullivan avoided models based on humanist discourse, while cementing the three-part composition of the Wainwright Building (Figure 5.18). Whatever other connotations one might attribute to Sullivan's term "artistically," it is the discourse of the tectonic that did not escape the attention of the progressive architects working in the Chicago of those decades.

The short English translation of Semper's *Style* (1889) was indeed available to Chicago readers; in it, the German architect discusses the importance of both construction, and the ethics involved in its artistic representation. Following Semper, and combining a logical analysis of the building's purpose with the need for ornamentation, Sullivan made every inch of the tall building "a proud soaring thing," as he put it. Also noteworthy is the concept of spatial organization (subdivision) that, in Sullivan's description, is based on an individual cell (room) framed by a window and two adjacent piers. The organic dialogue Sullivan establishes between form and function is in part motivated

5.18   H. Sullivan, The Wainwright Building, St. Louis, 1891. Exterior view. Photograph by author

by the vertical and horizontal repetition of these individual cells. This is evident from the artistic expression—that is, tectonic—of the building's soaring elements, which could be read simultaneously as columns and masonry mullions.

What makes Mies's approach to tall buildings different has little to do with the socioeconomic conditions that underpinned Sullivan's ethical approach to architecture. Mies's Seagram Building is a novel concept of spatial organization that is driven by an abstract and free space (open plan?) standing between two parallel slabs, not by the repetition of individual cells (Figure 5.19). Thus, in the Seagram Building, the placement of vertical and horizontal mullions is detailed to show how the cladding wraps around the building like a garment. The artistic expression of the cladding in Sullivan's Wainwright Building, instead, is still indebted to the classical vision of the façade, which more often than not is framed by a hefty corner pier. The abstract grid of Seagram's curtain wall, instead, assures the building's vertical posture with the suggestion of a void within. More important, and as far as the relation of architecture to the city is concerned, is the position of Mies's tower on the plinth, the perimeter of which is defined by the grid of Manhattan, and yet it resists fully engaging with the spatial-economic structure of the city. The plinth was for Mies the architectonics by which he hoped to re-enact the individual's disconnection from community that began in the Renaissance.[54]

5.19 Mies van der Rohe, Seagram Building, New York City, 1958. General view. Photograph by Bettman/Corbis

Whereas Sullivan's and Mies's buildings reveal a shifting architectonics within the development of the tall building, the OMA's CCTV building demonstrates a critical engagement with this process. Central to this design is the intention of undermining the verticality induced by the movement of elevators, plus other economic and technical considerations exemplified in the needle-high-rise typology. In his early work, Koolhaas had already explored designs combining two or three vertical and inclined bar-shaped volumes. In the Togok Tower (1996) in Seoul, for example, the building's three volumes are tied together, integrating each tower into a larger whole. The design employs a structural system that frees the building's soaring tendency from the vertical projection of a fixed ground-floor plan.

A different approach to figure-ground and the issue of verticality is suggested in Louis Kahn's design for the Philadelphia City Hall Tower (1956). The soaring posture of this unbuilt project is primarily informed by repetition of its space-frame module. Noteworthy in Kahn's project—and in the experimental structures developed by Kahn's collaborator, the French engineer Robert Le Ricolais, and by the British structural engineer Felix Samuely—is a system in which the structural strength is provided by the hollowing out or coring of solid blocks of matter; Le Ricolais described it as "where to put the holes." Thus was introduced the possibility to perceive the tall building as a hollow tube, the strength of which is assured by a thickening of the rim. In the conceptual shift from the structural system modeled on "plane" to that modeled on "space," the structural action moves to the periphery where the skin now addresses, at least partially, the forces of gravity.

Lost in the late 1950s experimentation with structures that operated like hollow tubes is the Miesian notion of "God is in the details," where the detail is expressed through the structural elements. Again, one is reminded of Kahn's proposed project for a welded tubular steel structure (Philadelphia), and also of the body of work developed by Konrad Wachsmann. However, in the recent renewed interest in applying science to structural engineering, and specifically the projects designed by Balmond, the ornamental nature of the vertical mullions of the Seagram Building's curtain wall gives way to the CCTV's diamond-bracing surface pattern, the primary function of which is to respond to the structural forces of stressing. If in the Seagram Building one could still pursue a Semperian understanding of the tectonic—in which artistic expression is sought in association with the constructed space—in the CCTV Headquarters, and in the Seattle Central Library, as noted earlier, the tectonic is transferred to the building's structured skin. The proliferation of diagrid and orthogonal tessellation patterns, according to Alejandro Zaera-Polo, "displays a general tendency toward antigravitational, uprooted, unstable, and differentiated *affects*, even if many of these patterns have in fact a structural function."[55] Architecture now draws its tectonics from the available technostatic experience. Thus, the exterior of the building "reveals how the construction is put together—not the actual construction, but a sort of echo of it; the inner structural network of triangles is made visible by steel beams sunk into the exterior façade, dividing the glass skin into diamond-shaped segments."[56] As in the work of engineering, where the duality implied in Semper's theory of the tectonic (the core-form versus the art-form) is subdued, the CCTV's cladding represents nothing—symbolically or otherwise—except the composing of the building's geometry with the diagram of structural forces.

An additional factor in the CCTV is the building's spatial organization. In Koolhaas's proposed designs for the National Library of France (1989) and the Sea Terminal in Zeebrugge, Belgium (1989), a concept of space is involved that is radically different from the one at work in both the Wainwright and the Seagram buildings. The floating volumes in these two projects simultaneously occupy and define the *big* volume of the building. They are similar to a horizontal section cut through the body: mutually dependent yet autonomous organs inform the planimetric organization of the library. Thus, what is similar yet radically different from Sullivan's tall building is Koolhaas's formalization of a different concept of spatial organization, not even available to Mies.

At a height of 230 meters with a floor area of about 400,000 square meters, the CCTV Headquarters combines TV-program production units with administrative and other public facilities. Instead of emphasizing verticality, the building is a continuous loop of horizontal and vertical sections, which together establish an urban site rather than a tower pointing to the sky. To avoid the single vertical posture of the traditional tower, a second building, the Television Cultural Centre (TVCC), is placed next to the main tower; it houses a hotel, a visitors' centre, a large public theater, and various exhibition spaces. The two buildings flow together morphing into one volume; this overall composition denies the verticality and horizontality that are central to the humanist figure-ground approach to design.

The CCTV's design involves the extrusion of a three-dimensional volume (void?) out of a rectangular tube: imagine two diagonally positioned vertical towers, each leaning towards the other at six degrees, both axes connected at top and bottom by an L-shaped volume. The building resembles neither a cubical box nor a vertical tower, and yet aspects of these geometries are included. The building's four main components add yet another paradox: the two towers, the base and what is called the "overhang" are composed in such a way as to deny the traditional three-part formula. This is not your postmodernist "both/and" pastiche either. Of interest here is the way the OMA conjugates the diagram of program analysis with the need for vertical and horizontal circulation. While the interior organization of the building lacks any homogeneous space of the kind expected from a public edifice, its loop-shaped figuration allows a direct exchange to take place between diverse spaces that are allocated/defined according to programmatic needs. The strategy allows for a planimetric organization

5.20   OMA,
The CCTV
Headquarters,
Beijing, 2002. Plan
drawing. Image
courtesy of OMA

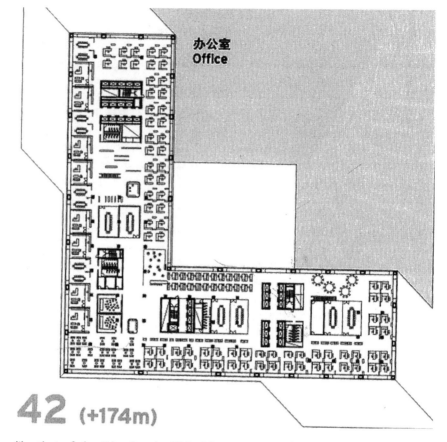

办公室
Office

42 (+174m)

like that of the Très Grande Bibliothèque, France where spatial organization is woven into the architectonic expression. Thus arises the possibility of plotting the building's planimetric organization in various forms: from an L-shaped geometry to two semi-square enclosures and then back to another L-shaped form (Figure 5.20). To what extent can these formalistic extrusions, motivated by the famous nine-square cube design problem, possibly have "urbanistic or representational significance," and this in reference to Frampton's referral to works such as the Eiffel Tower and El Lissitzky's *Wolkenbürgel* proposal for 1924, both inspirational precedents for the CCTV Headquarters?[57] Whereas El Lissitzky's tower was seemingly designed to be placed at the old gates of Moscow, Koolhaas's tower looks like an alien object having landed in a context where the processes of urbanization is taken for granted. Thus follows the legitimate question: if the critical significance of Étienne-Louis Boullée's work relates to the historicity of the Baroque, should the *big* architecture of the CCTV be considered in defiance of the expressionism permeating the parametric design, for example? And yet another concern: as an urban artifact, does it "provide conditional opportunities for development so that this impetus is not legible merely as an image making opportunity but also as a civic contribution to the real experience of the city"?[58] Or else, should we take the design's alien look for another proof of the farce, the claim made by most neo-avant-garde architects as the agent of historical transformation?

Gone also in the CCTV is the organic concept that was essential to Sullivan's artistic consideration of a techno-economic building type. Absent too is the Miesian esteem for abstraction, in which the building retains its objecthood at the cost of excluding the subject, that is, the subjective drive of the architect. What is involved in the move from the Wainwright Building to the Seagram is the aesthetic of abstraction: moving from the many facets of a building that could still communicate with the spectator to the Miesian "almost nothing," where every symbolic association gives way to a notion of anonymity informing the tectonic figuration. In the further mutation, and central to the historicity of the CCTV, one might argue that in late capitalism architects are hardly able to think buildings either as symbolic (Sullivan) or anonymous tectonics (Mies), but as a "subject" charged with a "look." No matter how surreal the CCTV might look, this does not compensate for the loss of the agent of architecture's critical rapport with the city, the plinth. An analogue of which can be found in Elia Zenghelis's Hotel Sphinx in Times Square (1975), in Ungers' numerous works in Berlin, and in the Dutch architect's projects produced in collaboration with the two.[59] Considering the present state of Chinese modernization, and Ungers' strategic approach to the city, the CCTV might be considered an approximation to what Frampton calls the "confrontation between place-form and the open city."[60]

In the present global culture where the people (read workers) unite to consume the aesthetic of commodity fetishism, architecture too has no choice but to internalize the same visual aesthetics. However, noteworthy in the work of a few contemporary architects is a conscious move to castrate the processes whereby architecture is subjected to the theatricality permeating the image-laden culture of late capitalism. Visiting most of Koolhaas's built projects, one can conclude that central to the aesthetic of the OMA's work is the montage of an embellished locale in the interior space (think of Vladimir Tatlin's corner reliefs, if not *trompe l'œil*), which in most cases stands in sharp contrast to its surrounding environment. Similar to the interior of the Euralille Convention Centre in Lille, France (1994), the available images of the CCTV's interior are also suggestive of Koolhaas's tendency for creating a theatrical visual ensemble where rough, exposed constructed materials are used next to the sensual quality of textures and reflective surfaces such as fabric, glass, mirror. His work is far different from both the totalized interiors of the art nouveau and the naked purity of early or late modernism. To twist Robert Venturi's problematic idea of "both/and" (1966), Koolhaas's design—more than any other contemporary architect's work—is centered on the sublime aesthetics of ambiguity evident today in the collapse of radical strategies of the historical avant-garde in the spectacle of mass culture.

However, it is plausible to suggest that two strategies run through the best of the OMA's work, including the released proposals for towers, the Mixed Tower (Jersey City, NJ) and the Museum Plaza Tower (Louisville, KY). These projects are perceived, firstly, to recode traditional typologies, and to tease out the lore of the aesthetic of commodity fetishism without rejecting the temporality essential to modernism. Architecture for Koolhaas, writes Aaron Betsky, "is no longer just a question of building, but of condensing data into form that is both insubstantial (modernist) and seductive (Manhattanist) enough to become mythic."[61] Secondly, the aesthetic visuality inherited from the traditions of Dutch modernism is often used by the OMA to modify the present aesthetic of spectacle. As the culture of late capitalism moves to occupy every landscape regardless of its political color, it remains to be seen to what extent the OMA's future projects can employ the theatricality underpinning Russian constructivism.

This longing for what might come next in Koolhaas's busy daily life might be something like "waiting for Godot." It does say, however, something about what has already taken place: the extent to which the architect has internalized Salvador Dalí's Paranoid-Critical Method as a way forward. In doing so, and like most neo-avant-garde architecture, the CCTV does not critically engage with the forces of contemporary urbanization. This is not to suggest that architecture should turn or return to iconography or symbolic languages associable with values that do not belong to the contemporary state of urbanization. To be critical, architecture should rethink aspects of the *polis* without dismissing the progressive forces of contemporary urbanization. Again, I am thinking of the plinth in the Seagram Building, which neither operates like a podium for the politics of the collective, nor reduces the work to "nothingness," the void left behind as the processes of abstraction and urbanization are further intensified. Evidently Koolhaas is aware of this even though the wish-image dimension of his work more often than not remains limited to the subtle visual recollection of formal solutions codified during the heroic period of modernism.

NOTES

1   On this subject see Gevork Hartoonian, *Ontology of Construction* (Cambridge: Cambridge University Press, 1994), 68–80.

2   Rem Koolhaas, "Cities within the City," *Lotus International* 19 (1978): 82–97. Also see Pier Vittorio Aureli, *The Possibility of an Absolute Architecture* (Cambridge, MA: The MIT Press, 2011), particularly the final chapter. And Kenneth Frampton, "O.M. Ungers and the Architecture of Coincidence," in K. Frampton and Silvis Kolbowski, eds, *O.M. Ungers: Works in Progress, 1976–1980* (New York: Rizzoli, 1951), 1–5.

3   Kenneth Frampton, "O.M. Ungers and the Architecture of Coincidence," 1951, 3.

4   Rem Koolhaas, "Cities within the City," 1978, 86.

5   Hal Foster, "Image Building," in Anthony Vidler, ed., *Architecture between Spectacle and Use* (New Haven, CT: Yale University Press, 2008), 164–79.

6   On this subject see Stanford Kwinter, "The Reinvention of Geometry," *Assemblage* 18 (1992): 82–5. And, Kwinter, "Spoke Check: A Conversation between Rem Koolhaas and Sarah Whiting," *Assemblage* 40 (1999): 36–55. Also, Veronique Patteeuw, ed., *What Is OMA?: Considering Rem Koolhaas and the Office of Metropolitan Architecture* (Rotterdam: Nai Publisher, 2003).

7   See Roberto Gargiani, *Rem Koolhaas-OMA* (London: Routledge, 2008).

8   Here I am following Benjamin H.D. Buchloh's reading of Thomas Hirschhorn's work in *Thomas Hirschhorn* (New York: Phaidon Publications, 2004), 40–93. See also Hal Foster, "Towards a Grammar of Emergency," *New Left Review* 68 (March/April 2011): 105–18.

9   Fritz Neumeyer, "OMA's Berlin: The Polemic Island in the City," *Assemblage* 11 (1990): 36–53.

10   Felicity Scott, "Involuntary Prisoners of Architecture," *October* 106 (fall 2003): 81.

11   Pier Vittorio Aureli, *The Possibility of an Absolute Architecture*, 2010, 180.

12   This I would suggest is the missing point in Pier Vittorio Aureli's analysis. See endnote 2.

13   See, for example, Gevork Hartoonian, *Modernity and Its Other: A Post-Script to Contemporary Architecture* (College Station, TX: Texas A&M University Press, 1997).

14   See R. Gargiani, *Rem Koolhaas*, 2008, 26.

15   Rem Koolhaas and Gerrit Oorthuys, "Ivan Leonidov's Dom Narkomtjazprom, Moscow," *Oppositions* 2 (1974): 96.

16   Benjamin H.D. Buchloh, "Thomas Hirschhorn: Layout Sculpture and Display Diagrams," in *Thomas Hirschhorn*, 2004, 88.

17   On the uniqueness of Rem Koolhaas's few designed houses, see Bart Verschffell, "The Survival Ethics of Rem Koolhaas: The First Houses by OMA," in Veronique Patteeuw, ed., *Considering Rem Koolhaas*, 2003, 153–64.

18   Rem Koolhaas, *Delirious New York* (New York: Oxford University Press, 1974), 203.

19   Kenneth Frampton, "Rem Koolhaas, Kunsthal a Rotterdam," *Domus* 747 (1993): 44.

20   Rem Koolhaas, "Introduction," *A+U* (May 2000): 19.

21   Peter Eisenman, *Ten Canonical Buildings, 1950–2000* (New York: Rizzoli, 2008), 216.

22   Peter Eisenman, *Ten Canonical Buildings*, 2008, 202.

23   R. Gargiani, *Rem Koolhaas*, 2008, 193.

24   Margaret Iverson, *Alois Riegl: Art History and Theory* (Cambridge, MA: The MIT Press, 1993).

25   See Lian Lefavivre, "Dirty Realism in European Architecture Today," *Design Book Review* 17 (winter 1989).

26   Fredric Jameson, *The Seeds of Time* (New York: Columbia University Press, 1994), 143.

27   From OMA's entry competition statement, "TGB (Very Big Library)," *A+U* (May 2000): 250.

28   Hubert Damisch, "Manhattan Transference," in *Skyline: The Narcissistic City* (Stanford, CA: Stanford University Press, 2001), 118.

29   Rem Koolhaas, *El Croquis* 53 (1992): 68.

30   Fredric Jameson, *The Seeds of Time*, 1994, 138.

31   The girdle was named after Arthur Vierendeel who used it in iron bridges erected around 1896. For the Kunsthal project see *El Croquis* 53 (1992), and 79 (1996).

32   On Cecil Balmond's cooperation with OMA, and his approach to structure see *A+U* 11 (2006), 246.

33   See Thomas Leslie, *Louis I. Kahn: Building Art, Building Science* (New York: George Braziller, 2005), 144.

34   Stanford Kwinter, "Politics and Pastoralism," *Assemblage* 27 (1995): 30.

35   Rem Koolhaas, *Delirious New York*, 1978, 72.

36   Fredric Jameson, *The Seeds of Time*, 1994, 139.

37   Rem Koolhaas, "Introduction," *A+U* (May 2000): 17.

38   I am reiterating Rem Koolhaas's reflection on the Russian architects. See Rem Koolhaas and Gerrit Oorthuys, "Ivan Leonidov's Dom Narkomtjazprom, Moscow," 1974, 103.

39   Fredric Jameson, "The Space of Post-Civil Society," *Assemblage* 17 (April 1992): 30.

40   Anthony Vidler, "Psychometropolis," in *The Architectural Uncanny* (Cambridge, MA: The MIT Press, 1992), 194.

41   Felicity Scott, "Involuntary Prisoners of Architecture," *October* 106 (fall 2003): 87.

42   See for example, Terry Smith, *What Is Contemporary Art?* (Chicago, IL: University of Chicago Press, 2009).

43   Gottfried Semper, *Style in the Technical and Tectonic Arts; or Practical Aesthetics*, trans. H.F. Mallgrave and Michael Robinson (Santa Monica, CA: Texts and Documents, The Getty Research Institute, 2004), 225.

44   Rem Koolhaas in an interview with Sarah Whitening, *Assemblage* 40 (December 1999): 49.

45   This is Spyros Papapetros's remark on Mies van der Rohe's glass tower, 1922. See Papapetros, "Animation, Animism, Animosity in German Architecture and Film from Mies to Murnau," *Grey Room* 20 (summer 2005): 26.

46   Cecil Belmond, *A+U* 6, 11 (2006): 264.

47   The quotation is by Jay Taylor and is cited in Lara Swimming, *Process: Seattle Central Library* (Seattle, WA: Documentary Media), 2005.

48   Quoted in Lara Swimming, *Process*, 2005.

49   Rem Koolhaas, *El Croquis* 134/135 (2007): 206.

50   Kenneth Frampton, *Modern Architecture* (London: Thames & Hudson, 2007), 62.

51   Rodolfo Machado and Rodolphe el-Khorury, *Monolithic Architecture* (Munich: Prestel-Verlag, 1995), 67.

52   See *El Croquis* 134/135 (2007): 226.

53   On this subject see Gevork Hartoonian, *Ontology of Construction*, 1994, 68–80.

54   Ludwig Mies van der Rohe, "The Precondition of Architectural Work," (1928) in Fritz Neumeyer, *The Artless Word: Mies van der Rohe and the Building Art* (Cambridge, MA: The MIT Press, 1991), 301.

55   Alejandro Zaera-Polo, "The Politics of Envelope," *Log* 13/14 (fall 2008): 201.

56   Edzard Mik, *Koolhaas in Beijing* (Amsterdam: Netherlands Foundation for Visual Arts, Design and Architecture, 2011), 94.

57   Kenneth Frampton, *Modern Architecture*, 2007, 345.

58   Pier Vittorio Aureli, in Pier Vittorio Aureli and Joachim Declerck, eds, *Brussels A Manifesto; Towards the Capital of Europe* (Rotterdam: NAI Publishers, 2010), 191–2.

59   I am drawing from the final chapter of Pier Vittorio Aureli, *The Possibility of an Absolute Architecture*, 2010.

60   Kenneth Frampton, "O.M. Ungers and the Architecture of Coincidence," 1951, 2.

61   Aaron Betsky, "Rem Koolhaas: The Fire of Manhattanism inside the Iceberg of Modernism," in Veronique Patteeuw, ed., *Considering Rem Koolhaas*, 2003, 39.

6

Zaha Hadid: *Proun* Without a Cause!

Much has been written about the influence of El Lissitzky's *Wolkenbügel* project on Rem Koolhaas's design of the CCTV, as discussed in the previous chapter. Equally well known is the extent to which Zaha Hadid's work, from her early pictorial drawings to her recent projects, is influenced by the visual culture of constructivism. Most of what she has produced thus far enjoys a level of theatricality and abstraction comparable to El Lissitzky's *Proun*. Central to this analogy is the creation of a dynamic visual field composed of elementary geometries. *Proun*, however, primarily sought to demolish "pictures," painting as such. El Lissitzky set the *Proun* in motion to move his work towards "neoplasticism." Conceived from various viewpoints, the object-looking drawings of *Proun* represent nothing more than facilitating the transformation of materiality to an object. El Lissitzky wrote, "The forms with which the Proun assaults space are material, not aesthetic."[1] Obviously, there are aesthetics involved in *Proun*. And yet, what El Lissitzky's statement meant was that aesthetics is not primarily driven by subjective desire and that *Proun* should be cleansed of any contextual or historical references.

The amalgamation of abstraction and dynamic composition is also evident in Zaha's graduation project prepared for the Architectural Association, London, 1977. Emulating aspects of suprematist composition, the final drawing of what was to be a hotel, designed for Hungerford Bridge, recalls the image of a spaceship floating at the edge of the earth, here the banks of the River Thames (Figure 6.1). Interestingly enough, the tectonics of this hotel were cut and dressed in reference to the brutalist forms of a 1950s art complex located on the South Bank. The implied vision of an architectural object has captivated the architect's best work today. What concern us here the most are the solid stone-looking form of *Proun* and its sober theatrical aesthetics. These characteristics will inform Hadid's work until a point in time, the 1990s to follow Patrick Schumacher,[2] when the architect submitted her design process to the logic of digital programming, parametric design. Even though her most recent projects still try to keep hold of the suprematist visuality, the association does not go far: absent in Hadid's work is the task Kasimir Malevich assigned to *Proun*, that is, the creation of a new political culture.[3]

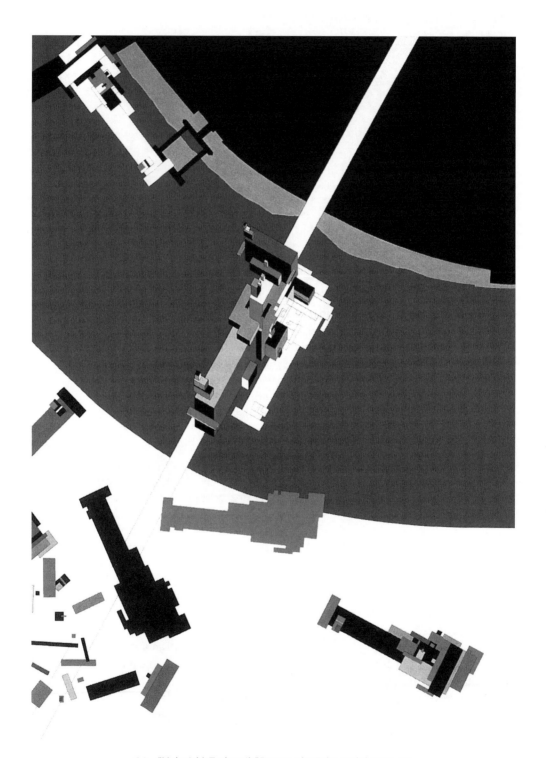

6.1   "Malevich's Tecktonik." Drawing by Zaha Hadid, 1976–77

Throughout this book, I have highlighted the historicity of the failure of the project of the historical avant-garde, and the need to make a distinction between theatricality and theatricalization. It is now important to say that the difference between these two states of playfulness is the result of two parallel developments which, at a point in time that can be associated with the 1968 student uprisings in Europe, crossed over each other marking the conditions of postmodernism in general, and the rise of neo-avant-garde architecture in particular. For reasons that do not fit with the objectives of this project, what should be stressed here briefly is the double nature of this transformation. On the one hand, mention should be made of the experience of a different level of abstraction permeating the production and consumption cycles of post-war capitalism. Although it is beyond the purview of this study to elaborate on the complex relationship between "exchange-value" and "use-value" of the commodity production system, the literature on this subject underlines the role "abstraction" plays in Marx's interpretation of a commodity form in capitalism.[4] On the other hand, it is the emergence of *image* as the medium of symbolic rapport nesting in the idea of "culture industry" as discussed by Theodor Adorno. Obviously *image* has been internal to the work of art for many centuries. What makes the contemporary turn to image different is that through abstraction the image is removed from its context and is charged with a second layer of signification, as discussed by Roland Barthes.[5] If one implication of the contemporary appropriation of image is suggested in the ways that American post-war abstract expressionism "stole" the agency of modern art,[6] 30 years later, the neo-avant-garde architects had difficulty disguising their historical delay in turning architecture into fragmented and abstract forms,[7] a collection of which was exhibited in the show "Deconstructivist Architecture," at the Museum of Modern Art (MoMA), 1988.[8]

Beyond the literal resemblance of "deconstructivism" to "constructivism," the architecture delivered by the preface "de" in the above mentioned show was expected to institutionalize the marriage between image and formal abstraction. This was sought as a necessary passage for the consolidation of both the modernist idea of progress and the aesthetic of theatricalization, if only to push the envelope of visuality beyond the historicism codified in Robert Venturi's notion of "both/ and." In MoMA's exhibition catalogue, Mark Wigley wrote: "The nightmare of deconstructivist architecture inhabits the unconscious of pure form, a slippery architecture that slides uncontrollably from the familiar into the unfamiliar, toward an uncanny realization of its own alien nature."[9] No wonder then that, upon entering the exhibition, the eyes of the crowd were first drawn to selected projects from the repertoire of Russian constructivism. If this was to show one aspect of the dialectics of "familiar" and "unfamiliar," another, unmentioned, had to do with the state of contemporary architectural crisis. If the internalization of the aesthetic of spectacle permeating late capitalism allowed the architecture of the pre-digital years to still look "familiar," another strategy of familiarization emerged through the organic informing most digitally produced forms since the turn of this century. Also in reference to the return of the organic in digital architecture, but also in consideration of the show's abuse of constructivism, we should recall the fact that at the dawn of the historical avant-garde, the tendency for "form-production," *Gestaltung*, was meant to overcome, among other things, the rift between mechanism and organism.[10]

It is significant that most of the architects discussed in this volume were prominent contributors to the 1988 MoMA exhibition. In retrospect, one can claim that Hadid's project, the Peak, was far more advanced than that of her comrades who had to struggle to show how their work differed from the formal and aesthetics of what was then labeled high modernism. Considering the fact that at the time of the exhibition digitalization was not yet available as a unifying technique, singular to Hadid's displayed project were her drawing skills, particularly her use of conceptual painting as a step towards the realization of playful architecture. Still, her early pictorial work made use of many aspects of both traditional and modern drawing techniques including layering, distorted perspectival views, and transparencies by which she would later manipulate "the ground plane by the means of cutting and wrapping."[11] These radical re-examinations of the pictorial world set the stage for the architecture of theatricality that should be distinguished from the visual effects of theatricalization permeating Frank Gehry's work discussed in the next chapter.

What makes Hadid's architecture different involves an understanding of the notion of field that is integral to her perception of object. Even for the design of a single building, the initial conceptual drawings usually start with abstract architectonic elements such as line (wall), surface (floor and/or roof) and enclosure, the dynamic composition of which opens up a *field*, landscape proper. What also

6.2   *Traits*, image courtesy of Abraham Bosse, La Pratique du trait, 1643, reprinted courtesy of the MIT Press from Robin Evans, *The Projective Cast*, the MIT Press, 1995, page 206

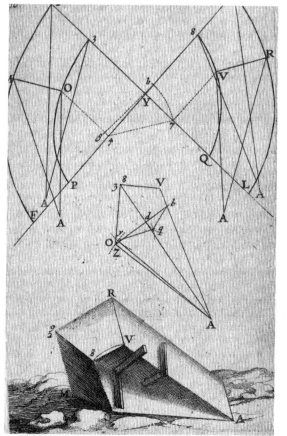

concerns us in this differentiation are the ways in which Hadid cultivates restless images, turning them into theatrical objects most of which are formed in concrete and with an eye on what can be called sculptured tectonics. The materiality delivered in her work is a reminder of tropes central to brutalism. Similar to this architecture of the post-war era, her tectonic cuts emulate the present turn to monolithic architecture, shortcutting the near past traditions of contemporary architecture, postmodernism proper. However, there are other layers of historical tropes in Hadid's architecture that demand equal attention.

Of these, on the one hand, we should consider strategies common among artists working within traditions of Islamic culture where representational arts have limited freedom. To compensate for these restrictions, these artists tend to recode the symbolic dimension of the artwork in *excess*. Of these strategies that have huge tectonic significance mention should be made of the colorful tiles used so excessively on the surface cladding of mosques that the entire edifice is turned into an artwork in its own right. On closer inspection of these surfaces, which are perhaps conceived in analogy to carpet and fabric, one also notices Qur'anic verses inscribed on the tiles. The aforementioned excess concerns both the layered cladding of tiles and the tattoo quality of letters. Both in Arabic countries and in Iran, calligraphy was, and still is, practiced as an art with the potential to turn the spectator's attention away from the meaning of the words to the playfulness of each letter and the work itself as ornament *par excellence*: a state of visual theatricality, if you wish, that takes on new life in Hadid's exposure to the images produced by Russian constructivist artists and architects.

On the other hand, Hadid's architecture should be historicized in the purview of another tectonic tradition. We are reminded of *trompes*, the most advanced theory of stonecutting used in part to defy the forces of gravity.[12] To facilitate additions to an existing building, *trompes* was appropriated as a structure in its own right. It was built out of drawings called *traits* where the geometric matrix of lines defines the stereotomic nature of the surface. The implied "shape" then would dictate the cuts to be made in various pieces of stone to be used in a *trompes*. Robin Evans's investigation highlights the perceptual contrast between the lightness of the geometry and the heaviness of stones depicted in *traits* (drawing) (Figure 6.2). In addition to discussing the tectonic merit of this or that style of pre-modern architecture, the significance of the art of stereotomy is associated with drawings containing two kinds of lines, one light and the other heavy; "the imaginary lines of geometrical construction and the lines indicating contours of the thing drawn."[13]

Through pre-modern theories of architecture it was believed that a structure should both look and stand stable. This rule was flouted by the idea of *trompes*, the most advanced theory of stonecutting developed in seventeenth-century France.[14] Again, Evans insists that stereotomy offered a means to differentiate the tectonics at work in classical buildings from those in Gothic. In most cathedrals, for example, the ribs were built first and the surface between them was filled later. A few architects, according to Evans, used stereotomy to refer to forms that were considered "ungothic and also unclassical," and not even Baroque. In the choir vault of Gloucester cathedral (1367), for example, the ribs look as if they are attached to a huge cambered sheet covering the entire choir (Figure 6.3). Gone in this cathedral is the emphatic distinction that could be made between the column and the wall, where *decorum* hinged on the tectonic rapport between structure and ornament.[15] Implied in this development is a notion of surface

6.3   Gloucester Cathedral, Gloucester, England, 1089– 1499. View of choir vault. Image from Robin Evans, *The Projective Cast*, the MIT Press, 1995. Photograph by R. Evans

6.4   Zaha Hadid,
The Peak Hong
Kong, 1982–83.
Photograph
courtesy of Zaha
Hadid Architects,
London

that is marked by the geometrical language detectible in Philibert de l'Orme's stone interlacing.[16]

These observations allow us to highlight Hadid's long-term pre-occupation with drawings, most of which deliver a pleasant image of lightness, dynamism, and the architectonics of *trompes*, made of concrete, but an ornament nevertheless. Furthermore, concepts such as fold and nonlinearity, as well as the popularization of digital software press for complex geometries, the architectonic of which, next to the tectonic, color the architecture of the closing decade of the last century.[17] However, the present shift to polished sculpted organic forms marks a departure from Hadid's concern for materiality and detailing detectable in most of her early work.

TECTONIC FIELDS

Hadid's architecture is successful when her semi-constructivist dynamic visual field is interwoven with topography. Two projects will be discussed briefly before taking up other projects that are significant for a critical discussion of the architect's turn to monolithic tectonics. With her winning competition entry project for the Peak Hong Kong (1982), Hadid entered the circle of the neo-avant-garde architects (Figure 6.4). The most intriguing aspect of this unbuilt project is—and is archaic to architecture—the tectonic figuration of the earth-work and the frame-work. Four frames, drawn perhaps in analogy to the high-rise buildings of Hong Kong, are composed in such a way as to deny the conventional frame structures where, to follow gravity forces, floors are stacked on top of each other like the layers of a cake. Of further interest are the ways the project's disjunctive composition is anchored to the earth and to the volumes buried underground. Added to this is the landscape of roads and highways. They thicken one's perception of this "club" to be experienced as landscape architecture *par excellence*. Thus difficult to highlight is the boundary between the land-form from the built-form.

The common thread running through the most vigorous projects submitted to the earlier mentioned 1988 MoMA exhibition was the strategy of attachment. To turn away the viewer's attention from fragmentation and distortion of otherwise familiar forms, these projects were conceived, in one or another form of prosthesis. Of these mention should be made of the object's attachment to an existing building, Coop Himmelb(l)au's Rooftop; additions and/or proximity to an existing building,

Peter Eisenman's, Frank Gehry's, and D. Libeskind's entries respectively. The ghost of something else haunted Koolhaas's design entry in which the proposed tower could not stand without a base, the Manhattan block. Exceptions to this general tendency were Bernard Tschumi's entry, and Hadid's reformulation of the tectonics of terrace making to the point where her project stood as a field of interactive terraces connected to each other through diagonal elevators and ramps. The most telling image of her design was a conceptual rendering that depicted the exploded landscape of the Peak. The sci-fi dimension of this pictorial drawing is convincing considering the collision shown between the tectonic of land-form and that of built-form. This aspect of Hadid's work is powerful whenever it meets either with an expansive field of programmatic requirements, and/or with a given infrastructure.

Of the first set of these examples, mention should be made of her allegorical plan for Manhattan that was conceived in criticism of Le Corbusier's vision for the city, and the West Hollywood Civic Centre (1987) where the building floats and intersects with the landscape. More successful but on a smaller scale is the Leone/Landesgarten Schau, Weil am Rhein, Germany (1996–99), an exhibition hall designed for an international gardening show (Figure 6.5). Of interest are the analogies the architect draws from landscape, especially her redefinition of formalist and abstract notions of "line" as a landscape contour. Starting with six parallel lines, the project's three main volumes expand the existing southern path turning it into a roof terrace that steps down gently at the other end. Whereas the so-called extended landscape path is a reminder of the ramp in Le Corbusier's Carpenter Centre, the overall configuration of the project draws mostly from Mies's experimentation with the element of wall, the Barcelona Pavilion for example. In contrast to the latter's over-dominant position of the roof, in Hadid's case, and perhaps after Tadao Ando, the wall is presented as a definitive tectonic element. In her project the line separating the volume from the landscape is blurred. Again

6.5   Zaha Hadid, Leone/ Landesgarten Schau, Weil am Rhein, Germany, 1996–99. General view. Photograph courtesy of Helen Binet, London

hard to define is the difference between the tectonics of land-form and the tectonic proper. Thus we have her sharp departure from the Carpenter Centre where the ramp, cutting through the two major volumes of the complex, becomes roof for a raised layer of the adjacent landscape.

Still, similar to the architecture of brutalism, Hadid's tectonic figuration does not solely invest in the formal consequences of the frame-structural system. Avoiding the axiom of the duality of skin and bone, for example, tropes such as theatricality and ornament attain sculptural dimension in her work. These tropes do not evolve out of a *poetic* thinking of the schism existing between the constructed form (the core-form), and the cladding (the art-form) either. This is one reason why the current

6.6   Zaha Hadid, The Vitra Fire Station, Weil am Rhein, Germany, 1990–94. General view. Photograph by author

turn to surface does not concern her work, at least in reference to projects discussed in this chapter. Even in her latest projects, where the materiality and detailing of the kind used in the Garten Schau are absent, the polished surfaces of these projects should be considered part of the traditions of material embellishment that go back to stereotomy. Another tectonic dimension of Hadid's work concerns tactile sensibilities flourishing the design's interior spaces. Putting aside the notion of *poché*, by which an architect differentiates the form seen from outside from the clad space inside, Hadid does her best to charge the interior ambience with the theatricalization that permeates the work itself. Thus, the interior space is approached as another field where movement is experienced through spaces most of which are embellished by materials such as exposed and painted concrete, wood, and metal, as well as by the play of natural and artificial lights.

The project where most of what has been said thus far is put to work is the Vitra Fire Station, Weil am Rhein, Germany, (1990–94) (Figure 6.6). Two double intersecting concrete volumes, and a wing-looking roof (canopy?) define the exit door of the fire station, now used for exhibition and other public events. The design's conceptual drawing comprises a series of parallel and intersecting walls in between and through which the building's interior space juts forward, as if a fire has forced the body of the building to reach out for open air! Recalling Louis I. Kahn's aphorism, Hadid's building wants to be a frozen motion, "suspending the tension of alertness, ready to explode into action at any moment."[18] The exit door canopy, the most theatrical element of the project, is cut in analogy to a broken wing that wants to take off. The image is held in place by 12 pipe-columns, a few of which are vertical the others inclined. The tectonic figuration of these columns is a reminder of both Alvar Aalto's Villa Mairea, where wooden columns are bundled together with rope, and the fluted columns of the early Gothic cathedrals. In addition to the perception of lightness, another detailing strategy concerns the metal screen grilles and the shape of the window cuts. These, and the cuts implemented in the massing of the Vitra make tectonic statements that concern movement and theatricality. Their playfulness, however, should be differentiated from early twentieth-century expressionistic architecture, Eric Mendelsohn's drawings and buildings, for example. The difference has to do with aspects of contemporary space/time experience that, in addition to the culture of image, involve infrastructures such as highways, fire, and high-speed train stations, building types not yet commercialized when the *Proun* was introduced.

This much is also evident from the Car Park and Terminus located in Strasbourg, France (Figure 6.7), where a concrete roof covering both the bus and tram station is cut and folded to transform the notion of the last stop to a departure point. The roof's partial cut defies the classical notion of frontality and *firmitas*, orienting the edifice towards the city. At the same time, the portion of the roof that is turned into a wall and then tucked to the ground directs one's attention to the car park located on the opposite side. Similar to other aspects of the design, the car park itself is an abstract statement about movement evident in the way cars are parked, and tectonic movement experienced as one leaves the car for the train station. Joseph Giovanni says about the project: as a gateway "choreographing and dignifying a mundane change of transportation modes, from car to tram and back, the design transformed the anomie of the edge of the city by articulating a parking lot and transport shed into a disciplined play of line, form and structure."[19] The strategy for transgressing the borderline separating the element of wall from the roof and landscape does two additional things: it conjugates the experience and feeling of heaviness with that of lightness, anchoring the flying roof to the earth. Thus the "wing" which seems to be trying to lift the Vitra Fire Station off the ground, is here tied to the earth just to resist the building's desire to move forward, toward to the city, tectonic configurations

6.7   Zaha Hadid, Car Park and Terminus, Strasbourg, France, 1998–2001. General view. Photograph by author

without which the floating roof, held up with trembling steel columns, would have suggested nothing more than a shelter. The implied difference is essential for differentiating the tectonic of theatricality from the aesthetics of theatricalization. Hadid is at her best when the design amalgamates purpose with the tectonics that is centered on the architecture's engagement with landscape.

Equally noteworthy is Hadid's design for the High-Speed Train Station, Naples, Italy (2003–) where, similar to the Garten Schau, the building sews the incision rail tracks made in the landscape. A band of glass wall, which then turns into the roof, holds together the station's split concrete volume. Hovering above the tracks, the longitudinal form of the building works like a bridge with downward access to the platforms and upward access to the commercial and public spaces located above the tracks (Figure 6.8). If the traditional design of the train station camouflaged the mechanical apparatus of arrival and departure behind a façade that was more often than not clad in the classical language of architecture, the dichotomy between the cultural (the civic?) and technological in Hadid's design is turned into a landmark, a gateway. The motion and emotion signified by the word gateway energizes the swirling body of the complex. Similar to the Heideggerian reading of a bridge's task (keeping the banks apart), Hadid's design highlights the cut introduced in landscape in reference to the cut underpinning the form of the building. The design neither reiterates the futurist enthusiasm for the roar of the machine, nor the nineteenth-century nostalgia for the picturesque. It, rather, recalls El Lissitzky's *Proun 1A Bridge* drawing (1919), which highlights the contrast between a three-dimensional deck connected to its massive base, and a two-dimensional flat surface ending at the opposite bank. In Hadid's project, the volume is stretched and elongated enough (at least when looking at the competition entry image that, similar to that of El Lissitzky's *Proun*, is drawn in an angle) to look like a stream, the spring of which remains subject to one's speculation as is the case with the origin of most passengers arriving at the train station.

6.8   Zaha Hadid, High Speed Train Station, Napoli-Afragola, Italy, 2003–12. General view. Photograph courtesy of Zaha Hadid Architects, London

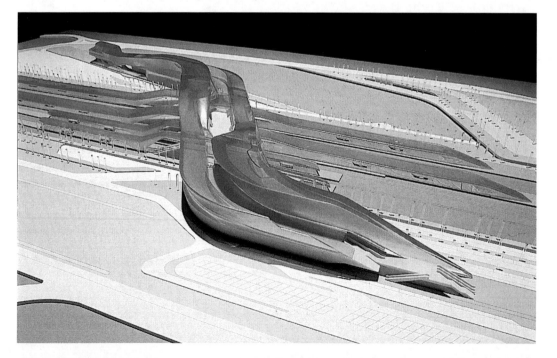

STONE-LIKE TECTONICS

The saying that "what goes up must come down" is part of our existential experience of the force of gravity. It also guides us in putting things together. The tectonic strives to address these so-called commonsense expressions of gravity through the conscious, and occasionally unconscious attempt of an architect making architecture distinct from utensil and sculpture. The tectonic does not concern the prejudice that "construction" comes first. It also does not mean that architecture should seem to be *standing firm*. Even though image is part of tectonic figuration, what is essential to tectonics is this: every constructive element of a building is already sought and developed through the long history of architecture as *tectonic*. In the culture of building, there are no floating walls, columns cut in midway, and roofs and floors positioned vertically, though these visual anomalies can be imagined and drawn.

6.9   Zaha Hadid, Phaeno Science Center, Wolfsburg, Germany, 2000–05. General view. Photograph by author

Of these coded tectonics we should recall the way a building responds to the ground. Starting with the generic potentialities of the Dom-ino system, the Phaeno Science Center in Wolfsburg, Germany, pushes the Semperian notion of the earth-work and the frame to a dramatic state (Figure 6.9). In many ways, Hadid's design is well orchestrated with the architectonic language of Alvar Aalto's Kulturhaus and Hans Scharoun's design for the city's theater, both located not far from the Phaeno Center. The building's semi-triangular floor plan provides an empty space for the hands-on examination and exploration of physical laws and scientific tricks. Both in its external form and interior spaces the building looks like a spaceship landed in Wolfsburg. And yet similar to the tram station in Strasburg, the Phaeno Center too seeks to revitalize the city's edge, which is marked by the train station. The placement of the building's ten pillions and the surface-cuts of this otherwise alien-looking object provide a public platform on the one side, stretching the building's body along the railroad tracks on the opposite side. The plan's third triangular side hangs over a ramp, which operates as both an emergency exit and a public path leading to a bridge crossing the rail tracks. The undulating wall facing the city, nevertheless, provides a backdrop for the public landscape in front, in association with the undulating façade of Aalto's building.

Standing above a buried volume, the Phaeno's ten hefty cone-shaped support piers hold up a concrete slab, the base for the building's walls, connecting the two-way spanning waffle slab structure of the roof and the floor. The underground volume, the car park, effectively acts as a raft, floating the whole structure above less than adequate subsoil for traditional pad and footing. Recalling Kahn's notion of an "empty column," the conical piers are conceived as part of the spatial organization of the volume. Informed by the major urban axis of the site, a number of these cones provides access to the elongated main volume of the building. Another is used for the lecture hall. Others house shops and exhibition spaces accessible directly from the main concourse level.

6.10   Zaha Hadid, Phaeno Science Center, Wolfsburg, Germany, 2000–05. View at piloti level. Photograph by author

Still, the pillars are detailed to appear as if rising from the sculpted ground plane, the earth-form (Figure 6.10). Their dynamic figuration, however, distinctively differs from the pilotis of the Marseille apartment block. Unlike the latter, the Phaeno's large volume is supported and structured by hollow cones, the skin of which seems shaped as if pushing the skin of the floor downward. The pilotis in Le Corbusier's building instead resemble arms holding up the mass. In Hadid's buildings, they follow a modest generic version of the dendriform columns of F.L. Wright's Johnson Wax Factory (1939). The theatricality of the entire volume, including the pleats and cuts of the concrete enclosure mark a distinct departure from the ethos of the new brutalism.[20] As in many other contemporary cases, Hadid has done her best here to animate and smooth the surface of concrete, presenting an alternative aesthetics against the dull and porous tactile qualities of most early industrial structures.[21] Contrary to the original examples of the architecture of brutalism, in the Phaeno Center, every cut and surface embellishment is used to exaggerate the animated body of the building. Along the southern face, for example, the technique of cut is used to express a glazed opening on the diagonal, accelerating the dynamic movement of the poised form. Even the massive interior truss system of the roof folds and bends here and there as if in dance with the floor whose undulating surface blurs the boundary separating the wall from the floor (Figure 6.11).

Call it "social construction of technology,"[22] the tectonic of theatricality attributed to the work under consideration here allows the heavy feeling of the concrete mass to appear as an agent of *light* architecture. The metamorphosis brings forth various dichotomies central to the transformational processes and versatility of building materials available today. In Hadid's hands, the heaviness of materiality (concrete) evaporates into an image that is in focus with the spectacle permeating the present culture, turning architecture into an ornament in itself. This aspect of contemporary architecture, elaborated on elsewhere,[23] is reiterated here to connect the subject with the art of stereotomy, mentioned earlier. Having roots in stonecutting, military engineering, mathematical geometry, and architectural composition, stereotomy cast a different light on the tectonics of column and wall, for example. It also provided a means to make a stylistic distinction between Gothic and classicism. This brief digression is made for two reasons. Firstly, instead of associating contemporary aesthetics with the Baroque, and this after Gilles Deleuze's text on "fold," the present tendency for theatricalization should be historicized in reference to those aspects of the discipline that are not driven by the style phenomenon, and/or considered part of the aesthetics attributed to a particular *Zeitgeist*. I say "and/or" because most tendencies in architecture today tend to associate contemporary aesthetics either with the perceptual horizon opened by the digital techniques, or with that of the Baroque to disguise their own historicist intentions.[24] Secondly, my own turn to stereotomy aims to show the historicity of image in architecture beyond the tectonics, and the move from mechanical to digital reproductivity. The latter transformation is, however, important and should be addressed, as has been attempted throughout this volume, particularly in reference to the discussed difference between the tectonic of theatricality and the aesthetic of theatricalization. Furthermore, my discussion of theatricality is dialectical, and I trust that I have clearly demonstrated the following adequately: that the tectonic of theatricality is part of the present turn to the digital mode of reproductivity, which paradoxically offers a useful strategic concept for critiquing architecture's drift into the field of image making.

6.11   Zaha Hadid, Phaeno Science Center, Wolfsburg, Germany, 2000–05. Interior view. Photograph by author

6.12   Marcel
Breuer, Begrisch
Hall, University
Heights, New
York University,
New York, 1961.
Photograph
by author

To historicize Hadid's work on a different level, we need to return to the Phaeno Center, where the idea of cut is implemented for an art-form (image?) that stands on the borderline of spectacle and theatricality of the kind we attributed to Koolhaas's Casa da Múscia. Specific to the tectonic fabrication of these two projects is the attempt to avoid two problems that "arose as soon as the illusion of imitating stone structures was abandoned; the first had to do with the exterior expression of the interior structure, and the second dealt directly with surface of the building."[25] During the 1950s, and by the proliferation of brutalism, in addition to its structural potentialities, what occupied architects the most was the aesthetic (appearance) of brute concrete. Consider Marcel Breuer's design for the Begrisch Hall (1967–70) the theatricality of which precedes the above two contemporary buildings (Figure 6.12). In the Begrisch Hall, the aesthetic is sought through stereotomic surfaces.[26] Similar to most monolithic forms, the exterior economy of Breuer's design is achieved "at the cost of formal and material excess and calibrated for intended effects."[27] The main volume of the Phaeno Center, for example, is evidently the result of cuts and pleats implicated in an otherwise rectangular prism, the Corbusian piloti system. The tectonic of theatricality (stereotomic surfaces) that informs Hadid's design, nevertheless, departs from both modern and classical traditions for which structure "was less a preoccupation of the collapse of buildings than a precaution against the collapse of the faith in the rectangle as an embodiment of rational order."[28] This is one reason why we should differentiate the Phaeno Center from one of Hadid's recent projects, the Cagliari Museum in Italy. The latter is Baroque and atectonic; its epidermal smoothness justifies the surface on its own terms.

Surface and its embellishment are important to the architect's perception of a building, during both the process of conceptualization and its gradual transformation into an edifice. We owe to Le Corbusier the contemporary formulation of surface as an autonomous aesthetic issue independent of the materiality of construction. This is evident from the white abstract façades of the French architect's early villas compared to the materiality of the Greek temples he most admired. Among other things, the implied difference speaks for the plan/ façade relationship. To emulate the modern aesthetic of abstraction, Le Corbusier's early work had to distance itself from the dictates of construction and its related spatial organization. The surface of the Cagliari Museum, instead, follows neither the aesthetics of purism nor those attributed to brutalist architecture. In this particular project of Hadid, the surface is conceived as a thin film attached to the body of the building, like a wetsuit, if not a coating of white chocolate! The best one could make of the computer-generated image of this project is to associate it with the polished, soft, smooth-looking forms of Greek sculptures. This is not the case with the Phaeno Center, and certainly not with Hadid's two institutional buildings, the one in Cincinnati and the other in Rome. In both these two projects, sectional investigation, rather than the plan-to-façade relation, allowed the architect to detail the edifice, and design its volumetric organization for particular effect.

Through section drawing the architect examines the internal circulation and the building's volumetric organization. Sectional investigation also reveals what lies between the interior and exterior cladding, allowing the architect to design relevant details in anticipation of construction. Mohsen Mostafavi includes Hadid's Contemporary Art Center (CAC), Cincinnati, among other works where "the section is used as both a concept and a drawing tool for choreographing the building's internal and even external vertical trajectories."[29] What draws one's attention to this project is the building's theatrical and crisscrossing interior stair, the steel handrail of which is painted in black, a polychromic choice repeated in the Maxxi Museum, Rome. Two vertical cubical volumes mark the interior of the CAC: one for service spaces, and the other for a small elevator used primarily by the staff whose offices are located on the third floor (Figure 6.13). To dramatize the presence of these two volumes and the three hefty concrete columns, the rear interior concrete wall is formed like a cyclorama, a large curtain or wall (often concave) positioned at the back of the stage-set area (Figure 6.14). Ascending the main stairway, one discovers

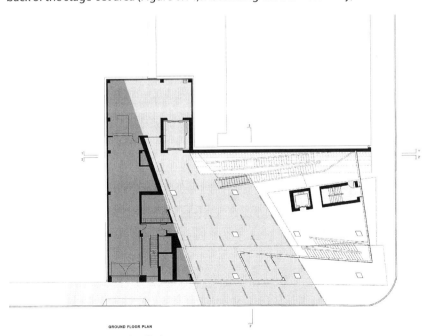

6.13   Zaha Hadid, Contemporary Art Center, Cincinnati, Ohio, 1997 2003. Plan. Drawing courtesy of Zaha Hadid Architects, London

GROUND FLOOR PLAN

other concepts that in return inform both the internal and external volumes of the building. Reaching the fourth floor we notice the sky and daylight pouring into the space, a glimpse of which is obtained when stepping onto the stair. In addition to a suspended volume that projects into the same floor, and because of the location of the main stair, one sees the diagonal alignment of the interior composition as determined with the fact that the building occupies a corner lot of downtown Cincinnati. "I wanted to bring the outside in, with the idea of an urban carpet,"[30] Hadid wrote. At the time of its realization, the CAC was almost an exception to the architect's résumé in the sense that its design scope was to a certain extent dictated by the tight spatial organization of Cincinnati's urban setting.

There are other ways to explain the rapport Hadid establishes between the building's interior space and its external volume. As a backdrop for the interior space, the cyclorama wall is extended to the exterior as seen from Walnut Street (Figure 6.15). The remaining volumetric composition of the building's free-façade, on the other hand, either emphasizes the presence of the cyclorama wall, or stresses the corner position of the building. While from outside one can hardly make a strong case for the placement of the various surfaces of the building's massing, the composition comes together reasonably well after the interior space is explored. One notes, for example, the correspondences between the third-floor window opening and the horizontal dark-colored box above and the interior spaces they cover (represent?) (Figure 6.16). Running parallel to Sixth Street, the same dark-colored rectangular box becomes a square posed against Walnut Street. The position of this volume, in reference to the concrete cyclorama wall, resonates with the placement of the main entrance. Approaching the building, one moves parallel to Sixth Street, entering the complex at a right angle to the cyclorama wall. The latter sets the stage for movement and the spatial comprehension of the project, as is the case with the wall in the Car Park and Terminus in Strasbourg.

6.14   Zaha Hadid, Contemporary Art Center, Cincinnati, Ohio, 1997–2003. Interior view. Drawing courtesy of Zaha Hadid Architects, London

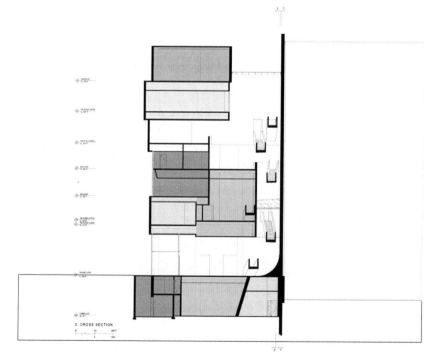

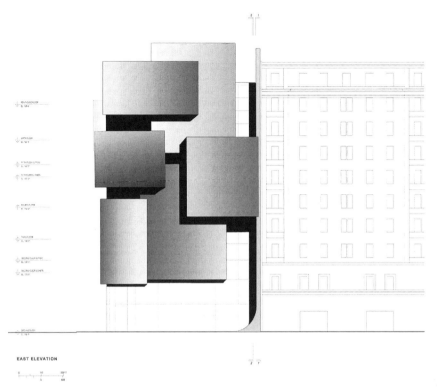

EAST ELEVATION

6.15   Zaha Hadid, Contemporary Art Center, Cincinnati, Ohio, 1997–2003. Exterior elevation. Drawing courtesy of Zaha Hadid Architects, London

As well as these departures from the classical canon of frontality, where one enters the building at a right angle to the main façade, mention should also be made of the lightness of the building's appearance and the weight felt in the interior. That the implied contrast might be consequential to the Dom-ino frame effect is one thing. Another point to be made is how an architect re-thinks the heaviness and lightness in tectonics. Comparing the Villa Savoye with the Ronchamp Chapel, one can speculate for the presence of two architects; one expresses lightness, the other heaviness. In addition to these explanations, the perceptual difference between heaviness and lightness suggests a state of interiority an architect chooses to bask in at a conceptual level. Consider this: every feature of the interior space of the Contemporary Art Center does its best to remind the spectator of the presence of an architect who against all odds wants to deliver her will-to-design. While this is manifested in every architect's design, what is involved in the CAC is the way in which the architect chooses to control the so-called will-to-design at the expense of comfort and use,

6.16   Zaha Hadid, Contemporary Art Center, Cincinnati, Ohio, 1997–2003. Walnut St. view. Photograph by author

and/or the sky and landscape. A case in point is the building's staircase leading to the lower level where the performance space, clad in dark wood, is located. The stair is narrow and runs at an angle. In contrast to the main stairway, this one is distractive, a reminder of the design's formalistic nature.

Similar to her other projects the CAC clearly shows Hadid's use of stairs and ramps for the effects of architectural promenade. Whereas Le Corbusier wanted the spectator to have the opportunity to explore the interior space from different heights and angles, he rarely used ramps and stairs as elements of visual spectacle without dismissing the need for the elegant and impressive presence of these architectonic elements. Moreover, his was against the background of two important moments in the use and abuse of stairway in architectural history: one is reminded of Charles Garnier's *grand escalier* in the Paris Opera House (1861–75) with its mixture of use and spectacle. Garnier's staircase is monumental, spacious, and comfortable. It is as much an object of interior display as is the building's exterior classical garment. Rising upward through three sweeping runs, the Opera's staircase reunites the four categories of opera fans, and "offers a processional denouncement to the public experience of arriving at the Opera."[31] Walter Benjamin wrote that Garnier's design focused as much on the performance hall as on the wide oval staircase on which ladies display their fashionable clothes and gentlemen meet for a casual smoke. This social life was what the opera was about.[32] The second moment concerns the stairs depicted in Gianni Battista Piranesi's prison etchings. Here catwalks, gangways, and stairs are dramatized in the anticipation of ruination of *place*, hinted at in part by the absence of the roof and the daylight pouring from the sky.

6.17   Zaha Hadid, Maxxi National Museum of 21st Century Arts Rome, 1998–2009. Aerial view. Photograph courtesy of Zaha Hadid Architects, London

Piranesi's exaggeration and fragmentation of the materiality of stone is consequential for the loss of space, and was in reaction to the lavishness permeating Baroque churches. Oddly enough, a stairway with a skylight at the top has become a generic element for contemporary commercial buildings. It is to this latter abuse that one should welcome Hadid's attempt to combine use, spectacle, and light in the design of the main stairway of the Contemporary Art Center.

One cannot fully grasp the importance of interior space for contemporary architecture without exploring Hadid's winning competition project, the Maxxi National Museum of 21st Century Arts, Rome (2010). Located on an ex-industrial site, just north of the city center, the building's tubular concrete volumes crisscross each other, first to accommodate the site's topography (Figure 6.17), and second to create flowing spaces that end at the main entrance (Figure 6.18). As a

6.18   Zaha Hadid, Maxxi National Museum of 21st Century Arts Rome, 1998–2009. Exterior view. Photograph courtesy of Zaha Hadid Architects, London

spectacle of movement, the element of stair forcefully returns in this building. Not only do the visitors' rambling and inspection of the artwork move smoothly, but so do the two main stairs that occupy the interior space. They are choreographed to move up and down, and crisscross each other occasionally. The pleasure of watching their movement is irresistible (Figure 6.19)! The ease with which the staircases turn up and down expands the display areas, most of which are calm, well lit, and spacious. Hadid's perception of space and movement in this project departs from historical precedents such as F.L. Wright's Guggenheim Museum in New York City, and Hans Scharoun's Library in Berlin, to mention two significant architectural works. Much like the former, the volume of the Maxxi is infused with its internal spatial organization. And yet unlike both buildings, the final result in the Maxxi neither configures a coherent and unified geometry, nor is *formless*. This much is evident from the three posed volumes of the Maxxi, which like a three-headed knot each pointing to one aspect of the topography of the site: one looks towards the main street, the second towards the courtyard of the complex, and the third towards the rear side of the building. Their position also forms a hypothetical triangle indicating the end and direction of the building's knotted interior space.

6.19   Zaha Hadid, Maxxi National Museum of 21st Century Arts Rome, 1998–2009. Interior view. Photograph courtesy of Hadid Architects, London

It is to Hadid's credit that the L-shaped footprint of the site is taken full advantage of, as are the possibilities of exploring a "linear structure by bundling, twisting, and building mass in some areas and reducing it in others—creating an urban cultural centre where a dense texture of interior and exterior spaces has been intertwined and superimposed over one another."[33] In the Maxxi, sectional investigation is edited to transgress both the classical and modern orthodoxies. Whereas in the architecture of early modern times (except in Loos's work), each floor replicates the

geometry and structural organization of the ground floor, and where in Le Corbusier the *tabula rasa* of the open-plan is sustained in its vertical repetition, Hadid uses the sectional cuts to transfer and elevate the wide ground-floor plan of the complex into a number of bar-shaped volumes (Figure 6.20). Only in this way could the architect have reiterated the visual dynamics of constructivism albeit in a culture where surface is abused to perpetuate the spectacle of late capitalism. And yet, unlike constructivist architecture, the dialectics of theory and practice force the architect to reiterate aspects of what we have called the culture of building. The reader has already noted Hadid's re-thinking of the open-plan, the stairs, and the element of skylight for particular aesthetic and formal ends. To these we should add Kahn's idea of "served and service spaces," noted in the pilotis of the Phaeno Center. To have the light pour from the sky, an idea that in the Maxxi attains both functional and aesthetic dimension, the ceiling has to be freed of mechanical accessories routinely stacked beneath it; thus the placement of most mechanical amenities in the thick, poured in situ concrete walls of the galleries. The architect's design statement suggests that, following the confluence of lines, the walls were considered the primary force of the site wherein their constant intersection and separation created indoor and outdoor spaces. The walls also play a major role in the organization of galleries, bridging and connecting various spaces to each other as needed.

6.20   Zaha Hadid, Maxxi National Museum of 21st Century Arts Rome, 1998–2009. Section drawing. Image by Zaha Hadid Architects, London

To further emphasize the strategy of breaking down a large volume into a number of tubular volumes, we need to check the Maxxi's skylight closely. Instead of detailing the rooflights with techniques providing a large double-glazed skylight, the space between primary beams, which spans across the galleries at 12.6-meter centers, is given over to an array of 2.2-meter-deep steel trusses clad in what is called glass fiber reinforced concrete (GRC).[34] This highly technical detailing does two things. It posits the aesthetic of line against that of the surface, achieved

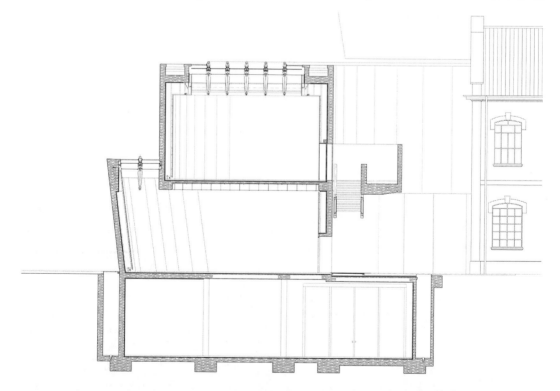

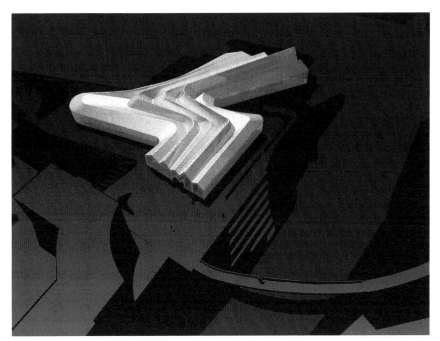

6.21   Zaha Hadid, Glasgow Riverside Museum of Transport, Glasgow, Scotland, 2004–11. Concept model. Image courtesy of Zaha Hadid Architects, London

by the intensification of linear expressiveness whilst breaking down the building's mass into smaller cubical volumes. In doing so the skylight turns into "wish-images" where its aestheticization of line recollects the image of skylight passages of the early last century where contemporary techniques of glass roof glazing were not available. In Felix Mara's words, "Its configuring of linear spaces, reinforced by graphic pattern of its parallel rooflights, is as old as the gallery building type, and it's important to remember that this is a museum of not only art, but also architecture. Perhaps its only flaw is that perfection in its external massing is sacrificed to the exigencies of internal planning."[35] One can extend his observation to Frank L. Wright's Guggenheim: both buildings radically defy contextualism and bring forth aspects of the context that otherwise would have remained unnoticed. Similarly, the internal flow of these two otherwise diverse buildings challenge the expected smooth association of the exhibited work with the modernist drive for spatial void. The architecture of void and *silence* is detectable not only in the Mies of his American period, but also in Kasimir Malevich's suprematist paintings, and in *Proun*, the dynamic aspiration of which Hadid had studied closely.

The suggested allegorical interpretation of the Maxxi's skylight (the infusion of the image of *old* into the *new*) can be applied to another Hadid project, the Glasgow Riverside Museum of Transport, Glasgow, Scotland (2011) (Figure 6.21). With its S-shaped form, the volume of this building connects the city to the river. The building works like a column-less passage mediating between the two flows of civilization (urbanism) and nature (the river). The architect's design statement reads:"The landscape, made up of stone slabs in a shadow path around the building and an informal open courtyard space, is designed to direct activities surrounding the building."[36] Similar to the old passages, the roof of this museum draws one's

6.22   Zaha Hadid, The BMW Central Building, Leipzig, Germany, 2001–06. Exterior view. Photograph by Werner Huthmacher, courtesy of Zaha Hadid Architects, London

attention to its two ends where the profile of each one is cut and embellished according to the roof's pleats. Whereas on the city side, the profile of the pleats recalls the trusses used in the nineteenth-century industrial sheds, on the waterside, it is dramatized in its vertical projections connoting a Gothic, gloomy setting especially if approached from the sea and at night. From a bird's-eye view, however, the roof looks like a rectangular cloth squeezed about the middle. As is the case with clothing, where the cut is decided based on the structure of the fabric, the roof's pleats, asymmetrical in their profile, speak for the present state of the art of engineering, manipulating and presenting the concrete roof as the most dominant element of this project, speaking aesthetically. The elementary nature of the project, which combines the roof with sidewalls, evokes the Miesian idea of "almost nothing." Hadid's project also recalls the German architect's design, the Concrete Office Building published in the first issue of G, the European avant-garde magazine of the previous century. Both projects are inspired by the Benjaminian idea of wish-images in that they transform the image of an industrial structure into a cosmopolitan edifice. These observations attain historical significance when the discussion is extended to the BMW Plant Central Building, Leipzig, Germany (2005) (Figure 6.22). Of particular interest is the generic factory type, the design of which is rarely, in recent times, commissioned to an architect of Hadid's stature.

In modernity and through the work of Peter Behrens, Walter Gropius, and many other architects, the factory was considered as both a symbolic expression of modernization and a civic work in its own right. Behrens famously applied an image of a Greek temple to the front façade of the AEG Factory in Berlin (1905), leaving the side elevation and the interior space to the dictates of the structural engineering of the time, and the functional and spatial organization of the production processes. The same dichotomy informs Albert Kahn's distinction between architectural art and what he called "business." Whereas the former would draw from the traditions of representation, the latter would accommodate the logic of industry. Similar to Behrens, Kahn treated the front entry part of his factories beyond its "functional concern."[37] In their joint effort, Gropius and Adolf Meyer, on the other hand, felt comfortable with the industrial look of the Model Factory (1914). Their main design effort, instead, focused on the administration section of the complex, charging it with aesthetics associable with the modernism of the time. I am thinking of the transparency and movement informing the corner stair, noted by most historians. In the Fagus Factory, built around 1913, the same two architects attempted to move the aesthetic aspects of the design of a factory beyond what Behrens had already established. Unlike the AEG, the side elevation of the Fagus building, and even the transparency of its corner design demonstrate the early modern architects' struggle with offsetting the vertical dictum of the structural in favor of the aesthetic of horizontality formulated by Heinrich Wölfflin. None of these issues and attributes is relevant to contemporary architects' design for industrial buildings. In addition to Hadid's previously mentioned project, one is also reminded of the UN Studio's Mercedes-Benz Museum, and Coop Himmelb(l)au's BMW Welt where the idea of civic has given way to an architecture of spectacle displaying cars as objects of desire.[38] This observation demands turning our attention once again to the notion of wish-images.

Both the production volume of the Model Factory, particularly the image included in N. Pevsner's *Pioneers of Modern Movement* (1936), and the entry volume of the BMW project emulates the architectonic of wish-images associable with the visual sensibilities of different historical moments. In the former building, one witnesses the juxtaposition (montage?) of the image of an industrial shed with the aesthetic of modernity, particularly the translucent glazing of the front façade. Having disbanded the modernist image of factory, Hadid's project attempts to express industrialization in the age of digital reproductivity. In David Cunningham's words, the formal abstractions employed in the Leipzig BMW plant "intensify the spatial experience of the modern program." It is a work of architecture that "self-consciously" articulates the experiences of modernity.[39] This is evident from the building's elongated and suspended volume where the cut for glazing emphasizes the separation between the elements of roof and the floor slab. Both in its tactility and window lines the glazing delivers an aura that is difficult to explain. Difficult because of its aesthetics— and this in consideration of its surface articulations and the materiality of the two above-mentioned elements, and the position of the concrete pilotis—none of which induces an ambience pertinent to modernity, nor the aura of surface spectacle permeating our digital age. Nevertheless, similar to most contemporary architecture, this one too endorses the return of the organic: I am reminded of the volume's animal like physiognomy when viewed from a particular angle. I am also referring to the ways in which the complex extends its arms to connect to the three existing buildings. In retrospect, Hadid's design gives the impression that the addition is oriented and animated by forces emanating from the central building.

The suggested connectivity delivers the aesthetic of theatricality, which in Hadid's most successful projects avoids organizing the complex into a single large volume. Crisscrossing each other, the internal elongated bar-shaped volume speaks for the organizational strategy of the BMW complex. The profile of the building's section is the telling story of this aspect of the design, and the interior space where the visitors view the half-made cars moving along tracks towards the production units located in the exiting building (Figure 6.23). The configuration follows "the cascading floor plates large enough to allow for flexible occupation patterns, thus opening more visual communication than with a single flat floor plate."[40] The section's profile and the architectonic elements included in this space are designed to accommodate the visitors, workers, and the assembly line. Together they create an ambience for experiencing weight and lightness, and the force of swirling linear elements that eventually are retracted in the dynamics of the bar-shaped volumes of the complex. The ambience is also suggestive that in a post-Fordist production system, both the workers and consumers contemplate the

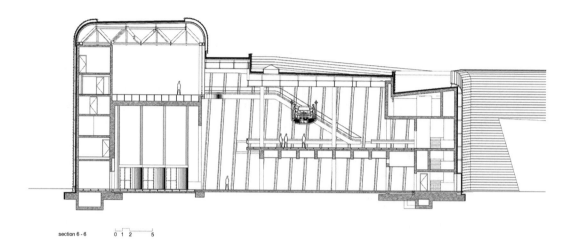

section 6 - 6   0 1 2   5

6.23   Zaha Hadid, The BMW Central Building, Leipzig, Germany, 2001–06. Section drawing. Image courtesy of Zaha Hadid Architects, London

product, i.e., the car as an alienated object of desire. The actual façade envelope, on the other hand, is pulled over to cover the top floor and projected out diagonally. The theatrical curvilinear forms at the top of the main entrance to the central building are further emphasized through the angled concrete columns, all leaning in the same direction. They pump movement into the previously noted projecting and animal-like volume.

The analysis of buildings presented in this chapter is of critical importance for a comprehensive understanding of the present state of architecture. On the one hand, it proceeds with the theoretical speculation that the idea of modernity experienced in late capitalism is transformative. On the other, the criticism intends to perpetuate a different understanding of the disciplinary tradition(s) of architecture. The trajectory of these two postulates underline the importance of the idea of parallax for a critical practice that is centered on the tectonic of theatricality. The latter could be considered the third state of architectural object next to the other two, which present themselves as either "purely functional" (modernism), or "purely aesthetic" (postmodernism).[41] In this sense the tectonic is universal in that its primary concern is focused neither on function nor on the aesthetic but on construction. Neither is it purely engineering. The tectonic of theatricality recodes the thematic of construction in the purview of available techniques and aesthetics in the consideration of two developments: firstly, that in late capitalism and thanks to the digitalization of architecture, the art of building has stepped into the realm of commodities, the world of image building; secondly that, whereas the general reception of the early modern architecture was limited, as was the case with abstract painting, the present public esteem for playful architectural forms should be considered part of what Slavoj Žižek calls "traumatic distortion."

Aside from the issue of the return of the organic, a few recent projects of Hadid herald a change in *style*. Patrik Schumacher, a director of Zaha Hadid Architects, claims that the expressionism permeating the most recent projects of Hadid must be considered the style that not only emulates parametric design, but also "forms a much more pertinent image and vehicle of contemporary life forces and patterns of social communication than the big Foster dome." Foster, according to Schumacher, is an architect who uses these techniques today, as do most architects.[42] Schumacher's observation relies heavily on the belief that in the prevailing corporate organization all contradictions are dissolved, and that scientific paradigms are in a better position to provide "a comprehensive unified theory" of architecture. This is a situation when "the thing itself can serve as its own mask—the most effective way to obfuscate social antagonisms being to openly display them."[43] That this style happens to be delivered by Hadid has little to do with the notion of artistic signature. Nor does it tally with an art historian's exhaustive research on the particular nature of contemporary architectural style. The style Schumacher has in mind evolves rather out of a research methodology that dumps "negative heuristics," for "positive heuristics," lending the aesthetics (style?) to parametric design.

Schumacher's theorization of architecture says little about the historicity of the style debate. His is a late note on the style debate without evoking the "late style." The latter, according to Adorno, loathes the *Zeitgeist* and lays down the seeds of something different.[44] The style to come, to follow Adorno, should step out of its time in the first place. Giorgio Agamben writes:

> those who are truly contemporary, who truly belong to their time, are those who neither perfectly coincide with it nor adjust themselves to its demands. They are thus in this sense irrelevant (in attuale). But precisely because of these conditions and precisely through this disconnection and this anachronism, they are more capable than others of perceiving and grasping their own time.[45]

Even Le Corbusier's work was not in complete harmony with the early modernism, even though historians such as Giedion presented it as such. The French architect's early work was indeed in sharp contrast with the existing landscape most of which was shaped by historicist styles. Even before historicism, there was never a uniform style attributed to each epoch. Even though most of the work of Hadid and most neo-avant-garde work is in harmony (both technically and image wise) with the spectacle of late capitalism, still the diversity of contemporary architecture cannot be neglected and it is as rich as when the international style of architecture was heralded.

Schumacher has uttered the last word, at least for now, in the sequence of theoretical annunciations of "ends" be it the author, history, or critical praxis. The turn to scientific system paradigms that attracted architects like Christopher Alexander during the 1960s has now gained a new momentum partly due to the exhaustion of theoretical ideas and concepts fashionably borrowed from the prevailing philosophical discourses of the time. With his propagandist rhetoric, Schumacher keeps us in the dark concerning the nature of the aesthetic of expressionism he wants to sell as the style proper to late capitalism. Should there be a *subject* (the architect?) involved in deciding what the final form of a project should look like? Or should the final form be left to techniques programmed to produce the kind of soft-forms that conform to the present aesthetic of spectacle where everything solid melts into air, to recall Marx's famous pronouncement. Whatever the answer to this and other questions already raised concerning Schumacher, Hadid's recent projects certainly indicate a perspectival shift in the tectonic discourse.

The critical analysis of Hadid's work presented in this chapter, nevertheless, intends to "rescue" those elements of the culture of building that in the present image-laden culture are anamorphically distorted.[46] There is a degree of anonymity in the tectonics that is not opaque and inaccessible. As *parallax* object, the tectonic communicates neither as a familiar sign of historical origin, nor as an image extraneous to the thematic of the culture of building, let alone the system theories Schumacher lists in the above-mentioned essay. The tectonic has the capacity to reach for a perception of surface-cladding that neither calculates the limits of load-bearing forces (to recall Banham), nor tallies with the skin-dressing of the organic forms of the kind produced by parametric design. In spite of this, Hadid's work is significant in its mutation between sculptured tectonics and theatricalization, the aesthetic of which denies materiality for a tectonic figuration that has disciplinary connotations. As for theatricalization, a case in point is the competition entry for the Beijing Central Business District (2010) where the main urban concept does not go beyond planting clone-like towers of various heights. Beside their uncanny look, the agglomerated towers do not challenge the utopian evident in Le Corbusier's and Hilberseimer's urbanism. For now, both on a local and urban scale, parametric design presents nothing but the old capital-driven commodity form dressed-up differently. Gone in lending architecture to digitalization is Hadid's early idiosyncratic work where imagination, drawing, and landscape were not approached systematically. Her most recent projects also suggest that the critical content and effectiveness of constructivism on contemporary architecture is exhausted. At least for now!

NOTES

1   El Lissitzky, "Prouns," in Sophie Lissitzky-Kuppers, *El Lissitzky, Life, Letters, Texts* (New York: Thames & Hudson, 1992), 347.

2   Patrik Schumacher, *Digital Hadid: Landscape in Motion* (Basil: Birkhauser, 2004), 6.

3   On this subject see Kasimir Malevich, *The Non-Objective World*, trans. Howard Dearstyne (Chicago, IL: Paul Theobald and Company, 1959), 39.

4   For a comprehensive discussion of this subject see Gail Day, *Dialectical Passions in Postwar Art Theory* (New York: Columbia University Press, 2011), in particular chapter 4.

5   Roland Bathes, *Mythologies* (New York: Noonday Press, 1972), in particular the final chapter.

6   See Serge Guilbaut, *How New York Stole the Idea of Modern Art* (Chicago, IL: University of Chicago Press, 1985).

7   Here I am thinking of K. Michael Hays in *Architecture's Desire: Reading the Late Avant-garde* (Cambridge, MA: The MIT Press, 2010).

8   Philip Johnson and Mark Wigley, *Deconstructivist Architecture* (New York: Museum of Modern Art, 1988).

9   Philip Johnson and Mark Wigley, *Deconstructivist Architecture*, 1988, 20.

10   Detlef Mertins and Michael W. Jennings, *G: An Avant-Garde Journal of Art, Architecture, Design, and Film* (Los Angeles, CA: The Getty Center, 2010), 5.

11   Patrik Schumacher, *Digital Hadid*, 2004, 10.

12   Robin Evans, *The Projective Cast* (Cambridge, MA: The MIT Press, 1995), 180.

13   Robin Evans, *The Projective Cast*, 1995, 206.

14   Robin Evans, *The Projective Cast*, 1995, 180.

15   Robin Evans, *The Projective Cast*, 1995, 220–39.

16   Bernard Cache, "Gottfried Semper: Stereotomy, Biology, and Geometry," *Perspecta* 33, Mining Autonomy, (2002): 86.

17   H.F. Mallgrave and Christina Contandriopoulos, eds, *Architectural Theory Volume II* (Malden, MA: Blackwell Publishing, 2008), 535–6.

18   Zaha Hadid, *Zaha Hadid: The Complete Buildings and Projects* (London: Thames & Hudson, 1998), 64.

19   Joseph Giovanni, Writing on the Occasion of Zaha Hadid's Reception of the Pritzker Architecture Prize, 2004.

20   I have elaborated on this subject in "Theatrical Tectonics: The Mediating Agent for a Contesting Practice," *Footprint* 5 (spring 2009): 77–95. See also *October* 136 (spring 2011), a special issue focused on new brutalism.

21   Jean-Louis Cohen and G. Martin, eds, *Liquid Stone* (Basel: Birkhauser, 2006), 7.

22   Jean-Louis Cohen and G. Martin, *Liquid Stone*, 2006, 12.

23   On this subject see the final chapter in Gevork Hartoonian, *Ontology of Construction* (Cambridge: Cambridge University Press, 1994).

24   See Antoine Picon, *Digital Culture in Architecture: An Introduction to Design Professions* (Basel: Birkhauser, 2010), especially the chapter titled "From Tectonic to Ornament."

25   Jean-Louis Cohen and G. Martin, *Liquid Stone*, 2006, 27.

26   See Isabelle Hayman, *Marcel Breuer, Architect* (New York: Harry N. Abrams, 2001), 155.

27   Rodolfo Machado and Rodolphe el-Khorury, *Monolithic Architecture* (Munich: Prestel-Verlag, 1995), 13.

28   Robin Evans, *The Projective Cast*, 1995, 212.

29   Mohsen Mostafavi, "Architecture's Inside," *Harvard Design Magazine* 29 (fall/winter 2008–09): 20.

30   Quoted in Hugh Pearman, "An American Beauty," *The Sunday Times*, June 15, 2003.

31   Christopher Curtis Mead, *Charles Garnier's Paris Opera: Architectural Empathy and the Renaissance Classicism* (Cambridge, MA: The MIT Press, 1991), 119.

32   Walter Benjamin in *The Arcades Project*. Here I am paraphrasing Slavoj Žižek, *Living in the End Times* (London: Verso, 2011), 272.

33   From the architect's design statement.

34   Information provided by Zaha Hadid Architects, London.

35   Felix Mara, *Architect's Journal*, London (September 2010): 63.

36   See Zaha Hadid, *The Complete Zaha Hadid* (London: Thames & Hudson, 2009).

37   David Leatherbarrow and Mohsen Mostafavi, *Surface Architecture* (Cambridge, MA: The MIT Press, 2002), 2.

38   See also Michael Cadwell's analysis of Coop Himmelb(l)au's BMW Welt in *Log* 21 (winter 2011): 47–52.

39   David Cunningham and Jon Goodbun, "Marx, Architecture and Modernity," *The Journal of Architecture* 11, 2 (2001): 178.

40   Zaha Hadid, *The Complete Zaha Hadid*, 2009, 128.

41   I am benefiting from Slavoj Žižek, "Architectural Parallax," in *Living in the End Times*, 2011, 274.

42   Patrik Schumacher, "Parametricism and the Autopoiesis of Architecture," *Log* 21 (2011): 62–79. See also Ingeborg M. Rocker's response to P. Schumacher's essay in the same issue of *Log*, 2011. For an early elaboration of his ideas see P. Schumacher, "Let the Style Wars Begin," *The Architects' Journal*, May 6 (2010). The author's ideas are extensively discussed in *The Autopoiesis of Architecture*, vol. 1 (London: John Wiley & Sons, 2010). For the review of Schumacher's book see *The Architects' Journal*, February 17 (2011): 2–6.

43   Slavoj Žižek, *Living in the End Times*, 2011, 253. For a critique of Schumacher see Douglas Spencer, "Architectural Deleuzism: Neoliberal Space, Control and the 'Univer-city,'" *Radical Philosophy* 168 (July/August 2011): 9–21.

44   I am benefiting from Edward Said in *On Late Style* (New York: Pantheon Books, 2006), "Introduction" specifically.

45   Giorgio Agamben, *Nudities* (Stanford, CA: Stanford University Press, 2011), 11.

46   I am benefiting from the concept of Parallax developed by Kojin Karatani, *Transcritique: On Kant and Marx* (Cambridge, MA: The MIT Press, 2003).

7

Frank Gehry: Roofing, Wrapping, and Wrapping the Roof[1]

A participant in the MoMA 1988 "Deconstructivist Architecture" exhibition, Frank Gehry has come a long way, securing both institutional and public support. He is one of the few contemporary architects with little interest in theorizing his own work, yet he shares the neo-avant-garde's tendency to renew architecture by borrowing from conceptual art. He says about his collaboration with artists and sculptors: "I have [been] very involved with their work; I think a lot of my ideas have grown out of it, and that there has been some … give and take."[2] During his collaboration with Richard Serra, Gehry noticed the expressive potential of the fish. In a biographical note he recalls: "Every Thursday through much of my childhood we would go to the Jewish market, we'd buy a live carp, we'd take it home … we'd put it in the bathtub and I would play with this … fish for a day … until she killed it and made gefilte fish." In the anti-Semitism that prevailed during Gehry's youth, the architect was given the ironic nickname "Fish" by "his tormentors, presumably to suggest bad odor, and he would not realize until much later that 'fish' was a Christian symbol. His ambivalent identity with the image, however, would last until exorcised in his fish sculptures of the 1980s."[3] Germano Celant also notes similarities between Gehry's work and Claes Oldenburg. According to him,

> Gehry, like Oldenburg, takes advantage of [the] Surrealist idea of the ready-made: The position that Gehry and Oldenburg seem to share must be examined by studying the relation to the contextual determinations that the object–icon has as it interacts with its context in reality. … This is how the meaning of Oldenburg's Bat Column and Flashlight may be understood in their dialogue with, respectively, Chicago and Las Vegas; the meaning of Gehry's fish may be deduced from its functioning with respect to the aquatic element that surrounds Manhattan.[4]

Still, according to Francesco Dal Co, Gehry has not been merely a passive recipient of ideas generated by contemporary artists. Rather, he "understands that it is possible to 'occupy' with architecture, the spaces that art is no longer able to dominate, assigning to architectural design the task of taking the experiments of the historical avant-gardes to their extreme consequence."[5] Throughout his long years of practice Gehry has pursued a self-imposed challenge: to avoid leaving any kind of personal signature on his work. He has taken every commission as an opportunity to generate something different. With the Disney Concert Hall, and later with the Guggenheim Museum in Bilbao, however, he has introduced a major note into the noisy debates on architectural theory and practice.

But what will be the next turn in his architecture after Bilbao? The question is an important one because the language of the Guggenheim Museum in Bilbao evolved out of a paradox in Gehry's own work, i.e., an "obsession" with the biomorphics of fish—as an emblem of formal autonomy—and a desire for regionalism, especially the element of roof and the workaday look of materials that were prolific in his early projects. Knowing about the role computer programming played in the Bilbao project, if there is some formal limitation to computer-aided design, a viable alternative would still seem to be a return to the orthogonal and the striated space of modern architecture.[6] This technical limitation has a theoretical corollary: how far can we stretch the formal implications of the "fold," another favored Deleuzian term in the neo-avant-garde vocabulary, beyond what Gehry and others have already achieved? These limitations are evident in the "repetition" haunting Gehry's recent projects: both the addition to the Corcoran Museum, and the Concert Hall for the Bard College are mini replicas of the Guggenheim in Bilbao, as is his proposal for the Guggenheim in Lower Manhattan (Figure 7.1).

I do not intend to discuss Gehry's complete work in this chapter.[7] Instead, I will focus on buildings and projects that are pivotal for the argument that theatricalization permeates present architectural practice. The metaphor of the fish, with its twisting and bouncing body, is suggestive of an architectural image whose space could be wrapped beyond the dictate of the "regulating lines" envisioned by Le Corbusier. To go beyond the horizontal and vertical datum of the tectonic, architecture might enter into the world of plastic arts where the tension between the art-form and the core-form, discussed by the nineteenth-century architect Carl Bötticher,[8] evaporates. In Gehry's recent buildings the neo-avant-garde tendency

7.1   Frank Gehry, Guggenheim Museum, New York, 1998. Model. Photograph by Wit Preston, courtesy of Gehry Partners, LLP

7.2   Frank Gehry, Guggenheim Museum, Bilbao, Spain, 1991–97. Entry plaza. Photograph by author

to deny architecture any purpose except a formal one takes a different turn: his work is informed neither by images from the mainstream of pop culture, nor by the metaphysics, issues that preoccupy most architects who have read Jacques Derrida's deconstruction theory. From a certain angle, the Bilbao building stands as a phantom-like image comparable to visual effects seen in the best Hollywood movies (Figure 7.2). It is an exuberantly modeled three-dimensional space. Here architecture is not a stage-set, around and within which an event could take

7.3   Frank Gehry, Housing Project, Kalamazoo, Michigan, 1981. Drawing courtesy of Gehry Partners, LLP

place, but the event itself. Again, the idea is to ponder a distinction evident between Gottfried Semper's discourse on architecture of theatricality and the theatricalization of architecture—one representing tradition materialistically, the other drifting tradition into the phantasmagoria of a world of commodity. Here I am alluding to the term phantasmagoria as discussed by Walter Benjamin. Borrowing Karl Marx's articulation of the deceptive appearance of commodities (fetishism of commodities), Benjamin highlighted the optical illusions stimulated by the spectacular look of Paris. According to Susan Buck-Morss, Benjamin's point of departure "was a historical experience rather than an economic analysis of capital, the key to the new urban phantasmagoria was not so

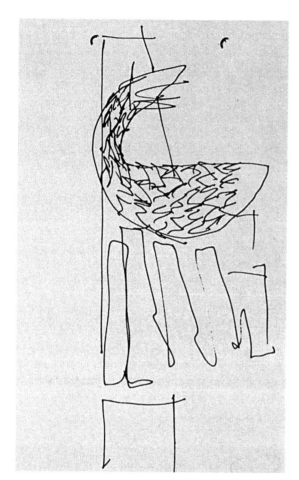

much the commodity-in-the-market as the commodity-on-display, where exchange value no less than use value lost practical meaning, and purely representational value came to the fore."[9] It is not far-fetched to say that the design of contemporary museums and other corporate institutions have inherited the visual allure of the world exhibitions built around the 1850s. In the context of the nineteenth-century cities, the Crystal Palace, for example, enjoyed a level of phantasmagoria comparable to the commodities displayed in its interior space.

The argument presented here is that the surreal quality of the Guggenheim in Bilbao, a found-object with discrete charm, evolved out of Gehry's move from regionalism towards a montage of fragmented masses and volumes. In this mutation the year 1981 is important: in a housing project for Kalamazoo in Michigan, the entire landscape is marked and dominated by a freestanding hotel envisioned in the shape of a vertical fish (Figure 7.3). Here we witness the return of a childhood memory of fish as the emblem of both formal perfection and the "other" that is charged with therapeutic function. "The fish evolved further," Gehry recalls in an interview, and continues, "I kept

7.4   Frank Gehry, Fishdance Restaurant, Kobe, Japan, 1986–87. Drawing courtesy of Gehry Partners, LLP

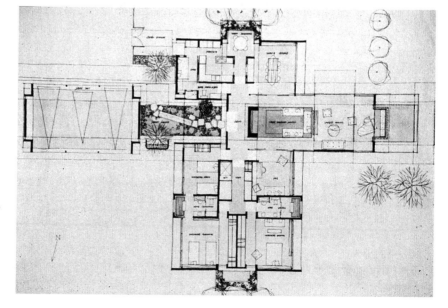

7.5   Frank Gehry, Steeves Residence, Brentwood, California, 1958–59. Plan drawing. Image courtesy of Gehry Partners, LLP

drawing it and sketching it and it started to become for me like a symbol for a certain kind of perfection that I couldn't achieve with my buildings. Eventually whenever I'd draw something and I couldn't finish the design, I'd draw the fish as a notation." Speaking of his participation in Tigerman's call for the Chicago Tribune Competition, Gehry recalls again that, "since I was never able to finish the Tribune drawing, I started making the colonnade with the eagle. And then I decided—well I should

have more columns. And that's when I drew the fish standing up …"[10] (Figure 7.4). Hence the proposition that Gehry's architecture evolved out of a dialogue, at times confrontational, between a montage of fragmented forms and the plastic quality of folding surfaces that is analogous to the bouncing body of a fish.

7.6   Frank L. Wright, Robie House, Chicago, 1909. Main view. Photography by author

ROOFING

Consider the Steeves House and the Ronald Davis Residence, built almost ten years apart. In both buildings the roof stands out as an architectonic element responding to the landscape and the region's vernacular tradition. The crucifix plan of the Steeves House (Figure 7.5) recalls the planimetric organization entertained by Frank Lloyd Wright, with the difference that the hearth (where two perpendicular arms of the plan come together) was for Wright the existential nucleus of dwelling whose architectonic presence is stressed either by the vertical expression of the chimney in the façade (the Robie House) (Figure 7.6), or by a hovering roof that shelters the house like an umbrella (the Ward Willis House). Gehry, instead, approaches the

7.7   Frank Gehry, Steeves Residence, Brentwood, California, 1958 59. Bird's-eye view. Image courtesy of Gehry Partners, LLP

7.8   Frank Gehry, Davis Studio and Residence, Malibu, California, 1962–72. Photograph courtesy of Gehry Partners, LLP

7.9   Frank Gehry, Davis Studio and Residence, Malibu, California, 1962–72. Interior view. Photograph courtesy of Gehry Partners, LLP

crossing point of the Steeves House pragmatically. Here the crossing point makes room for the main entrance, keeping the bedroom wing apart from the other three wings. The horizontal roof of this house (Figure 7.7) is another element that should be associated with Wright's design in the Goetsch-Winkler House built in Okemos, Michigan. Again, absent in Gehry's approach is the importance Wright would assign to the roof, not only at a tectonic level, but also at a metaphysical level. In the Goetsch-Winkler House, the roof attains its particular form by being anchored to the entrance. Should the absence of narrative of the kind Wright would weave in tectonic forms be considered a weakness in Gehry's architecture? Even a positive response to this question can't deny the attention Gehry gives to the client's needs and the local landscape, thus endowing the architecture with regional qualities. In the Steeves House the roof stretches out to make openings for a patio and a pergola above the living room. The split body of this roof generates a draft that cools the patio, and also allows light to penetrate indirectly into the living room and the garage.

Gehry's vernacular sensibilities attain a different level in the Davis Studio and Residence (Figure 7.8). A two-bedroom house with a painting studio, this house is conceived almost like an overturned box, with several volumes that are connected to each other by wooden stairs (Figure 7.9). The space between the shell and the interior volume acts as a passage, overriding the conventional distinction between inside and outside spaces. The posts, connecting the wood joists to the partition walls below, stress the detachment of the roof from other parts of the house. The exposed wooden structure of the roof floats over the interior volumes while its sloping form echoes the mountains of Malibu. Here Gehry combines the image of an American ranch house, a single freestanding object in the midst of the landscape, with spatial sensibilities derived from modern architecture. Germano Celant writes: "the

O'Neill Hay Barn and the Ron Davis House pay tribute to the architectural tradition of the Indian of the Northwest. … The architectural language of the Ron Davis House is linked to the craftsmanship tradition of tribes living from California to Alaska, who consider the shaping of their environment to be one of the highest artistic expressions."[11] Rosemarie Haag Bletter, instead, considers Gehry's sensibilities in part derived from "toying with a conflation of the world of perception and conception … "[12] The expressive quality of the roof in the Davis Studio, however, is in part a regional element utilized previously in the architect's non-residential buildings such as the Public Safety Building and Merriweather-Post Pavilion, both built in Columbia, Maryland. In Davis's Studio Gehry uses corrugated galvanized steel and exposed plywood, charging the building with an industrial/vernacular look. The tactile sensibilities experienced in this building are indeed rooted in the tradition of modern architecture. We are reminded of R.M. Schindler's DeKeyser House in Hollywood, where the living room volume is entirely sheathed in a green rolled roof which projects over the lower floor (Figure 7.10). More compelling is Schindler's Armon House in Mt. Washington, California, where an expressive roof and exposed wooden structure shelters an otherwise disjunctive plan where three volumes penetrate each other. This work anticipates Gehry's own house.

According to Margaret Crawford:

> Like Schindler, Gehry tended to develop interior spaces independently from exterior facades. Directly antithetical to the modernist insistence on the legibility of the interior on the exterior, this produced interesting slippages that Schindler exploited to create complex spaces and Gehry to produce complex exterior forms. Paradoxically, the influences between Schindler and Gehry are reciprocal; if Schindler made Gehry possible, Gehry's work illuminates Schindler's in new ways. For example, Gehry's far more dramatic use of exposed studs (as in his own house) to reveal the nature of wood frame construction make it possible to see Schindler's less explicit and more integrated use of exposed studs (as in the living room of the DeKeyser house) in a new light.[13]

Using inexpensive and ordinary materials such as chain link, corrugated metal, and unfinished plywood, Gehry's own house brings together two design themes essential to his departure from regionalism. Fredric Jameson has noticed the spatial qualities of Gehry's house, suggesting that it makes a departure from modernist understanding of the dialectics between interior and exterior spaces. More interesting is Jameson's idea of "wrapping" versus the modernist tendency for "grounding": whereas one stresses the figure/ground relationship derived from the force of gravity, the other envisions floating forms comparable to dancing figures in a surrealist artwork, if not similar to the floating nature of commodities in late capitalism. Jameson describes the "wrapping" intervention into the old house thus:

7.10   R.M. Schindler, DeKeyser House, Los Angeles, California, 1935. General view. Photograph by Grand Mudford

both the now sunken living room and the dining areas and kitchen opened up between loosely draped external wrapper and the "withering away" of the now seem to me the thing itself, the new postmodern space proper, which our bodies inhabit in malaise or delight, trying to shed the older habits of inside/outside categories and perceptions still longing for the bourgeois privacy of solid walls (enclosures like the old centered bourgeois ego), yet grateful for novelty of the incorporation of yucca plants and what Barthes would have called Californianity into our newly reconstructed environment.[14]

For Jameson, the idea of wrapping is a formative theme for postmodern architecture. My following remarks on the importance of "clothing" in Gehry's architecture, instead, intend to demonstrate the architect's departure from regionalism and the popularity of his recent work (Figure 7.11).

In several interviews Gehry has expressed his fascination with the unfinished quality of painting, sculpture, and even buildings under construction: "I was interested in the unfinished—or the quality that you find in paintings by Jackson Pollock, for instance, or de Kooning, or Cézanne, that look like the paint was just applied. ... We all like buildings in construction better than we do finished—I think most of us agree on that."[15] The fact that contemporary painting can mediate with the outside world through the use of paint and even sometimes by the use of plain metal and wood evokes primitive tactility rooted in vernacular arts. In Gehry's house the juxtaposition of the unfinished wood studs with highly articulated white cladded surfaces could be associated with the aesthetic sensibilities of the idea of both/and discussed by Robert Venturi. Criticizing what he calls the "tradition of either-or," in orthodox modern architecture, Venturi emphasizes a contradiction and hierarchy that "yields several levels of meanings among elements with varying values. It can include elements that are both good and awkward, big and little, closed and open, continuous and articulated, round and square, structural and

7.11   Frank Gehry, Gehry's Residence, Santa Monica, California, 1977–78. Exterior view. Photograph courtesy of Gehry Partners, LLP

spatial."[16] In Gehry's hands, the thematic dualities such as inside/outside or old/
new do not end in either/or resolutions. His own house marks a departure from
what one might call architecture's interiority[17] for a way of thinking in which
architecture is perceived as "modeling." Comparing Aldo Rossi with Gehry, Giovanni
Leoni suggests that, Rossi perceived architecture analogous to stage construction,
and concludes that, "the anti-architectural force of Gehry's architecture, which is
perhaps what makes it appeal so much to the general public, can on the contrary
be called modeling." According to him, Gehry's buildings "seem to be architectures
which live in complete serenity within the world of the form, and with their
procession of dancing objects … " Aware of Gehry's lack of interest in tectonics,
he continues: "It is not necessary to quote either Semper or Mies to assert that
modeling denies architecture as technique, while construction as assembly denies
architecture possibly to be an individual creative act."[18] I will address the problems
implicit in Leoni's view shortly; first, I would like to introduce the idea of formal
playfulness as another theme important for Gehry's departure from regionalism.

Having considered programmatic requirement and the situation of the site,
Gehry's design embarks on an open-ended path of formal experimentation similar
to that of scientific research; it is the gestalt of compositional elements that informs
each stage of decision-making design. Gehry wrote, "I guess, I approach architecture
somewhat scientifically—there are going to be breakthroughs, and they're going
to create new information. It's adding information to the pot—not necessarily
regurgitating other, older ideas."[19] Gehry's interest in spontaneity of design process
ends in a distillation of his architecture from metaphysical considerations. At the
same time he avoids engaging with issues such as the pleasure of the body in space
pursued by Peter Eisenman and Bernard Tschumi respectively. Also unattended in
Gehry's architecture is the duality between construction and appearance, a crucial
theme for the tectonic. Considering his interest in the "unfinished," however, one
might suggest that Gehry's design paradigm is rather similar to that of an artist;

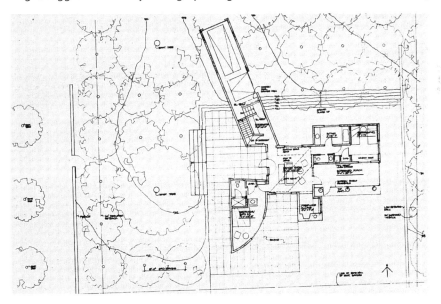

7.12   Frank Gehry,
Winton Guest
House, Wayzata,
Minnesota,
1982–87. Plan
drawing. Image
courtesy of Gehry
Partners, LLP

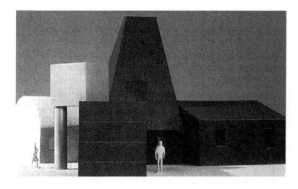

7.13   Frank Gehry, Winton Guest House, Wayzata, Minnesota, 1982–87. Model. Image courtesy of Gehry Partners, LLP

no one except the painter, for instance, knows why a painting is considered finished at a certain point in time.

The formal implications of a design informed by the aesthetic of unfinished and spontaneous playfulness is best demonstrated in the Winton Guest House built in Wayzata, Minnesota (1982–87) (Figure 7.12). This house embodies some architectonic elements both from the past and from what would become formative for Gehry's future architecture. The Winton House employs the idea of montage and theatricalization of architecture simultaneously: each room is perceived and shaped based on programmatic needs and clad with different materials without addressing any particular narrative (Figure 7.13). One bedroom is clad with local kasota stone, while the other is sheathed in painted metal panels. These boxed volumes are playfully arranged around a core (the living room) built next to a house designed by Philip Johnson in 1952. This theatrical composition, however, dismisses the serenity of regional sensibilities, in particular the element of roof. The design also lacks the kind of animation permeating his later projects. The Winton House is, indeed, an extension of ideas already at work in the California Aerospace Museum where dreamlike images collide with each other to express their formal autonomy (Figure 7.14). Also noticeable in these two buildings is the central void, whose presence is stressed by a vertical volume rising above other elements. The living room (the void) of the Winton House is shaped by the surrounding volumes and a truncated cone at the top. With metallic flesh and the void within, the truncated cone of the Winton House can be associated with the vertical figure of a fish. If this last observation seems subjective, the fact remains that the architectonic of a truncated cone compromises the line separating the roof from the wall.

The implied pyramidal form of the living room of the Winton House is a reminder of the ancient Egyptian temples which according to Semper,

> … rose chiefly from that element we have called the enclosure, … The other element, the roof, manifests itself in a twofold way: at times symbolically in the sekos as a pyramidal headpiece. …, and second, as the flat cover over the courtyard. There

7.14   Frank Gehry, California Aerospace Museum, Los Angeles, California, 1982–84. Section drawing. Image courtesy of Gehry Partners, LLP

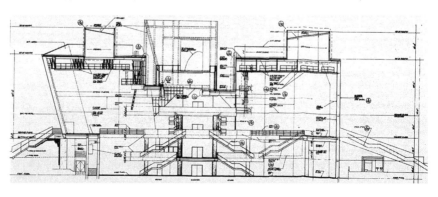

7.15   Egyptian Temple of Edfu. From J. Gardner Wilkinson, *The Manners and Customs of the Ancient Egyptians*, 1837

it ceased to appear from the outside, but inside, as an unfurled sail, it fell into the province of the wall filter, the motive to which it originally belonged.[20]

For Semper, the element of roof and its support evolve out of a conscious tectonic response to the essential act of walling (Figure 7.15). The reference to Semper and the tectonic rapport between the roof and the enclosure is not meant to put limitations on formal creativity. The intention rather is to underline the importance of the image of the fish in Gehry's work and the way such an image induces a world of pure figurative forms that raises questions about the tectonic rapport between the enclosure and the roof. Obviously, a certain kind of "image" occupies a particular place in the architect's mind, to the point that, like a craftsman, he/she attempts to correspond the final form of design with that particular image. What is important, however, is the way an image is recoded to probe issues internal to architecture as well as those forces framing architecture within a material and aesthetic network of a given production and consumption system.[21]

The discussion thus far is not primarily concerned with the atectonic architecture of Gehry. What needs to be emphasized here is that he does not produce an architecture that, in one way or another, stands against the drive of commodification of culture and its aesthetic connotation for architecture. Kenneth Frampton for one has presented the tectonic as essential for a "critical practice" in postmodern conditions when the "novum" has lost its validity. He writes, "While the crisis of the neo-avant-garde derives directly from the spontaneous dissolution of the new, critical culture attempts to sustain itself through a dialectical play across a historically determined reality in every sense of the term."[22] In raising this point, however, I am aware of the difficult task I am imposing upon Gehry, or any contemporary architect: How would one develop a critical practice in a situation when the production and consumption of images have become essential for the culture? This is important because it says something about the present situation when "everything is cultural, and that the economic dimension, for example, is no longer visible independently," but is rather expressed in the fact that the subject has lost the ability to recognize his/her marks on the object.[23]

THE TECHNIQUE OF SPECTACLE

Giovanni Leoni is right to remind us of the anguish caused by combining "aura and market." Nevertheless, he is wrong to conclude that architecture survives in Gehry's work through "new expressionism."[24] Architecture has been thriving under the pressure of the commercialization of landscape since the 1960s, most tangibly in America. The anguish was first theorized by Robert Venturi and Denise Scott Brown in the language of "complexity and contradiction," and then domesticated in their own lessons drawn from Las Vegas.[25] Neil Leach has this to say about the architectonic implications of *Learning from Las Vegas*:

> once one enters an argument of "form for form's sake" where form is abstracted
> from other concerns, it is not easy to "resynthesize" these concerns into form in
> the final design. It is this principle of aestheticization, then, that allows Venturi,
> Scott Brown, and Steven Izenhour to remain so oblivious to the socio-political
> questions at the heart of Las Vegas, to anaesthetize it, and to adopt an approach
> that is epitomized by their celebration of the advertising hoarding.[26]

If we see architecture's survival in the expressive language of tele-communication technology, as does Leoni, then we stop short of learning a lesson from the experiences of the 1960s, as well as being unable to distinguish theatricalization that is taking over current architecture from the expressionism of the 1920s. The same can be said about Kurt W. Forester who makes analogies between the playfulness of Gehry's architecture and that of Francesco Borromini.[27] I will discuss the analogy between the current esteem for "expressionism" and that of Baroque later in this chapter. It is necessary to add here that analogies made between the theatricalization of current architecture and either the Baroque or expressionism of the 1920s surpass the modernist historicism, but also stop short of stressing the historicity of current architecture. According to Alan Colquhoun, historical analysis would have to reconcile "the uniqueness of our culture, which is the product of historical development, ... with the palpable fact that it operates within a historical context and contains within itself its own historical memory."[28] In search of the lost spirit of the war years, expressionism, for example, envisioned fantastic forms that "would suspend the forces of gravity and overcome the obstinate solidity of matter ... "[29] If the utopia of glass architecture was the representational mode proper to a class of disenchanted modernists, then one could say that irony and rhetoric are tools by which postmodernists disguise the entering of architecture into the realm of the "culture industry." Is it history's irony that today we can witness how expressionism (a familiar language, though of a high culture) smoothes the passage of architecture towards the aesthetic of commodity fetishism? Francesco Dal Co makes a similar assessment by suggesting that, by updating techniques used by the historical avant-gardes, Gehry makes "significant innovations in professional and design practice, because this program can be realized only when the constructed work is assigned the task of establishing a relationship not to a public of users, but with an audience of spectators. In this way architecture tends to mutate, to change its nature, eschewing usage and becoming entertainment."[30] The implied turn resonates with Fredric Jameson's periodization of art into three modes of "realism," "abstraction," and the fetishism of commodity production, wherein each period marks an aesthetic appropriation of art and architecture proper to a particular stage of modernization.[31] Following George Simmel's "Philosophy of Money," published in 1920, Fredric J. Schwartz also underlines the presence of "spectacle" as an important element smoothing an artifact's way to the realm of consumption.[32] We are reminded of the popularity of Gehry's architecture, and the fact that the dancing body of his architecture reconciles the biomorphics implied in the image of the fish with animation internal to most products of parametric design.

The impact of technology on architecture is not new. I do not intend to examine the issues here.[33] What should rather be stressed here, albeit briefly, is the way the technification of architecture (to use Theodor Adorno's term) empties the tectonic of any import for architecture. Using techniques developed outside of architecture's interiority reduces architecture to an appendage of technique.[34] Discussing the technification of music, Adorno casts light upon Gehry and other architects who use computer techniques not just as a means but also as a force to shape the end itself. According to Adorno, "extramusical technique is no longer present to act as a corrective but becomes instead the exclusive authority. The whole official music culture is moving in the direction of fetishizing of means, and it is even celebrating a triumph among its enemies in the avant-garde."[35] If at the turn of the last century, architecture enjoyed a unique sense of cosmopolitanism inaccessible to other cultural products, the aesthetic homologies unfolding through digital technification is detectable in the metallic, sensuous, and puffed-looking latest design of cars as well as the theatricalization that permeates the Disney Concert Hall building. What is involved here, speaking architecturally, is the role of sectional investigation in design. Whilst the façade is liberated from the plan through the frame-structure, and its surface can be articulated based on the design of its own plan, in the architecture of theatricalization, the section has turned out to be the site where the relationship between cladding and the frame is exploited, subjecting the former to a vision of aesthetics that has the least connection to function, type or model, and the frame.

There are two reasons for introducing the subject of technification of architecture here. First, the introduction of industrial techniques made it impossible to conceive architecture according to the classical notion of techné. This development also had repercussion for the work of historians and critics. Briefly, and at the risk of dismissing many significant details, I would like to suggest that major contemporary architectural discourses, in one way or another, are framed by the multiple consequences that modernization has forced on architecture. I am reminded of Demetri Porphyrios's insistence on the tectonic of stone architecture inherited from the classical tradition, as the sole language to be practiced today. Without pushing the envelope to this extreme, Manfredo Tafuri has persuasively launched a relentless critique of modernity and its implication for architecture, in a way that makes contemporary architecture seem like a by-product of a schizophrenic mind, a situation when one has no choice but to enter the dead-end alley of modernization as the only escape from modernity itself. Alberto Pérez-Gómez, on the other hand, projects the crisis of architecture back to the time when the poetic rapport between *logos* and *mythos* disappeared. His position can be characterized as a vision of modernity whose objective and subjective forces have never attained hegemony.[36] The missing issue in their discourses is the architecture's interiority and its potential to resist commodification, a process that uproots architectural production and reception from its craft-based domain, subjecting the art of building to the laws of a capitalist market economy. The second reason for highlighting the notion of technification has to do with the changing socio-political nature of contemporary avant-garde work. If the historical avant-garde embraced technology in order to construct a utopian enclave whose cultural matrix remained "high art" and inaccessible to the masses, the fusion of electronic technologies within everyday cultural production and consumption has adorned reification—induced by the project of modernity— with a mysticism shared by everybody.

To the embarrassment of Peter Eisenman and many others, you no longer have to know the philosophical implications of the "weak form" in order to appropriate his or Gehry's architecture. It is enough to watch pop culture on MTV or in Hollywood's latest blockbuster movies and get tuned with the morphed temperament of deconstructivist architecture. "Hey," an excited Venturi exclaims, "what's for now is a generic architecture whose technology is electronic and whose aesthetic is iconographic—and it all works together to create decorated shelter— or the electronic shed."[37] This populist view suggests that the distance once felt facing the abstract aesthetic of early modern art and architecture is neutralized in part by computer generated images which have been grafted onto every aspect of the life-world. Again, it should be stressed that Semper's idea of dressing and his concept of theatricality differ from the phantasmagoria of the postmodern world. For Semper, the dressing of the core-form, even when negating the material basis of building, comes to life out of a rapport between the roof and the enclosure, or the earth-work and the frame-work. Accordingly,

> ... the correct relation of the enclosure to the enclosed should, moreover, be apparent in the fact that the former (in all its formal properties and colors) forcefully emphasizes and supports the effect of the latter. The enclosed should present itself unmistakably as the principle theme and be placed upon a suitably chosen background. But, again, this goal will be achieved only by using precisely those properties of ornamentation that develop a priori from the formal concept of the surface as such.

Semper continues, "these properties should at the same time be easily depicted or produced and should derive from techniques first used in the production of such surface dressing (namely textile)."[38] In this line of consideration, one is reminded

7.16 Frank Gehry, Walt Disney Concert Hall, Los Angeles, California, 1997–2003. Entrance view. Photograph by author

of the German architect's emphasis on the theatricality of the afterlife of an event. According to Semper, "The monuments were scaffolding intended to bring together," not only various cultural artifacts, but "the crowds of people, the priest, and the processions."[39] One is reminded of Jean-Jacques Rousseau's description of a non-theatrical public spectatordom:

> But what then will be the objects of these spectacles? What will be shown in them? Nothing, if you like. With liberty, wherever abundance reigns, well being reigns as well. Plant in the middle of a square a pole crowned with flowers, bring the people together there, and you will have a festival. Do better still, make the beholders the spectacle; make them actors themselves; make each of them see himself and love himself in the others so that they will all be more closely united.[40]

The challenge to maintain Semper's notion of theatricality today has to do with the fact that spectacle, discussed by Guy Debord, has overtaken the collective space.

WRAPPING

7.17   Frank Gehry, Vitra International Design Museum, Weil am Rhein, Germany, 1987–89. Photograph by author

In the context of the above theoretical considerations, and taking some exceptions into account, it can be argued that, since the Winton House, Gehry's architecture has moved further away from the form-giving potentialities of construction to the point where the element of clothing has emerged as the formative means for his most recent work. This development is forcefully expressed in Gehry's Walt Disney Concert Hall project where an icon of mass culture and music orchestrate

the theatricalization of architecture (Figure 7.16). The Disney Concert Hall, in evolution since 1989, is an important work that needs to be experienced in order to complete the evolutionary chain leading to the Bilbao building, if not for any other particular reason. The project marks a definitive departure in Gehry's design: it resolves the conflict between the montage of fragmented forms and an expressive clothing whose many layers come together to emphasize the vertical void in the middle. In the Vitra Museum, completed in 1989 (Figure 7.17), we have already witnessed the presence of undulating surfaces that are intermingled with fragmented volumes, anticipating the formativeness of the element of wrapping in the Disney project. At Vitra, the element of roof, mostly covered by titanzink, is presented as another enclosure wrapping a cluster of fragmented volumes. Only when inside the building can we experience the presence of the roof; a situation that recalls

7.18   Frank Gehry, Fishdance Restaurant, Kobe, Japan, 1986–87. Photograph courtesy of Gehry Partners, LLP

Semper's observation about ancient Egyptian temples. Meanwhile, during the years separating the Winton House from the Disney project, the fish metaphor continued to occupy a visible place in Gehry's oeuvre. Besides being the subject of several artistic installations erected between 1983 and 1986, the metaphor leaves the two-dimensional realm of Gehry's drawing board and attains major architectonic form, first in the Fishdance Restaurant built in 1987 (Figure 7.18), and later more forcefully in the Vila Olimpia built in Spain (1992). In this last project, a 160 ft long and 100 ft tall fish obtains its visibility and landmark position by hovering above a complex of commercial buildings (Figure 7.19).

Gehry's design for the Disney Concert Hall skews the postmodern fascination with historical images and the architecture of spectacle. By doing so, Gehry sounds an off-note in the tectonic thinking. The Concert Hall project is fashionably dressed-up to designate a volumetric mass that denies any coherent and hierarchical order, and yet relates the building to its site heterogeneously. Seen from Hope Street, the main body of the central hall sits on a horizontal volume that houses the servant

7.19   Frank Gehry, Vila Olimpia, Barcelona, Spain, 1989–92. Photograph courtesy of Gehry Partners, LLP

spaces. This *parti* was also used in the Jung Institute for Los Angeles in 1976. The sketches of this project depict an L-shaped rectangular box whose roof is marked by a number of playful and independent volumes (Figure 7.20). According to Kurt Forster, Gehry was "obviously discovering something important at this stage, when he relaxed, and even

7.20 Frank Gehry, Jung Institute, project, 1976. Perspective drawing. Image courtesy of Gehry Partners, LLP

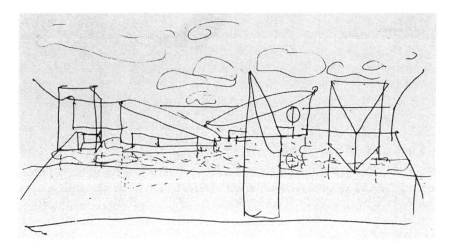

severed, the links that had hitherto locked the various parts of a building into a single whole."[41] This observation is paralleled in Gehry's design for the Familian Residence and his own house. In the Jung Institute and the Disney Concert Hall, we witness a disintegrated whole that is not achieved through fragmentation but through a compositional distinction between what is necessity and what is excessive. In the Disney project, the rational articulation of the base stands in contrast to the vertical and dynamic configuration of the central volume. The podium in these two projects holds up a vibrant form evoking the relationship of a dancer to the stage. The seam connecting the building to the ground in the main façade, on the other hand, is treated more in line with the dressing of the concert hall. Here, the fragmented and twisted surfaces are dramatized by cuts that mark the main entrance. This figurative gesture is stressed by rotating the plan of the amphitheater against the main axis of the site (Figure 7.21). The inflection projects the figure of the main volume forward and up, as floors are stacked on top of each other. Seen from the angle of the main entrance, the vertical cut through the enclosure makes room for a glazed volume to jut out, disclosing the central void. Through the same opening we can see the structural columns, whose form indicates a distinction between what is dressing and what is constructional. Each column has a short, tree-trunk base from which structural, vertical elements stretch out to support the enclosure. The cuts on the body of the amphitheater emulate the idea of "ruin in future," a visual sensibility fashionable in the "grunge" style of dress of urban youth circa 1980s. However, it is to Gehry's credit that he makes use of the space between the metal wrapping and the "shoebox" amphitheater with terraces, gardens, and other programmatic requirements, an arrangement that saves the project from being a mere postmodernist "decorated shed."

The metaphoric analogy between dress and the vertical configuration of the central volume in the Disney Concert Hall recalls the posture of a dancer. There is an intriguing dialogue between the disintegrated seam in the front part of this building and the soaring volume of the concert hall. Somewhat similar to a ballet dancer, the vertical volume appears to be defying the force of gravity. This "theatrical posture" does not, however, simulate total weightlessness. The building's configuration

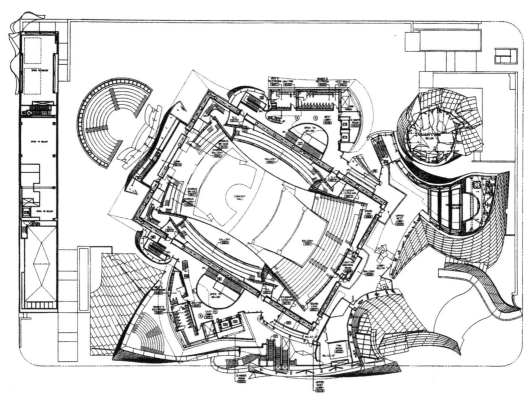

7.21   Frank Gehry, Walt Disney Concert Hall, Los Angeles, California, 1997–2003. Floor plan. Drawing courtesy of Gehry Partners, LLP

evokes the posture of a dancer who, after soaring up and twisting around, eventually stands firm and maintains minimum contact with the ground. The fragmented and torn surfaces of the amphitheater could also be associated with the fabrics used to cover carnival scaffolding and, of course, tent architecture. This analogy is important not because of the twist that might be given to the debate on the origins of architecture, but because of the importance of textiles for architecture (whether implied in Semper's idea of dressing or derived from the architecture of the tent) and the concept of fabrication as a way of seeing and making that is implied in the word fabric. The art-form of the Disney Concert Hall suggests that the perceived spatial envelope is literally a fabrication; the etymology of the word suggests both the style and the plan of construction and woven material. Reminding his readers of that ambiguous moment of intersection between gravity and the unconscious, particular to the animated world of cartoons, Michael Sorkin makes the following observation that "the Disney project is also a distortion, a cartoon that inflates the unseen ideal form: those shapes in the Disney hall are both dancing flowers or hippos but also dancing not-cubes and not-rectangles, distorted away from the familiar but not so far as to cease affinity." Sorkin's reminds us of a particular aspect of filmmaking that is important to Gehry's work. According to Sorkin, "both cartoons and films evolved out of a process of bringing single frozen cuts or images together by animation." In this process, however, there is no limit in the act of distortion as far as the familiar object and its image is not totally washed out. "While Mickey resembles a mouse but looks like no mouse we've ever seen, nevertheless, the cartoon holds its familiarity to our eye as long as Mickey plummets to earth when being conscious of walking in air."[42] The implied defamiliarization in Sorkin's statement discloses a formalistic approach to architecture, one that would free the enclosure from any constraint, including the geometry induced by the structural logic, which results in the absolute autonomy of form.

The discrepancy between the art-form and the structural logic for the tectonic is convincingly discussed in Hubert Damisch's structuralist reading of Viollet-le-Duc.[43] Of further interest is Frampton's discussion of Jørn Utzon's Sydney Opera House, where we are reminded of two historical occasions when the gap between structural logic and architectonic form comes to closure. According to Frampton, "The first of these occurs during the high Gothic period, while the second arises in the second half of the nineteenth century with the perfection of ferro-vitreous construction."[44] Nevertheless, Gehry does not address the suggested gap and fails to articulate the rift between the formal (sculptural) and the structural beyond a postmodernist either/or resolution. We might speculate that Gehry utilizes the analogy between fabric and dressing in spite of the nineteenth-century tectonic discourse. We might also suggest that his architecture folds the tectonic thinking back to a state of primitivism when architecture, according to Adolf Loos, was realized by putting up four carpets, and the structural elements were seen as auxiliary; they just support the carpets. Loos used the metaphor of carpet to stress the importance of cladding and the architect's intelligence in choosing material that suits particular spatial effects.[45] And yet, was not the idea of the Dom-ino frame (and its consequences for the free-façade and the free-plan) in part motivated by tent architecture, whose regulating lines still refer to the importance of cubes and rectangles, even seen through the distorted lens of postmodernity? By investing "fabrication" and demystifying the classical discourse on construction, Gehry's design entertains an early modernist vision in which a primitive sense of freedom was sought as a means of rebuffing, even if temporarily, the constrains forced on architecture by modernization. The "actualization" of past through the present (what Walter Benjamin termed allegory) reaches a critical dimension in Gehry's appropriation of the aesthetic of fabrication. The aesthetic appeal of the wrapping surfaces of the Disney project is a reminder of the "mystical" character of commodities whose fetishism speaks of the dissociation of the commodity from its use-value.[46]

The theatrical character of Gehry's design, its allusions to the posture of the dancer and the expressive falseness of its dressing, are suggestive of an architecture of spectacle. As a metaphor, "spectacle," in this particular case, stands for the programmatic and iconic connotation of the Disney Concert Hall. In Kahn's words, Gehry's building wants to be the architecture of event that has no reference point, and yet, by bringing together the spectacle (the stage) and the spectator, the building itself becomes part of the culture of spectacle. The idea is given a new pitch in the Guggenheim Museum in Bilbao, Spain (Figure 7.22). This building is, indeed, Gehry's ultimate statement in defying Semper's theory of dressing, i.e., *Bekleidung* favoring the aesthetic of dressed-up.[47] While the former is achieved by

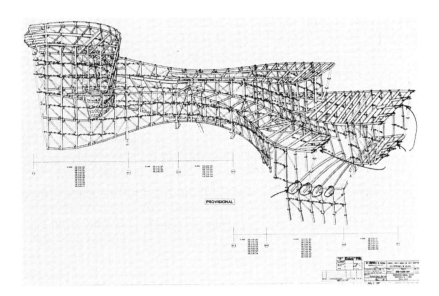

7.22   Frank Gehry, Guggenheim Museum, Bilbao, Spain, 1991–97. Computer drawing of the steel structure. Image courtesy of Gehry Partners, LLP

the embellishment of a constructed form and its poetic expression in cladding, the dressed-up, instead, suggests a vision of wrapping that is implied in the formal and aesthetic freedom embedded in the frame-structure that has been used since the inception of the Dom-ino frame. The Bilbao building also recollects two themes important for Gehry's work: first, the image of the fish, which, in this particular project, attains a contextual quality, partly owing to its waterside location, and second, the specifics involved in a sculptor's vision of the object at hand.

7.23   Frank Gehry, Guggenheim Museum, Bilbao, Spain, 1991–97. Entrance view. Photograph by author

While the overall form of the Bilbo building discloses nothing short of an image of spectacle, the building's relation to the site is of most interest here. The tactile qualities of the metallic cladding and the formal energies pumped into different parts of the building connote the restless situation of the body of a fish wanting to free itself from the hook. The significance of this analogy, though presented in visual terms, should be elaborated in architectonic terms. What is involved here is the dichotomy between the site plan and the overall volume of the building (Figure 7.23). While most published pictures of the project emphasize the sculptural nature of the volume and its allusive geometry, the site plan instead discloses the way in which Gehry has skillfully infused aspects of the idea of land-form architecture into his design. This much is clear from the location of the main entrance where we are invited first to step down to the level of the adjacent river, and then to climb back up almost to street level

7.24 Frank Gehry, Guggenheim Museum, Bilbao, Spain, 1991–97. View from the adjacent bridge. Photograph by author

and from there to the upper galleries. Thus the Semperian idea of earth-work and terrace making, and its essentiality for the building grounding in the site. Also of interest, as far as the issue of land-form is concerned, is the volume of the gallery (the largest one houses the work of American artist Richard Serra) the body of which is extended to occupy the underground of the highway above. It is to Gehry's credit that he combines architecture with infrastructure, the highway and the river, marking the building as a pleat where what was once "natural" has to be folded into that of the city, the spectacle. The implied dichotomy is legible in the montage of the overall volume of the complex where the sculptural form seen from the city is balanced with volumes whose form is edited in reference to the surrounding landscape (Figure 7.24).

This aspect of Gehry's architecture, the building's relation to its context, has been interpreted differently. Rosemarie Haag Bletter reminds us, as early as in 1986, of the importance of the idea of constant change invested in Kurt Schwitters' Merzbau (1933) and Gehry's house in Santa Monica: "Schwitters' sculpture gradually grew from inside out to absorb the old house," Bletter observes. Gehry, "works from the outside in by entrapping the original bungalow of his Santa Monica house within a new shell."[48] Dal Co has picked up on the Merzbau to discuss the Bilbao building.[49] What is intriguing in the Merzbau, however, is the endless transformation of the project to the point that the work precludes any possible representational dialogue between material, construction, and representation. According to Dal Co, the "operative" technique utilized by Schwitters "makes its constituent elements imperceptible: the only presence it permits is the continuously evoked presence of its artifice."[50] An artifice indeed, but one that is more in tune with the language of parody than the tectonic, even when the incompleteness of the final form is wrongly taken for the filmic technique of montage. The "operative" technique is the form-giving principle in the Guggenheim's titanium dressing whose overall envelope reveals no trace of the steel frame beneath (Figure 7.25).

To underline my concern for the rapport between a constructed form and the clothing, it is important to draw the reader's attention to Claes Oldenburg, an artist dear to Gehry's heart. In Oldenburg's entry for the Chicago Tribune Tower Competition of 1968, a skyscraper is envisioned in the form of Lorado Taft's sculpture *Death*. Here, Oldenburg wraps the body of his work with fabric, stressing the flesh and evoking a sense of verticality and ruin. Oldenburg's skyscraper recalls Gustav Klimt's painting *The Kiss*, where the physicality of the depicted body

7.25   Frank Gehry, Guggenheim Museum, Bilbao, Spain, 1991–97. Three-dimensional rendering of steel structure frame. Image courtesy of Gehry Partners, LLP

disappears behind a wrapping cloth. However, equally important to my concern for the tectonic is the way Jørn Utzon draws analogies from both the visual arts and the natural world in the design of the Sydney Opera House. According to Françoise Fromonot, the repetitive coil in the wavy hair of Venus in Botticelli's *The Birth of Venus*, or the fanned pleats falling from the shoulder over the protruding knees in the figure of *Christ*, found on the Tympanum of Vézelay, encouraged Utzon to make visible what is load-bearing and what is cladding. In doing so, he avoided the temptation of indulging in expressionistic forms such as clouds, instead, favoring standardized elements that would shape the dialogue between cladding and "the primary tectonic order of building."[51] This last observation does not suggest that Gehry's design world is empty of imagination. I rather want to stress a problem inherent in the interiority of architecture: since the experience of the Dom-ino frame, the frame-structure has provided a chance for the architect to avoid the tectonic dialogue between structure and the element of wrapping.[52] The pictures taken during construction of the Bilbao building suggest that the steel framework was entertained primarily as a supportive mechanism to hold up a pre-conceived shell. The expressive freedom charged to the clothing of Gehry's recent building recalls Gilles Deleuze's association between the idea of "fold" and Baroque architecture. According to Deleuze "Baroque architecture can be defined by this severing of the façade from the inside, of the interior from exterior, and the autonomy of the exterior, but in such a condition that each of the two terms thrusts the other forward."[53] And yet long before Deleuze's text became the textbook for deconstructivist architecture, Hans Sedlmayr had recognized the "artistic structure" of Borromini's San Carlo in the repetition of an undulating wall four times in the plan. Here, "structure is found paradoxically in a surface element without structural function." According to Christopher Wood, "the deliberate, paradoxical reversal of

the structure–surface hierarchy characteristic of baroque or rococo architecture became in effect the fundamental maneuver of *Struktur-analyse.*" We could follow Sedlmayr's "*Struktur-analyse*" to discuss the dialogical relationship between the roof and the enclosure as the "structure"; a design principle informing Gehry's work, and the recent work of the neo-avant-garde architects.[54] I would like to suggest that, independent of structure the element of wrapping has become the form-giving impulse in the Bilbao building. Gone in Gehry's vision is the Miesian tectonic that is revealed in the dialogical relationship between column and wall, and the earth-work and the frame-work. Gehry also dispenses with Kahn's attempt to reveal the way a space is conceived and constructed. Instead, Gehry says, "I have been interested in expressing feelings in my work, that means you don't distill them with rationalization. You solve the practical stuff but don't take the juice out while you are doing it." The "juice" perhaps refers to

7.26   Frank Gehry, IAC Interactive Corp Headquarters, Manhattan, New York City, 2007. Photograph by author

the protein of the formal voyeurism rested in computer-generated images, which Gehry appropriates so skillfully.

We are also reminded of Gehry's two recent projects in Manhattan, the language of which tries to break away from the major formal and aesthetic issues informing most of the projects discussed here. In the Inter Active Corp Headquarters (IAC), located on the West Side Highway, the building's cladding defies any importance the detailing has for tectonics, to the point that the crystal-looking form of the building offers a seamless envelope with no expressive joints (Figure 7.26). Moreover the building does not address issues whose experience might lead to a critical understanding of architecture's rapport with the political economy of Manhattanism, to recall Koolhaas. The IAC's dressing is a deliberate attempt on the part of the architect to present the corporate spatial organization as an obscure object of desire. Recalling the notion of "juice" mentioned earlier, Reinhold Martin writes: "Liquidity, juice: the very definition of capital, and therefore appropriate enough to describe this instance of corporate architecture. Anything more solid— geological rather than fluid or atmospheric—implies indifference (or resistance?) to capital's inexorable, circulatory pulse and therefore might seem behind the times, out of sync."[55] Similarly to Christo and Jeanne-Claude's installation in Basel (1997–98), the skirt-like pleats of the IAC's dressing suggest the presence of a wider structure at street level with setbacks as the structure soars up. However, the mysterious looking objects of Christo's wrapped trees give way in the IAC to a security device protecting the invisible privatized workplace in the era of

7.27   Frank Gehry, Residential Tower, New York City, 2011. Photograph by author

corporate global capitalism. The building's envelope confirms that, when "energy and security concerns have replaced an earlier focus on circulation and flow as the content of architectural expression."[56] To highlight the obvious difference between architecture and sculpture, the IAC's envelope offers elusive horizontal transparencies, through which the interior spaces can have a glimpse of the surrounding landscape. In spite, or perhaps because of this, the expected natural flow between the inside and the outside is curtailed and the building looks like a soft crystal armor.

The implied formal and spatial anonymity is carried through Gehry's design for a tower located in Lower Manhattan. A 76-story residential tower, clad in a wrinkled looking stainless-steel skin is placed upon a six-story base clad in brick with openings sized to its structure (Figure 7.27). The so-called pedestal is the only part of this rather inaccessible tower that can be associated with the surrounding buildings at street level. "Inaccessible" because the main entrance to the residential part of the tower is not accessible from the street level, it is discreetly located underground. The flat south façade of the tower, with its regular window openings, is in sharp contrast to the playful geometry of the rest of the envelope that takes its cue from the waves of the Hudson River. The building's setbacks induce a sense of verticality delivered through the notion of towering evident in Cass Gilbert's Woolworth building (1913) located within walking distance. The setbacks of Gehry's tower are further stressed by its discontinuous surfaces and sharp-edged lines, which make the cladding resemble a glossy chiseled cloth. Even though the design adds a new look to the Manhattan skyline, it nevertheless fails to do two things that Mies established in the Seagram Building. First, Gehry's tower debunks tectonic figuration at the expense of dragging architecture into the world of spectacular tall buildings, a *collection* that in subtle ways perpetuates the hegemonic position of the corporate culture in Manhattan. Second, as an urban artifact, neither of these last two projects intervenes, nor tries to change the given urban structure as the plinth of the Seagram Building does. The plinth not only provides a public entry space to Mies's tower, but also defies the economic-spatial structure of the block. Furthermore, in connecting the Seagram Building to its urban structure, the Miesian plinth "affects not only one's experience of what is placed *on* the plinth, but also—and specifically—one's experience of the city that is *outside* the plinth."[57] For Pier Vittorio Aureli the uniqueness of Mies's urban architecture is the way the building relates to *that* (urbanism) which the building is already separated from.

A resistance to critically engaging with, and making meaningful additions to the present urban structure is perhaps the common thread running through the work of most architects discussed in this volume; they either maintain a cynical position against the failure of the project of modernity, or try to capture that aspect of the age of digital reproductivity that we have associated with the architecture of theatricalization.

NOTES

1   A version of this chapter was first published in *The Journal of Architecture* 6, 1 (spring 2002): 1–31. It is slightly revised and edited for this volume. The original essay was written before Hal Foster's essay, "Master Builder," in *Design and Crime* (London: Verso, 2002), 27–42.

2   Stated in an interview with Peter Arnell in P. Arnell and Ted Bickford, eds, *Frank Gehry: Buildings and Projects* (New York: Rizzoli, 1985).

3   Thomas Hines, "Heavy Metal: The Education of F.O.G.," in *The Architecture of Frank Gehry* (New York: Rizzoli, 1986), 11–24, and 13–14.

4   G. Celant, "Reflections on Frank Gehry," in P. Arnell and T. Bickford, eds, *Frank Gehry*, 1985 .

5   Francesco Dal Co, "The World Turned Upside-Down: The Tortoise Flies and Hare Threaten the Lion," in Kurt W. Forester and Francesco Dal Co, eds, *Frank O. Gehry* (New York: Monacelli Press, 1998), 42.

6   Gilles Deleuze and Felix Guattari, "The Smooth and the Striated," in *A Thousand Plateaus* (Minneapolis, MN: University of Minnesota Press, 1987), 474–500.

7   See for example, Kurt W. Forster and Francesco Dal Co, *Frank O. Gehry*, 1998.

8   On the subject of theatricality see Chapter 2 in this volume.

9   Susan Buck-Morss, *The Dialectics of Seeing: Walter Benjamin and the Arcade Project* (Cambridge, MA: The MIT Press, 1989), 81–2.

10   See endnote 2, above.

11   Germano Celant, "Reflections on Frank Gehry," in P. Arnell and Ted Bickford, eds, *Frank Gehry*, 1985.

12   Rosemarie Haag Bletter, "Frank Gehry's Spatial Reconsiderations," in Thomas Hines, ed., *The Architecture of Frank Gehry*, 1986, 26.

13   Margaret Crawford, "Forgetting and Remembering Schindler: The Social History of an Architectural Reputation," *2G* 7 (1998): 129–42.

14   Fredric Jameson, *Postmodernism, or the Cultural Logic of Late Capitalism* (Durham, NC: Duke University Press, 1991), 115.

15   B. Diamonstein, *American Architecture Now* (New York: Rizzoli, 1986), 36.

16   Robert Venturi, *Complexity and Contradictions in Architecture* (New York: The Museum of Modern Art, 1966), 31.

17   By architecture's interiority I mean tropes that are accumulated through the history of architectural theories and practice. I am thinking of ideas concerning inside/outside, the tectonic rapport between the column and the wall, and the tectonic achieved by the symbolic embellishment of a constructed form, or that of the earth-work and the frame-work as discussed by Gottfried Semper. My discussion of architecture's interiority differs from Peter Eisenman's reflection on "interiority of architecture" where he presents a formalistic understanding of architecture. See Eisenman, *Diagram Diaries* (New York: Universe Publishing, 1999), 27–43.

18   Giovanni Leoni, "Modeling Versus Building," *Area* 41 (1998): 4–5.

19   See B. Diamonstein, *American Architecture Now*, 1986, 37.

20   Gottfried Semper, "The Four Elements of Architecture," in *The Four Elements of Architecture and Other Writings*, trans. Harry F. Mallgrave and Wolfgang Herrmann (Cambridge: Cambridge University Press, 1989), 115.

21   It is important to recall the criticality of images of silos and liners for the aesthetic dimension of Le Corbusier's architecture, and that of the hut for Mies van der Rohe. It is equally important to remember how each of these two architects re-articulated architecture in reference to earth, sky, and the impact of the metropolis on architecture.

22   Kenneth Frampton, *Studies in Tectonic Culture* (Cambridge, MA: The MIT Press, 1995), 25.

23   Fredric Jameson, *The Hegel Variations* (London: Verso, 2010), 128.

24   Giovanni Leoni, "Modeling Versus Building," 1998, 2.

25   For a critical reflection on Robert Venturi, and Denise Scott Brown, see Kenneth Frampton, "America 1960–1970: Notes on Urban Images and Theory," *Casabella* 359–60, 25 (1971): 24–38. For Dennis Scott Brown's response to Frampton's charges, see *Casabella* (1971): 39–46.

26   Neil Leach, *The Anaesthetics of Architecture* (Cambridge, MA: The MIT Press, 1999), 63.

27   Kurt W. Forester, "Architectural Choreography," in Kurt W. Forester and Francesco Dal Co, eds, *Frank O. Gehry*, 1998, 9–38.

28   Alan Colquhan, "Three Kinds of Historicism," in *Modernity and the Classical Tradition* (Cambridge, MA: The MIT Press, 1989), 16.

29   Fritz Neumeyer, "Nexus of the Modern: The New Architecture in Berlin," in Tilmann Buddenseig, ed., *Berlin 1900–1933: Architecture and Design* (Washington, DC: The Smithsonian Museum of Design, 1987), 52.

30   Francesco Dal Co, "The World Turned Upside-Down," 1998, 42.

31   Fredric Jameson, *Postmodernism*, 1991.

32   Fredric J. Schwartz, *The Werkbund: Design Theory and Mass Culture before the First World War* (New Haven, CT: Yale University Press, 1996).

33   See the first chapter of my *Ontology of Construction* (Cambridge: Cambridge University Press, 1994), where I discuss the historical transformation from *technè* to the tectonic and montage. See also the final chapter of *Modernity and Its Other: A Post-Script to Contemporary Architecture* (College Station, TX: Texas A&M University Press, 1997), where my reflection on technology and architecture draws from Theodor Adorno's discourse on the subject as presented in his *Aesthetic Theory* (London: Routledge and Kegan Paul, 1984).

34   The subject was central to the nineteenth-century rationalist approach to architecture, and was sterilized later by those who underestimated the creative and representational dimension of architecture. At a theoretical level, Reyner Banham's *Theory and Design in the First Machine Age* (1960), and his emphasis on Richard Buckminster Fuller, presents ideas that can be associated with Hannes Meyer's "antipathy to composition in architecture," to use Kenneth Frampton's words. Noteworthy also is Walter Gropius's prefabricated Torten Housing of 1926, where the final layout and the design's form were dictated by the technologies of the assembly line. As I will discuss below in the main text, contemporary architecture's infliction by technology has touched the historical vision of authors like Sigfried Giedion and Banham. For a collection of essays looking at this subject see, Peter Galison and

Emily Thompson, eds, *The Architecture of Science* (Cambridge, MA: The MIT Press, 1999). Frampton's quotation above is cited in *The Architecture of Science*, 1999, 354. Also see Alan Colquhoun's review of Banham's *Theory and Design*, in Colquhoun, *Essays in Architectural Criticism: Modern Architecture and Historical Change* (Cambridge, MA: The MIT Press, 1981), 21–5. The original text of Banham was published in *British Journal of Aesthetics* (January 1962): 59–65.

35   Theodor Adorno, "Music and Technique," in *Sound Figures* (Stanford, CA: Stanford University Press, 1999), 202.

36   Alberto Perez-Gomez, *Architecture and the Crisis of the Modern Science* (Cambridge, MA: The MIT Press, 1983).

37   Robert Venturi, *Iconography and Electronics upon a Generic Architecture: A View from the Drafting Room* (Cambridge, MA: The MIT Press, 1996), 11.

38   See Gottfried Semper, *Style in the Technical and Tectonic Arts; or Practical Aesthetics*, trans. H.F. Mallgrave and Michael Robinson (Santa Monica, CA: Tests and Documents, The Getty Research Institute, 2004), 127–8.

39   Gottfried Semper, *Style*, 2004, 65.

40   Quoted in Michael Fried, *Absorption and Theatricality* (Berkeley, CA: University of California Press, 1980), 221.

41   Kurt W. Forster, "Architectural Choreography," in Kurt Forster and Francesco Dal Co, eds, *Frank O. Gehry*, 1998, 24.

42   Michael Sorkin, "Frozen Light," in Mildred Friedman, ed., *Gehry Talks: Architecture + Process* (New York: Rizzoli, 1999), 31.

43   Hubert Damisch, "The Space Between: A Structuralist Approach to the Dictionary," *Architectural Design Profile* 3–4 (1980): 84–9.

44   Kenneth Frampton, *Studies in Tectonic Culture*, 1995, 273.

45   Adolf Loos, "The Principle of Cladding," in *Spoken into the Void* (Cambridge, MA: The MIT Press, 1982), 66–9.

46   I am alluding to the idea of commodity fetishism and the possibility of relating architecture of the spectacle to fetish, "an object endowed with a special force or independent life." See Hall Foster, "The Art of Fetishism: Notes on Dutch Still Life," in Sarah Whiting, Edward Mitchell, and Greg Lynn, eds, *Fetish* in *The Princeton Architectural Journal* 4 (1992).

47   I have discussed Gottfried Semper's theory of *Bekleidung* and Adolf Loos's idea of dressing in *Ontology of Construction*, 1994, 20–25. See also Gevork Hartoonian, *Modernity and Its Other*, 1997, 178.

48   Rosemarie Haag Bletter, "Frank Gehry's Spatial Reconstruction," in Thomas Hines, ed., *The Architecture of Frank Gehry*, 1986, 25–63, and 47.

49   Francesco Dal Co, "The World Turned Upside-Down," 1998, 39–61.

50   Francesco Dal Co, "The World Turned Upside-Down," 1998, 40.

51   Francoise Fromonot, *Jørn Utzon: The Sydney Opera House* (Berkeley, CA: Gingko Press, 1998), 167. According to the author, Utzon's fan-shape glass walls were sought in analogy to the wings of a seagull in flight.

52   On this subject see Gevork Hartoonian, "The Limelight of the House-Machine," *The Journal of Architecture* 6 (spring 2001): 53–79.

53 Gilles Deleuze, *The Fold: Leibniz and the Baroque* (Minneapolis, MN: University of Minnesota Press, 1993), 28. The separation of the façade from the interior in Baroque architecture speaks for the independence of the element of wrapping from the structural. This of course marked a departure from the classical language of architecture where there is a one-to-one correspondence between the façade and the plan, and the organization of the interior space. On this last subject see Gevork Hartoonian, *Ontology of Construction*, 1994, 12.

54 Christopher S. Wood, *The Vienna School Reader* (New York: Zone Books, 2000), 32–3.

55 Reinhold Martin, "The Crystal World," *Harvard Design Magazine* 27 (fall 2007–winter 2008): 1–4.

56 Alejandro Zaera-Polo, "The Politics of the Envelope," *Log* 13/14 (fall 2008): 196.

57 Pier Vittorio Aureli, *The Possibility of an Absolute Architecture* (Cambridge, MA: The MIT Press, 2011), 37. On this subject, and Mies's dialectical understanding of the organic and mechanics, see Detlef Martins "Architecture, Worldview, and World Image in G," in Detlef Martins and Michael W. Jennings, eds, *G: An Avant-Garde Journal of Art, Architecture, Design, and Film, 1923–1926* (Los Angeles, CA: The Getty Research Institute, 2010), 71–99. The author reminds us of the fact that Mies owned a copy of Karl Bötticher's *Die Tektonic der Hellen*, and his work was influenced by Bötticher's distinction between *Kernform* and *Kunstform* (Martins, 2010, 76).

8

Steven Holl: Fabrication Detailed

This book highlights major shifts taking place in the achievements of the architects under consideration. More often than not, this change follows a diversion in theory, either in reference to a larger pool of theoretical paradigms available through interdisciplinary work, or in reference to revisions the architect introduces to his or her own design philosophy. This opening statement for a chapter focusing on Steven Holl's architecture is convincing. And yet, the distinctive mark of his work, both written and built, concerns the culture of building. Typological investigations, for example, underpin both his early research, published under the heading of *Pamphlet Architecture* (1978),[1] and a recent competition entry for the Museum of Human Evolution, Burgos, Spain, 2000 (Figure 8.1). This latter project will be examined later. For now it is important to note the design's superimposition of a theatrical image of the body on a courtyard building type. The implied excess, often explored in the architect's conceptual watercolor work, is another persistent theme of Holl's architecture. This aspect of his career is a reminder of Le Corbusier's daily schedule: attending painting during the early morning and architecture and related business during the rest of the day. The difference between these two architects, however, is significant. If a modernist visuality underpinned Le Corbusier's simultaneous rapport with painting and architecture, what most interests Holl is the phenomenological depth and its various implications for architecture, the understanding of which demands recalling Maurice Merleau-Ponty's reading of the experience of looking at a painting of Cezanne. A phenomenological transformation of form is thus the third constant responsible for the shift(s) taking place in Holl's architecture that this chapter would like to examine. Cutting through these commonalities, this chapter will attempt to single out projects that bring forth the complex task of intertwining phenomenological excess with the tectonic.

After completing his undergraduate degree at Washington University, Holl continued his architectural research in Rome during the 1970s. Like Louis I. Kahn, Holl could not dismiss the typological vigor of Rome's rich classical heritage. Influential for these two American architects was what Le Corbusier had already

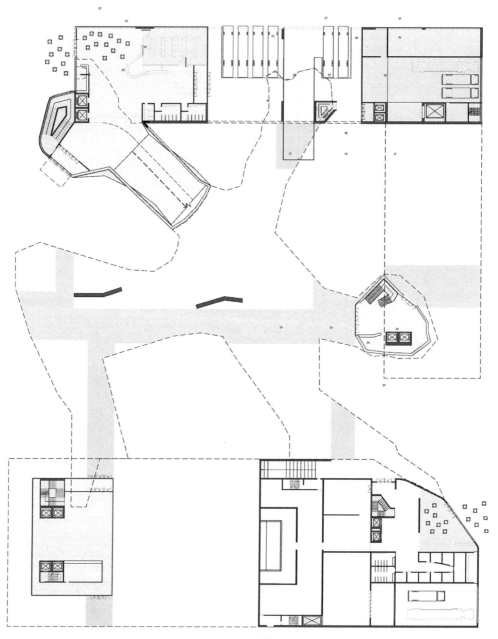

8.1   Steven Holl Architects, Museum of Human Evolution, Burgos, Spain, 2000.
Second floor plan. Drawing courtesy of Steven Holl Architects

recognized almost half a century earlier: drawing from Greek monuments, he had suggested that, "architecture is the masterly, correct and magnificent play of masses brought together in light," and that form is revealed through the interplay of light and shade.[2] Holl writes, "The perceptual spirit and metaphysical strength of architecture are driven by the quality of light and shadow shaped by solids and voids."[3] No wonder then that the work of Kahn and Holl remained focused on the two tropes of typology and light, although each of the architects came to a different conclusion. The difference is perhaps generational, or because Holl studied his graduate degree at the Architectural Association (AA), London, where he came across the work of Rem Koolhaas, Bernard Tschumi, and Zaha Hadid, other protagonists of this volume. In retrospect, the fact that the work of these radical architects of the AA was balanced by Dalibor Vesely's phenomenological approach to architecture suggests that Holl's work has since oscillated between the *common ground*, the centrality of the body for the phenomenology of architecture, and the burden of constant change forced by capitalism, the aesthetic implications of which are the major occupation of this book.

Before attending to Holl's work, it is useful to touch on the architectural discourse in Italy of the late 1960s. Like other European countries, reconstruction and national restitution were topical subjects with ample political and cultural ramifications for Italy. In his capacity as the editor of *Casabella*, Ernesto Roger laid out the cornerstone for typological investigation, underlining the importance of the theme of history for architecture. In an entry essay for a book titled *A New Europe* (1964), he highlighted the active presence of history in European cities. Making swift remarks about the need, for what was coined the second generation of architects, to maintain a balanced rapport with tradition, he then presented examples from the past to establish that, "if there is anything inherent in the European spirit (God keep me from making racial distinctions!) it is a feeling for history, for the simple reason that Europe is the laboratory of history."[4] For him that aspect of history that concerns the built environment had already taken on an architectural form, type—a cumulative collective experience—and it was the task of architects to come to terms with the traditions of the art of building by analyzing buildings based on the notion of type.[5]

Out of this concern for architectural history emerged the *Tendeza* group. Among its prominent members, Aldo Rossi and Vittorio Gregotti gave a radical twist to the role history plays in architecture. Enough has been written about the Italian architecture of the 1970s, and about the influences of Rossi and Gregotti on American architects, especially those critics and historians who gathered in the Urban Studies Center and contributed to its magazine, *Oppositions*. The fact that the most radical architectural work at the time in America was carried out by the New York Five Architects indicates how much hold Holl had over the intellectual ambience of Italy when he returned to America in the late 1970s. This is in consideration of another fact, that the Five's horizon of tradition did not go beyond what Le Corbusier had worked out, nor the formalism inherited from the historical avant-garde. Nevertheless, we have already noted in previous chapters on Tschumi and Koolhaas the generative potentialities of Manhattan as a radical substitute for

8.2   Steven
Holl Architects,
Gymnasium
Bridge, South
Bronx, New York,
1977. Image
courtesy of Steven
Holl Architects

what Roger called the "laboratory of history." In this mutation, according to Holl, the publication of *Pamphlet Architecture* was an attempt to advance an alternative point of view to "a weary Modernism" polemically "tousled by historicism."[6]

TYPE LIBRE

A closer inspection of the issues of *Pamphlet Architecture*, edited by Holl, demonstrates the impact of Manhattan on the architect's typological investigation. As was pointed out in Chapter 4, what Ernest Bloch called the "empty lot," a distinctive byproduct of capitalism's spatial and territorial expansion, was and perhaps still is more tangible in Manhattan than in any European city. There was also the difference between "rural and urban house types," to recall the title of *Pamphlet* number 9, edited by Holl (1983), at the time when the alleged difference was already disappearing. In two other edited issues of the magazine, Holl focused on the edges of the larger New York Island, especially sites left behind as capitalism selectively expanded its domain of production and consumption cycles. Thus in *Pamphlet* 1 (1977) we are presented with the design of a bridge to revitalize an area on the southern edges of the Bronx (Figure 8.2). The rectangular volume of the bridge connects its site to the park on Randall's Island. This two-story steel truss volume, clad in translucent white insulated paneling, is theatrically hinged onto another bridge that houses water-related activities. The animated formal dialogue between the latter's painted concrete mass and the main bridge draws programmatically from what in the Russian constructivist repertory was called "social condenser." The design also speaks for an early example of the architect's interest in intertwining the tectonic of heavy structure with light ones. This tectonic image will indeed recur in the best work Holl has produced to date.

The two themes of "empty lot" and "bridge" are revisited in a project sought to revitalize an otherwise abandoned elevated rail link in the Chelsea area, west of Manhattan, now "High Line" designed by the Diller Scofidio+Renfro firm. In what is called the "Bridge of Houses" (1981), various housing types are placed upon the elevated rail structure. Here the Semperian notion of theatricality is delivered in the design's articulation of the earth-work and the frame-work. Of interest is the radical twist given to the tectonics of structure (the houses and the structure of the rail), and the "ornamental portions of the rail bridge which pass over the streets remain open."[7] Holl's engagement with the edges of Manhattan suggests ways in which urban architecture should trigger and transform one's mental map of a given context. Against the background of semiotic theories permeating the 1960s, the American Kevin Lynch had already highlighted the city's edges and landmarks as two important urban venues for establishing a dialogue between people and the built environment. Lynch wrote, "in the process of way-finding, the strategic link is the environmental image, the generalized mental picture of the exterior physical world that is held by an individual." He continued, "the image is the product of both the immediate sensation and of the memory of past experience, and it is used to interpret information and to guide action."[8]

This turn to morphology is evident from a number of Holl's proposed projects designed for the edges of cities like Manhattan (New York), the Netherlands project (2001–02), Dallas-Fort Worth (Texas), and Phoenix (Arizona). The last two date from 1989–90. In addition to the edge issue, these projects share the following: first, the diagrammatic elements of a tower, be it the vertical bar in the Manhattan project, an intertwined horizontal and vertical bar in the Netherlands and Phoenix projects, or a cube made out of bars in Dallas-Fort Worth, are cut and manipulated to the point where the geometry implied in these three typologies is disbanded. Second, and because of such a radical deconstruction of a given type, the final form conveys an image of theatricality that in most cases resembles the living body of an organic creature. In the case of the Phoenix and Netherlands projects, this takes the shape of an intertwined courtyard type volume, where forms seem to be locked horizontally, and soar up at one end like a snakehead. The suggested theatricality is dramatized by the choice of material and the construction system. The watercolor of the Netherlands project shows three suspended volumes looking out from the top ends of the vertical bar, called the "cactus tower." The glazed frontal surface of the tower is sandwiched between two vertical concrete walls of equal dimension to the horizontal volume. Noteworthy is Holl's transference of watercolor techniques of materiality to what I will discuss later as the technique of "cut," a strategy used to postpone the theatricalization underpinning both digitally produced forms and the aesthetic of the fetishism of commodities that Hal Foster has eloquently discussed in terms of "image building."[9]

We will return to the technique of cut shortly. For now attention should be given to the ways in which Holl takes liberty in recoding historically received types. The architect's heuristic approach draws from a given program, in line with either Kahn's famous phrase, "what the building wants to be," or ideas with phenomenological connotation. Of the first set, mention should be made of the Museum of Human Evolution, Burgos, Spain (Figure 8.1). Here a zoological form whose organs are twisted and stretched to reach different parts of the plan, shores up a fragmented courtyard plan. It is interesting to note that this "creature" volume houses most of the vertical and horizontal circulation of the complex. In addition to a few public spaces, the stretched out volume works like a "servant" space feeding various sides of an otherwise fragmented rectangular mass. As the architect suggests, one reason for animating the form is that it points to "the phenomenon of the body moving through spaces."[10] From a bird's-eye view, the central crisscross figure recalls a series of Pablo Picasso's drawings where human bodies float weightlessly; or Bacon's depicted tortured bodies. Perhaps, what makes the return of the organic in Holl's work singular, and this in consideration of blob architecture, is the architect's conceptualization of the dialectics involved in art and science where the ontological dimensions of architecture are excessively stressed to balance the aesthetic of theatricalization induced by the commodification of culture.

Related to this museum type, and for the above suggested second set of projects, we should turn to the competition project for the Palazzo del Cinema, Venice (1990), where a "thick wall" brings together a horseshoe-shaped plan, the internal void of which is *packed* with seven cinemas of different sizes and plan-forms (Figure 8.3). This project is a "decisive shift in Holl's preferred morphological strategies," writes Kenneth Frampton.[11] It breaks away from the earlier geometrically informed types for open-ended morphologies. The two wings of the design seem to hold together the volumes of cinemas otherwise floating in the palazzo's void. Yet, each stone-looking volume of these seven cinemas is cut to sustain its theatrical composition

8.3   Steven Holl Architects, Palazzo del Cinema, Venice, Italy, 1990. Image courtesy of Steven Holl Architects

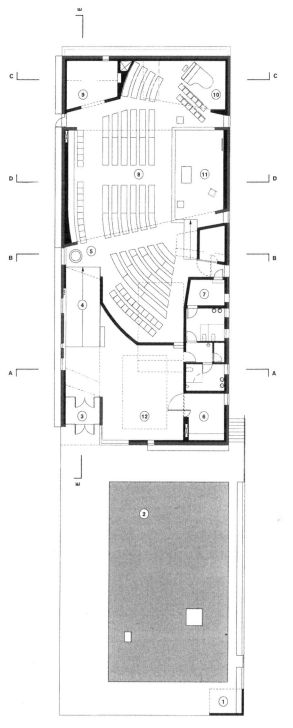

8.4   Steven Holl Architects, Chapel of St. Ignatius, Seattle, Washington,
1994–97. Plan drawing. Image courtesy of Steven Holl Architects

allowing the interplay of shadow and light "as programs to be achieved parallel to solving functional aspects."[12] The project's uniqueness relates to the ways in which it brings together the phenomenological experience of architecture with the filmic, an art for which deliverance of emotional power is indispensible. What informs architectural experience is "the passage of time; light, shadow and transparency; colour phenomena, texture, material and detail."[13] The section of the Palazzo del Cinema, where each movie theater is conceived as a filmic frame, strongly supports the suggested association between architecture and film.

The idea of a void compacted with other volumes, like objects filling a carpenter's toolbox, recalls the architect's watercolor prepared for the Chapel of St. Ignatius, Seattle, wherein seven volumes are jammed into a stone caret. From this conceptual model evolved a tight rectangular plan (Figure 8.4). Morphologically, the Chapel's plan is divided into cells with no analogical references to nature of the kind visible in the best of Alvar Aalto's planimetric organization. Window cuts in the lateral walls of the plan of the Chapel keep apart the gathering and the altar, and the spaces between them. These cuts, which in part become the regulating lines articulating the interior surfaces, project a sense of closure distinct from the exterior volume of the building. One is reminded of the same distinction evident in Utzon's civic projects such as the Bagasvaerd Church (1976), and the Sydney Opera House, to mention two prominent cases where both the external form and its cladding differ from the interior. In Holl's hands, however, these interior surface cuts are used to dramatize the interplay of light and shadow, creating an ambience similar to that achieved by the Russian filmmaker Andrei Tarkovsky, mentioned by the architect in his previously cited essay. The analogy between film and architecture should be supplemented with a discussion that concerns the essentiality of the concept of cut in clothing.

Throughout this volume Semper's theory of dressing is recalled on several occasions. Fundamental to his theory of architecture is the importance of textile for a number of reasons including the phenomenon of polychromy in Greek architecture, and the essentiality of enclosure and detailing for the art of building. Obviously the theme of enclosure emulated both the custom of covering the body and the craft of joining things together, the latter evident in the knot as the ontological origin of detailing in architecture. According to Semper, "we find the first efforts to embellish functional objects through conscious choice of form and decoration." He maintains that the cut and pleats sought for covering should highlight the properties of what is covered.[14] Therefore, both in clothing and the covering of architectural space, the surface does not operate as a neutral skin, but is conceived according to the purpose and convenience expected from what is covered. In clothing, the cut principally follows the figure of the body, both in reference to practical considerations, and its final look. This is one reason why the fashion industry promotes different *cuts* each season. Furthermore, surface cuts in clothing have an aesthetic dimension; otherwise there would be no idea of fashion as such. Throughout history, architects have attended the element of surface, introducing cuts with both aesthetic and theoretical purposes.[15] The columns inscribed in the façade of the Palazzo Rucellai (1446–51) are a good example.

They stand for Leon Battista Alberti's theorization of column as ornament *par excellence*. Even in the whitewashed surfaces of modern architecture,[16] fenestrations were used for theoretical and occasionally phenomenological experiences of a particular building. Of the first, mention should be made of Le Corbusier's use of cut to theorize the "horizontal window." In Ronchamp (1953– 55), instead, fenestrations of various sizes were used to convey "a vessel of intense concentration and mediation."[17]

Now, in addition to the seven inscribed cuts of the entry door, the interior dressing of St. Ignatius is adorned with cuts that frame and reveal the positions of fenestrations (Figure 8.5). Other apron-like vertical and horizontal surfaces are cut to diffuse both daylight and the artificial lights installed behind them. The intention was, the architect explains, to achieve a "twofold merging of concept and phenomena."[18] The excess, theatricality, experienced in this project is not meant to produce visual theatricalization. It is, rather, controlled and modified by a system of making, cut and raised concrete panels (Figure 8.6). The strategy can be traced in early projects where the interior cladding is embellished using the cubist technique and where the line reveals the edges of both cut and pasted surfaces. In the refurbishment of an apartment in Manhattan (1983), the studio and the bedroom are designed in planar mode. In what should be considered homage to the De Stijl interest in planar compositions, the vertical panels of the same apartment are cut to create both L-shaped doors and pivoting

8.5   Steven Holl Architects, Chapel of St. Ignatius, Seattle, Washington, 1994–97. Interior view. Photograph by author

8.6   Steven Holl Architects, Chapel of St. Ignatius, Seattle, Washington, 1994–97. Exterior view. Photograph copyright Paul Warchol

8.7 Steven Holl and Vico Acconci, Storefront for Art and Architecture, Manhattan, New York City, 1993. Photograph by author

wall segments. The operation aims to make a distinction between the vertical dressing and the collared surface of the ceiling perhaps suggesting blue sky. According to Frampton, "these neo-Suprematist elements activate the existing structural frame by causing it to dilate within the blue depth of metaphorical sky."[19] The same applies to another alteration, an apartment on the upper floors of the tower of the Museum of Modern Art (1986). Following a "hybrid illumination of X, Y, Z directions,"[20] lines and colorful surfaces are employed to make the entire interior space look like a planar fabrication. This *tekton*-oriented operation of Holl comes full circle in the Storefront for Art and Architecture, New York City (1992–93) (Figure 8.7).

Greek in origin, *tekton* denotes the work of an artisan skilled in the materiality of wood, used in boat making, carpentry, and joinery. From the assemblage of objects to that of building parts, the correct handling of material and artisanal roles, the final product is not devoid of aesthetic considerations. As soon as "an aesthetic perspective—and not a goal of utility—is defined that specifies the work and production of tekton, then the analysis consigns the term 'tectonic' to an aesthetic judgment."[21] The passage is relevant to the concept of excess and the aesthetic of theatricality highlighted throughout this volume, and the design of the Storefront, a small triangular exhibition space located in lower Manhattan. Designed in collaboration with the artist Vito Acconci, the final result draws from both art and architecture. Thus, the street façade is as much a work of joinery as a work of art, especially when the store is closed. Drawing from the original use of the main wall of the space, the surface of the street façade is furnished with graffiti: lines cut in various geometric forms, which are then turned into hinged panels of various sizes. Not only is the element of wall deconstructed into various operable panels (itself a work of art), but gone is the strict separation between the inside and the outside of the gallery space. Holl returns to a *tekton* mode of operation not only in the aforementioned Seattle Chapel, but also in a recent house, the "Planar House" (2002–05), designed for a couple with a large contemporary art collection.

These last two projects and the 1983 apartment in Manhattan discussed earlier demonstrate Holl's interest in geometry and mathematics, exploring their architectonic manifestation in the three elements of line, plane, and volume. Comprising a number of projects, and still focused on typology, his first theoretical book, *Anchoring* (1989), speaks of the architect's turn to the phenomenological interpretation of architecture. To depart from a Cartesian perspective, Holl saw his task as intertwining concept and form with material, detailing, and light. Whereas his typological phase was merely focused on rethinking the historically derived types, the competition entry project for Porta Vittoria Milan, Italy (1986) shows one important architectonic consequence of his turn to phenomenology. Among four diagram drawings, the two that are crossed out show the plan and perspectival view of a building type with eight parallel rectangular wings placed symmetrically along the central axis of a circle. The second pair of drawings shows a plan composed of a number of rectangles, a square, and a circle, the organization of which is dynamic, multi-directional, and non-symmetrical. From this emerged a semi-rectangular volumetric organization, a generic diagram that recurs in the architect's various projects designed since then. Holl writes: "the conviction behind this project is that an open work—an open future—is a source of human freedom." And he explained his theoretical intention for the XVII Triennale, Milan, thus: "To investigate the uncertain, to bring out unexpected properties to define the psychological space, to allow the modern soul to emerge, to propose built configurations in the face of (and fully accepting) major social and programmatic uncertainty."[22] No wonder then that the final rendering of the project is a surrealist *tour de force*. The most compelling element comprises a crooked café/lounge and a wiry truss connecting a footbridge to a suspended chapel! The design is indeed an urban manifesto, perhaps in recollection of the work of Russian constructivists. It also speaks for the uncertainty delivered by the conservative politics of the Reagan era, and the postmodern tendency for the simulation of historical forms. This latter development might be one reason why the architect inclined towards intertwining architecture with the existential condition of the 1980s.

Holl's further exploration of what can be called typological liberation is further evident in the competition entry for an addition to the Amerika Gedenk Bibliothek, Berlin (1988) (Figure 8.8). Unless seen from a bird's-eye view, the implied square type plan of the last floor is held together loosely by fragments of rectangular and square geometries similar to the diagram drawing prepared for the Milan project. These extractions line up the complex with its urban context and the rectangular mass of the existing building. The strategy of lifting up the two wings

8.8   Steven Holl Architects, Amerika Gedenk Bibliothek, Berlin, 1988. Photograph courtesy of Steven Holl Architects

of an otherwise hollow cube, made of bar-shaped elements, offsets the expected visual and formal effects of "addition": the existing building seems to penetrate the proposed addition. The picture is complete considering the children's library, a translucent bridge that, again, similarly to what we saw in the Milan project, is suspended over the existing building. The image recalls Adolf Loos's consideration of the cross as the first ornament with erotic origin.[23] The design is also a plausible precedent to the OMA's tower discussed in Chapter 5. Most importantly, it says something about Holl's inclination for the tectonic of heaviness and lightness conceptualized in the weight of the "old" building, and children's preoccupation with *play*. The metaphor of youth achieves its tectonic figuration in the lattice truss structure of the children's library, which is clad in sandblasted glass with vision panels. The same material is used in other parts of the complex, although in different colors and for tactile and functional reasons. One is reminded, for example, of the top of what can be called a vertical circulation tower, which, according to the architect, "offers a public observation point—a lens focused on the city—and supports the children's library."[24] The tower rises up from a two-story horizontal wing evenly dimensioned, the overall composition of which anticipates the theatricality noted earlier in the architect's projects for the edge city. The Berlin project is a canonical work in Holl's *curriculum vitae*. According to Frampton, the project "brilliantly synthesized two themes that would continue to play a key role in his subsequent architecture; first an open-ended contrapuntal urban form that he had envisioned in his 1986 proposal for Porta Vittoria, Milan, and second, an equal contrapuntal attitude that he adopted for the internal *promenade architecturale* of the same project."[25] No wonder then, that the architect revisits the planimetric organization of the same work for the design of the Makuhari Housing project in Chiba, Japan. The theatricality evident in this project's volumetric composition and its planimetric organization will be taken occasionally to its extreme state of animation in most of what the architect has produced since then.

Consider the plan of the School of Art and Art History Building located on the campus of the University of Iowa, Iowa (1999–2006).[26] The design draws from two morphologies, the grid of the Iowa City and the organic formation of the adjacent limestone cliff. Even though the recent flood has detracted from the natural aging process of this building, one cannot but agree with Frampton that it is

8.9   Steven Holl Architects, School of Art and Art History Building, University of Iowa, Iowa, 1999–2006. Photograph copyright Tom Jorgensen

> ... *a topographic work opening out onto the pond, together with a stand of trees, and turning its orthogonal "back," containing classrooms and offices, to an access road coming off the suburban pattern and eventually linking across the river and into the city. There is something about this form, its finish and its placement on the site that suggests that it has always been there.*[27]

Mention should also be made of the deforming of an otherwise semi L-shaped plan in a composition that evokes the image of a creature: a curved head with an arm extended towards the lagoon and with a short leg (tail?) expanded outward from a two story rectangular spine that houses offices. These rooms are clad in translucent glass planks with clear operating windows considered for each room. The final configuration of what for the architect connotes "a hybrid instrument of open-edge and open center" is conceived in homage to Pablo Picasso's sculpture, a broken guitar (Figure 8.9). Entering from the curved head and perpendicular to the arm over the lagoon, a Piranesian steel stairway floats in the entry forum's void resonating with the theatricality of the building's planimetric organization (Figure 8.10). The suspended and playful figure of the stair resonates with the fire-exit stair dropped down from the belly of the bridge although it is twisted to land on the adjacent lawn. The section drawing through the interdisciplinary volume of the complex is suggestive of Holl's phenomenological interpretation of *promenade architecturale*. It also articulates a fine note on the fragility of the tectonic dialogue between support and gravity forces. This tectonic experience is expressed in the contrast between the bridge wing's concrete slab and support, and the volume's steel and glass cladding (Figure 8.11).

One cannot but suggest here that the entire design hinges on what might be called "suspending the weight." This is evident both from the aforementioned library arm that hovers over the pond, and the Piranesian stair, which is partially suspended from the ceiling and from the floor slabs placed at different levels. The

8.10 Steven Holl Architects, School of Art and Art History Building, University of Iowa, Iowa, 1999–2006. Interior stair. Photograph courtesy of Eric Dean

8.11 Steven Holl Architects, School of Art and Art History Building, University of Iowa, Iowa, 1999–2006. Exterior view. Photograph courtesy of Eric Dean

extended arm is tacked to the main body of the building at an angle exposing the interior space to the adjacent cliff. The untamed quality of the cliff next to the corten steel and glass cladding of the building evokes a sense of ruination, adding a new dimension to the suggested idea of suspending the weight. The concept can be traced in most of the detailing, cutting, and binding of the various materials that similar to most of Holl's architecture, insinuate the porosity of the volume, reminding one of the materiality of the surrounding environment including the building itself. Nowhere better than at the interior end of the library does Holl show his mastery of detailing, not only in putting together various materials, but in evoking a sense of interiority that is understood in dialogue with light, sky, and landscape. With its exposed crisscross structural elements, this space is also remarkable in its evocation of the tectonics of suspension. Finally, the ambience recalls Holl's design for the entry head of what is called the Cranbrook Institute of Science (1993–98) where a few formal achievements of the De Stijl are recoded, although with exceptional emphasis on materiality and detailing.

TECTONIC CUTS

We have already noted in this chapter and on various occasions throughout this volume the tectonic significance of the concept of cut. From Semper's discussion of clothing to my remarks on the technique of montage, and the discussion of stereotomy presented in previous chapters, these observations indicate the usefulness of *cut* for a critical practice. In what follows and in the context of Holl's architecture, the concept of cut is taken up once more to highlight the aesthetic dimension involved in tectonics. In clothing, for example, the cut has both aesthetic and technical connotations. It involves the transformation of fabric into a shape, more often than not, with anonymous references to the contours of the body, and its embellishment through pleats and lines lending a particular appeal, sometimes seductive. Speaking aesthetically, architecture, unlike fashion since its inception, should not be seductive. Alberto Perez-Gomez might be right in saying that, "it is only through seduction that we can enact compassion."[28] However, when architecture is drawn into the aesthetic world of commodity fetishism, how could one today see "seduction" as exclusive to a phenomenological interpretation of experience?

I will attempt to respond to this question later. For now, what should be underlined is the significance of cut as a strategy for postponing the theatricalization detectable in a number of Holl's works. This is important because since the architect's turn to phenomenology, his design is exposed to a particular realm of excess. This is a plausible charge if we step out of the timelessness implied in the phenomenological perception of the world. This said, one should salute Holl's endeavor in intertwining material, light, and space. Nevertheless, does every architect's interest in materiality, light, shadow, and space necessarily end in tectonics? And, is it enough to aspire to a romanticist notion of poetics, centered on individual creativity, as indicated in the aforementioned essay of Perez-Gomez, when the magnitude of the crisis architecture is facing today surpasses that of the nineteenth-century's historical departure from classical wisdom? Still, one should cautiously agree with Juhani Pallasmaa's suggestion that "the authenticity of architectural experience is grounded in the tectonic language of building and the comprehensibility of the act of construction to the senses."[29] However, the operative domain of aesthetics in late capitalism is so pervasive that one's experience is already informed by the overwhelming power of "image making," to recall Foster again. And this in consideration of Semper's theory of the tectonic where the rapport between the core-form and the frame-work is not transparent but anonymous. It is the anonymity informing the tectonic cuts in Holl's architecture that most interests this author.

In discussing Frank Gehry's work we noted the architect's fascination with the unfinished state of buildings under construction. One can expand his observation to include the aesthetic appeal of scaffolds most of which are erected for practical purposes, providing a measure for the contours of the as yet unfinished building. There is a fascination with this kind of temporary structure even today. Perhaps these scaffolds remind us of Sigfried Giedion's suggestion that construction was the unconscious of the nineteenth century, or else, one should take it for the theatricality evident in the Russian constructivist projects discussed in Chapter 1. There is another dimension to scaffolding: its temporary life is in sharp contrast to the everlasting character of architecture. Together with, and in recollection of Semper's interest in festive structures, scaffolding helps us to understand the tectonic of heaviness and lightness and this in comparing a masonry construction system with steel and glass architecture.

This much is clear from the Berkowitz House, Martha's Vineyard, Massachusetts (1984) (Figure 8.12), where the overall form is an abstract derivative of the Camel Shut Gun house type popular in Florida. In its original type, the house comprised a long continuous corridor with doors opening into rooms lined up along the corridor. In Holl's hands, the Camel Shut Gun type is modified in many ways, for example, by the placement of the entrance next to a double height volume, and also by the fact that, in the Berkowitz House, the one-story elongated volume of the entrance side becomes a two-story volume at the opposite end. Located on the top of a deep terrain, the vertical cubic volume anchors the building into the ground, orienting the building towards the visitor in one direction and the Atlantic Ocean in the other. Drawing from Melville's *Moby Dick*, the 2 × 4 wooden balloon structure of the house recalls a whale's skeleton used by the original settlers of the site. The lightness of the exposed wooden structure of the veranda is experienced through the shadows it casts on the adjacent wooden volume. For Frampton, "this awareness accounts for the tattered framework that crosses the verticals of the exposed balloon frame, a decorative, playful brise-soleil that already evokes its eventual ruin."[30] One might go further and suggest that the inside-out balloon frame of the house is a tectonic reversal of Semper's idea that the architect should think of the enclosure first, and the support system later. The interlocking of light, material, and detailing pursued by Holl in this project speaks for that stage of his work when typological logic yields to the tectonics of the earth-work and the

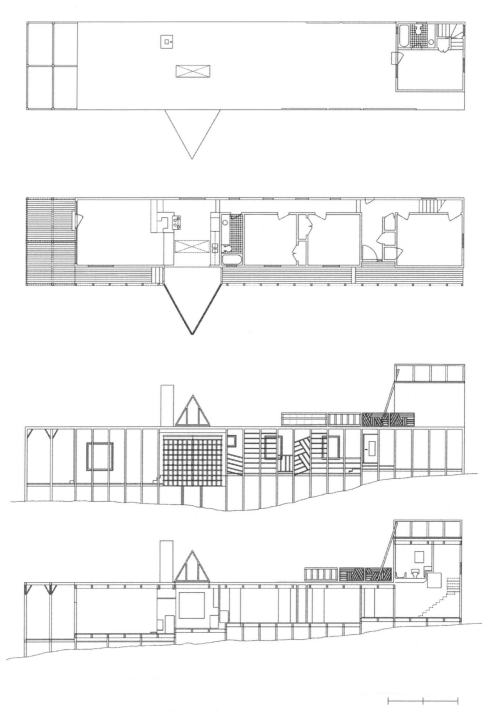

8.12   Steven Holl Architects, House at Martha's Vineyard, Massachusetts,
1984–88. Drawing courtesy of Steven Holl Architects

frame-work. It is this aspect of Holl's work that makes his typological investigation different from the neo-rationalism of Aldo Rossi.

If the extraverted skeleton of the Berkowitz House anchors the house in the site, in the Stretto House, Dallas, Texas (1989–91), it is the nearby dam and river that inform the theatrical tectonics of the four concrete-block masses adorned with playful roofs (Figure 8.13). And yet, the dialogue established between these two main architectonic elements of the house can be associated with the two main aspects of any tectonic figuration that is the earth-work and the frame-work. The four heavy-looking volumes are extended terraces reaching high to hold the steel tube lightweight "bones" of the roofing. What the architect metaphorically calls "stone and feather" is a successful essay in recollection of the nineteenth-century tectonic dialogue concerning a masonry construction system that is prepared to receive iron structural elements discussed in Chapter 2. Still, the playful arrangement of the house's heavy volumes recalls Mies van der Rohe's Brick Country House (1923), a derivative of Theodor van Doesburg's painting, *The Russian Dance*, composed of parallel and animated lines. Holl's design here is also in homage to Wright's notion of breaking the box and the tectonics he established between the walls of the Robie House and its flying roof. For Holl, however, the initial concept of his design was motivated by Béla Bartók's quartet, *Music for Strings, Percussion and Celeste*. Thus we have the analogy of the percussion for the heaviness of the four volumes and

8.13   Steven Holl Architects, Stretto House, Dallas, Texas, 1989–91. Exterior view. Photograph copyright Paul Warchol

the strings for the lightness of the element of the roof. Convincing though this analogy might be, the empty fourth volume and its adjacent terrace raise questions concerning the transparent rapport the architect establishes between the four segments of the music and the four volumes. Nevertheless, if the shadows projected by the exposed structure of the Berkowitz House anticipate ruination, as noted by Frampton, it is the spatial void and the emptiness of the fourth volume and its position next to the pool of the house that recall a classical sense of ruin. Putting this house next to the Berkowitz House, it is convincing to suggest that Holl's tectonic figuration presents the skeleton and *void* as the subconscious of architecture.

Still, and in reference to Semper's observation that dance and music are cosmic arts, Holl's design is a pleasant note in the tectonic articulation of structure and ornament. As with dance, where figurative excess is not an addition to the body, the Stretto House is successful in intertwining materiality with space, anchoring the building to the ground. The playful and elegant morphology of the plan defies the expected conventions of house-type; each of the four volumes houses various aspects of what can be considered service areas, the spaces between which are given over to various activities during both day and night (Figure 8.14). In contrast to the masonry block volumes, these latter spaces are enclosed by glass and metal partitions. Of further morphological importance is the circulation. In analogy with both a Paul Klee painting and music notation, where parallel and horizontal lines structure the

8.14   Steven Holl Architects, Stretto House, Dallas, Texas, 1989–91. Drawing courtesy of Steven Holl Architects

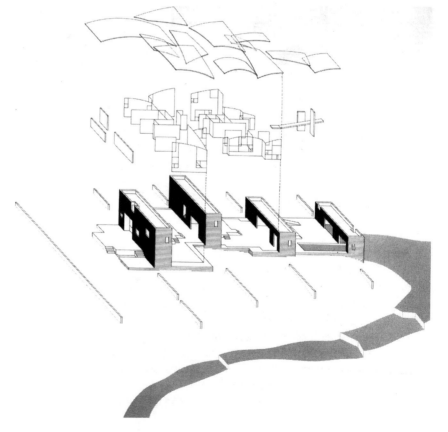

visible disorder of the written notes, the four heavy volumes of the Stretto House are brought together by the horizontality of the interior circulation, moving from the space framed by two masonry volumes into another space. Whereas architects usually can and should get inspired by ideas extraneous to the art of building, what stands out in the house under examination here is the final image: approaching the entry porch of the house, one cannot help but recall Wright's residential work where a *porte-cochère* preludes the move from the outside to the inside.

Of the design strategies used to deconstruct given types, mention should be made of the notion of light and lightness for Holl's tectonic thinking. The theatricality of the Chapel of St. Ignatius, for example, has as much to do with the architect's deconstruction of the conventional rapport between the element of roofing and the enclosure, as it is part of the transference of the motive of seven burning candles into the architectonics of light-catchers. Thus, the roof is conceived as a tectonic element in its own right where the structural and the ornamental are intertwined for the simultaneous covering and revealing of the interior space. Of these latter effects, the phenomenological rapport between earth and sky leads one to recall the idea of cut as discussed earlier. This is clear from the Chapel of St. Ignatius where the cut achieves tectonic dimension in interlocking concrete panels around the windows, which are intertwined with the extension of three vaulted roofs each designating transitions taking place in the plan. The idea of cut here is also meshed with the surface cladding where hooks, used to lift the panels into an upright position, are capped with bronze (Figure 8.6). The detailing used here recalls Otto Wagner's Post Office Savings Bank, Vienna.[31] Whereas Wagner's design was polemically addressing the designs of the secessionist artists, the cuts of the St. Ignatius Chapel are sought against the current tendency for the theatricalization of surface. In doing so, the façade is divested of its classical connotation of the "face." And yet, unlike most contemporary architecture where the façade is metamorphosed into animated surfaces, the cuts in the Chapel of St. Ignatius emulate the building's section. The project seems to have developed out of an orthogonal projection of its section, rather than the plan, as is the case with the architecture of humanism conceived in reference to the body, face, and frontality.

Obviously Holl is not interested in the humanist discourse on the subject of the body and architecture,[32] but in a phenomenological discourse that has been central to the development of his work. If light and the perceptual horizon of space and its haptic dimension were formative themes for the realization of his early work, in Holl's most recent projects the body is introduced as the uncanny living phenomenon, with architectonic implications more complex than the organic permeating digital architecture. In contrast to the latter, in Holl's work, the profusion of excess fundamental for animating form is curtailed abruptly. Central to his strategy is the concept of cut, which was implemented in the architect's early interior alterations, and in the Chapel. In the following projects, the strategy of cut is taken to suggest the incompleteness of form, and/or to allude to the act of castration.

One is reminded of the Helsinki Museum of Contemporary Art (1998) (Figure 8.15), where the dialogical relationship between the concept of cut and the organic seems essential for the final editing of the building's geometry. Here too, the final

8.15   Steven
Holl Architects,
Museum of
Contemporary Art,
Helsinki, Finland,
1992–98. General
view. Photograph
copyright Paul
Warchol

design accommodates the major form-giving elements of the site: the cityscape with its historic monuments in the west, and the infrastructure of Eliel Saarinen's Helsinki Station, in the east. If the building's response to the site is a reminder of Frank Gehry's Bilbao project discussed previously, the association goes no further. Using the topography of site, the project seems to have evolved out of knotting two rectangular volumes at a point where a cut is introduced to allow spatial continuity between the two sides of the building. A second cut is introduced to sustain separate identities for the same two volumes where each accommodates a different function. These two cuts establish a circulatory void the presence of which is felt as one ascends the ramp located next to the main entrance. With their transparent glass walls, the upper floor galleries link the exterior to the exhibition space. Back to the ground floor one cannot dismiss the notion of Kiasma in the way the rectangular mass of the museum is intertwined with its curved shape. The vertical circulation of the building is architectural promenade *par excellence*. The observer's movement through the space is indeed filmic.

Furthermore, one might speculate concerning the three intertwined factors informing the geometry of the building, where a larger curvilinear volume shelters and protects a smaller one. We are reminded of the need to cover the two circulatory voids; the urge to orient the building towards the aforementioned existing historical edifice; and the decision to integrate the site's topography into the building's tectonics. This last requirement is evident from the curved roof of the larger volume the cuts of which work towards two tectonic configurations. On the one hand, the cut eludes the existing topographic drop, allowing the office rooms to have operable windows. Also this flat vertical surface may be conceived as being in dialogue with the main façade of the Post Office building located across the street. Together they create an urban space. On the other hand, the same cut defies the line demarcating the roof from the wall. To further emphasize this last tectonic articulation the curving volume is at one point cut sharply, the traces of which are expressed in the vertical surface articulation of the morphing volume.

Here again one is reminded of the importance of sectional study in Holl's work, which in most cases is coordinated with the tectonics. One consequence of this can be followed in the planimetric organization of the Helsinki Museum. Not only are permanent artworks located in the relatively small rooms of the smaller volume, but temporary artworks, and public lecture rooms are placed in the larger volume. This morphological set-up speaks for the phenomenological association the architect makes between *room* and the notion of permanence, and between temporality and *open-plan*. These latter spaces are mostly *poché* and conceived in response to the curving roof. According to Frampton who has written extensively on Holl's architecture, in the Helsinki Museum "sectional amputation also curtails the form at its greatest width, at the northern end facing out over the water. Here the cropped section assumes the form of a relief-façade lined in copper."[33] Similar to the idea of cut in cinematography is the final form of the museum, which "appears" incomplete although the project fully accommodates the programmatic requirements.

The uncanny animation entertained in Holl's work suggests the anonymity of the tectonic. What this means is that the form seems to be cut from something whose presence is not perceivable, and that the form is incapable of fully releasing (realizing) its own internal energies. Of the first operative dimension of cut, in addition to the Helsinki Museum, mention should be made of the Swiss Residence (2006). Located in a rectangular lot, Washington, DC, the residential quarters of the complex seems to be merely the remains of the extracted volumes. Not only is the final geometry of the main residence conceived in reference to the "red-cross," but the latter's iconic presence is delivered by changing the materiality of cladding. In contrast to the painted exterior surfaces, the L-shaped cut-outs are clad in sandblasted glass. The second operative aspect of the cut can be pursued in the work's resistance to fully engaging with the prevailing aesthetics of theatricalization. Whereas in most contemporary architecture the surface plays a critical role in wrapping the space and presenting the final form as part of the visual culture of spectacle, in Holl's architecture the cut subscribes to a concept of surface that cannot be fully appreciated in terms of either cladding or wrapping. More often than not, the surface configuration reveals the trace of the very act of cutting where every element is detailed and embellished to excess.

The excessive attention Holl gives to detailing and surface articulation tallies with the designs and products of the arts and crafts movement. Whereas the latter was an attempt at the dawn of modernization to keep alive the craft-based traditions of the art of building, the aesthetic challenge Holl has taken on is to navigate through and to resist the prevailing visual culture of late capitalism. Not only is this evident in the theatricality of most projects thus far discussed, but in particular the articulation of the northern end of the Helsinki Museum reveals a new tendency in Holl's work. It presents the linear and planar elements informing the surface articulation of his early interior alterations, and in the context of the current turn to surface. The northern façade combines horizontal and vertical lines with surfaces that directly or indirectly correspond to the interior organization of the project, embracing the contours of the curving volume. From this tectonic detailing one can move to the entry lobby of the addition to the Cranbrook Institute of Science, called the "Light Laboratory." In the tradition of De Stijl, the cubic volume of the south facing entry is cut in front and at the corner to highlight the entrance of the complex. According to the architect, "different phenomenon of light such as refraction and prismatic colour are displayed on the lobby walls as the sunlight changes."[34] The articulation is a three-dimensional artwork in its own right although it has elements which recall Carlo Scarpa's fascination with the embellishment of a detail to the point that the *object* looks like a fabrication. One might speculate that singular to Holl's work is the constant mutation from artificiality to artifact. This is evident from the Y House in the Catskill Mountains, where the split body of the house (domesticity!) opens itself into the landscape through apertures that resemble a late Mondrian painting. Contrary to the painterly analogue, each painted metal and glass area of the fenestration is sought in reference to the position of the body in the interior space. The artificially constructed domestic enclave, however, is in sharp contrast with the implied split view of the world outside. The difference is experienced through what was noted earlier: the design's subconscious juxtaposition of frame and void, here the balconies and their metal vertical support posts.

There is another dimension to Holl's phenomenological approach that also concerns the dialogue between artifice and artifact. In most of his tectonic cuts, the plan's classical stronghold is questioned so the *cut* can emulate the building's sectional organization. One is reminded of the Bellevue Art Museum, Seattle, Washington (1997–2001), a didactic example where the section dictates the overall composition of the volume (Figure 8.16). Starting from the metaphor of the "three-fingers" of the top floor level, the geometry of the lower floors follows the building's sectional contour. Thus six cuts of various shapes and sizes transform the rectangular plan of the top floor into three single volumes connected to each other at opposing ends. Whereas two volumes house the museum's galleries, and are exposed to south-light and north-light respectively, the major cut of the third floor is experienced in a void placed within the rectangular form of the two lower levels. The void becomes the phenomenological fulcrum for the architect's interest in intertwining daylight with nightlight. The remaining cuts of the third floor can be associated with the main sectional organization of the building as one moves around the building. In a conscious attempt to avoid what Pallasmaa calls the "bias towards vision,"[35] Holl continues to work with strategies that engage the senses. The architect's early design for the Bellevue Museum explores concepts such as the "right hand motor role," and different perceptions of time carried out through physical models and conceptual watercolors. Thus we arrive at the incised cubic finish of the building. The four orthogonal façades are clad in dark red "special 'shot concrete' construction,"[36] while the exposed angular cuts are clad in light collared modular tiles. Consequential to these design strategies is the "dialectic between regular outline and internal complexity."[37] That the organizing ideas here remain so visible in the final form highlights Holl's rejection of the domination of the visual

in contemporary architecture and the all-encompassing role digitalization plays in the production of the architecture of spectacle.

Holl revisits the aforementioned metaphor of "stone and feather" in the Nelson-Atkins Museum Expansion project (1999–2007). The generic concept of this project draws from both the Bellevue Art Museum and the Seattle Chapel. Similarly to these two designs, the extension to the Nelson-Atkins Museum proceeds from a section drawing where an enclosed container provides the seat to be topped with luminous theatrical volumes. One is reminded of Mies's National Gallery in Berlin where the building's tectonic dialogue between the earth-work and the frame-work is revisited for steel and glass architecture. From what has been said thus far we can suggest that in most cases Holl's projects attempt to recode the Semperian tectonics phenomenology, and in the light of the prevailing visual spectacle. Thus, an irregular elongated concrete volume, half buried underground, is used for terraces upon which six independent luminous volumes (lenses) with different cuts are placed (Figure 8.17). The remaining terraces are covered with grass and pathways to further infuse the new extension with the forecourt sculptural garden of the existing neoclassical building built in 1933. The addition is, thus, as much a museum building as it is a work of landscape and art conceived in dialogue with the sculptures crowning the large landscape of the museum. Positioned on the east side of the ground of the Nelson-Atkins Museum, Holl's extension has an eye to the morphology of Kansas city, the major commercial district of which is located to the west of the existing museum and along what is called the Plaza, a commercial strip with buildings tattooed in fresco. Seemingly Holl used the best of his architectural vocabulary to posit a *fabricated* alternative to the spectacle permeating the nightlife of the city's commercial strip.

8.16   Steven Holl Architects, Bellevue Art Museum, Seattle, Washington, 1997–2001. View from southwest. Photograph copyright Paul Warchol

8.17   Steven Holl Architects, Nelson-Atkins Museum of Art Bloch Building, Kansas City, Missouri, 1999–2007. General view. Photograph by author

Elsewhere I have promoted the idea of architecture as a stage-set in front of which the events of everyday life can take place.[38] This observation, which was taken from Walter Benjamin's suggestion that, contrary to other artwork, architecture is historically appropriated in a distracted mode,[39] is echoed in Jeffery Kipnis's eloquent reflection on Holl's extension. He writes: "A principle part of the job of any contemporary architecture for a museum is to set the stage for that fragile encounter. It must be able to guide and direct attention without imposing its will too insistently, be generous but have an opinion—a museum is, after all, only human—while encouraging other opinions."[40] Among these other "opinions" Holl's design communicates in two interrelated languages. Firstly, it is the building's austere and elegant aesthetic of neutrality in comparison to the classical language of the original building. Secondly, the addition is experienced and empathically understood through the ways in which it relates to the existing building, the sculptural garden, and the landscape of the site. This last dialogue is better understood when the complex is approached from Rockhill Road in the east

8.18   Steven Holl Architects, Nelson-Atkins Museum of Art Bloch Building, Kansas City, Missouri, 1999–2007. Photograph by author

(Figure 8.18). Approaching from the north, instead, one cannot miss Holl's contribution to deconstructing the classical notion of "entrance." A reflective pool preludes the existing museum's separation from the Bloch Building (the single standing volume of the addition), marking a choice of either entering the old building, or the new addition. Approaching the addition by car, on the other hand, is no less exciting. It is to the architect's credit that he turns the dark underground image of the car park into a space of structural clarity wherein artificial lighting intermingles with the luminous water reflection pouring down from small, round skylights placed under the pool (Figure 8.19).

Speaking generically, the five lenses of the extension draw from the existing building, an elongated rectangular volume with three projections. Whereas the old building's projections are intended to mark its main entrance and the two ending poles, the new lenses depart from the classical language of architecture. The five lenses dominating Holl's design are indeed five machines for observation. What do we observe through them? Consider the entry volume where, upon entering, one is moved by the interplay of the different modalities of light and the location of ramps and stairs. This entry volume can be called the "circulatory lens," which, interestingly, draws from the generic type of the architect's design for the Kiasma. Here too, a staircase on the right, and an elegant space in front waiting to be discovered marks an elongated space. Similarly to other lenses, this one opens into a visual field through which one comes to the understanding of architecture's relation to the displayed art, landscape, sculpture, and the existing building. The sum total of these relationships operates like a stage-set conceived for a particular event waiting to be revealed. As does theater, the fabricated stage-set, the architecture of museum, dramatizes the experience of the displayed work.

8.19   Steven Holl Architects, Nelson-Atkins Museum of Art Bloch Building, Kansas City, Missouri, 1999–2007. Photograph by author

To fully assess these aspects of Holl's extension, we need to agree with Kipnis that Holl's five lenses are not pavilions.[41] The latter is a freestanding edifice for arrival and departure. A pavilion also shelters the end point of a journey. The five lenses of the Bloch Building, instead, are the manifestation of an invisible structure, the aforementioned elongated volume of the extension. The vertical segmentation of the exterior volumes is indeed subdued by the addition's continuous interior space. As was suggested in our discussion of the Stretto House, these lenses too are conceived in part as the continuum of the act of terrace-making that in Holl's hand is used for the reconstruction of the site. But *site* is a measurable entity with a particular geometry and orientation that has to be transformed into a cultural artifact. It is through the tectonic articulation of the relationship between the earth-work and frame-work that the architect comes to a critical differentiation between site, place, ground, and land. If one dismantles the phenomenological prejudice that place holds the seed of all identities, then Kipnis's observation is apt. He writes, "we regularly seek to transform place by changing the land, … the expansion seeks to transform the place of the Nelson-Atkins Museum by changing its ground."[42] Like all architects sensitive to landscape, Holl also knows that to erect a building one has to dig into the land, and then refabricate the ground for the architecture to sit on. It is indeed through this reconstructive process that architecture gets the opportunity to depart from the metaphysical and material properties of land and site. It creates its own site, and terraces the land. What is impressive about this building of Holl is that, underground, one is always taken by various openings reminding us of the sky, earth, and the surrounding landscape. And yet, underground, one's feeling is constantly fuelled by the presence of a solid mass extruded here and there to accommodate the design's circulatory elements, and enclosed spaces that contain artwork. These openings, cuts, and enclosures however, bring forth what contains the volume, the walls, columns, and T-shaped structural canopies (Figure 8.20).

Considering the measurable spatial and sculptural dialogue Holl establishes between the existing neoclassical building and the new extension, it is difficult not to recall its impact for the design of a private residence, the Oceanic Retreat (2001) (Figure 8.21). Located at the top of a hillside in Kaua'i, Hawaii, with views to the ocean, the design emulates organic metaphor that occasionally occupies the architect's imagination. Not only are the two separate concrete masses of the house conceived in sculptural tectonics, but the L-shaped massing of the second floor of both volumes is cut and embellished to look like two creatures in upright position, heads turned, staring at each other. The main house and the guest section seem to want to talk to each other. Holl says of this tectonic configuration. "Like two continents separated from each other by tectonic shift, an imaginary erosion creates two L shaped forms: a main house and a guest house."[43] Although these two parallel houses are off-centered from each other, when seen from a distance they still speak to each other in tectonic language. The upper level of each segment is cut, shaped, and embellished in reference to tongue-and-grove wood detailing. The sharp and narrow ending of one mass seems ready to join the balcony opening of the opposite volume. The visible cuts and erosions marking the body of these two stereotomic objects allude to a historical time when together they were part and parcel of a larger and perhaps meaningful world. The implied wish-image can be extended to Holl's entire

8.20   Steven Holl Architects, Nelson-Atkins Museum of Art Bloch Building, Kansas City, Missouri, 1999–2007. Interior view. Watercolor courtesy of Steven Holl Architects

repertory, suggesting that, in spite of the architect's phenomenological tendency, his architecture is free of the existentialist weight that is delicately articulated in Peter Zumthor's work. "Fabrication Detailed" is indicative of a chapter in Holl's work where the Benjaminian wish-image is activated as he maintains a constructive rapport with the artificiality of the current culture of spectacle.

8.21   Steven Holl Architects, Oceanic Retreat, Kaua'i, Hawaii, 2001. Image courtesy of Steven Holl Architects

Considering what has been said in the previous chapters, Holl's Oceanic Retreat is a fine note in contemporary architecture's shift to sculptural tectonics. The few discussed examples of the present turn to monolithic architecture are of further interest: in sculptural tectonics, the strategy of cuts has the potential to shortcut the postmodern interest in communication. The historicist architecture evident in formalistic, typological, or imitative modes of contemporary architecture tends to establish a transparent rapport between architecture and its modes of appropriation. Still, the anonymity implicit in a monolithic form (its un-approachability), a few examples of which are highlighted throughout this volume, is of critical importance in reference to contemporary architects' euphoria for the spectacular images that garnish digital architecture. Like a stone diverting the flood, contemporary sculptural tectonics are gravitational forces standing here and there against the liquidation of architecture enacted in our global age of digital reproductivity.

NOTES

1   For the first ten volumes of the journal see *Pamphlet Architecture 1–10* (New York: Princeton Architectural Press, 1998). Steven Holl edited Pamphlets nos. 1, 5, 9 on "Bridges," "The Alphabetical City," and "Rural and Urban House Types," respectively. Other issues of the journal were edited by various architects, including Zaha Hadid and Rem Koolhaas.

2   Le Corbusier, *Towards a New Architecture* (New York: Dover Publications, 1986), 29.

3   Steven Holl, "Archetypal Experience of Architecture," in S. Holl, J. Pallasmaa, and A. Perez-Gomez, eds, "Question of Perception," *Architecture and Urbanism* (July 1994), special issue, 63.

4   Ernesto N. Rogers, "The Phenomenology of European Architecture," in Stephen R. Graubard, *A New Europe* (London: Oldbourne Press, 1964), 433.

5   Jorge Otero-Pailos, *Architecture's Historical Turn: Phenomenology and the Rise of the Postmodern* (Minneapolis, MN: University of Minnesota Press, 2010), xxiii.

6   See Steven Holl's short entry essay in *Pamphlet Architecture 1–10*, no page number indicated.

7   Steven Holl, *Pamphlet Architecture 7* (July 1981).

8   Kevin Lynch, *The Image of the City* (Cambridge, MA: The MIT Press, 1960).

9   Hall Foster, "Image Building," *Artforum* (October 2004): 270–74.

10   Steven Holl in a conversation with Juhani Pallasmaa, published in *El Croquis* 108 (2001): 12.

11   Kenneth Frampton, *Steven Holl Architect* (Milan: Electa Architecture, 2003), 19.

12   Architect's statement, see S. Holl, J. Pallasmaa, and A. Perez-Gomez, eds, "Question of Perception," *Architecture and Urbanism*, 1994, 147.

13   Steven Holl, "Archetypal Experience of Architecture," in S. Holl, J. Pallasmaa, and A. Perez-Gomez, eds, "Question of Perception," *Architecture and Urbanism*, 1994, 41.

14   Gottfried Semper, *Style in Technical and Tectonic Arts; or Practical Aesthetics*, trans. H.F. Mallgrave, and M. Robinson (Santa Monica, CA: Texts and Documents, The Getty Research Institute, 2004), 126.

15   See M. Mostafavi and D. Leatherbarrow, *On Weathering: The Life of Building in Time* (Cambridge, MA: The MIT Press, 1993).

16   On this subject see Mark Wigley, *White Walls, Designer Dresses: The Fashioning of Modern Architecture* (Cambridge, MA: The MIT Press, 1995).

17   Quoted in Christian Norberg-Schultz, *Meaning in Architecture* (New York: Rizzoli, 1981), 213.

18   Steven Holl, *Architecture Spoken* (New York: Rizzoli, 2007), 56.

19   Kenneth Frampton, "On the Architecture of Steven Holl," in Steven Holl, *Anchoring* (New York: Princeton Architectural Press, 1989), 5.

20   Steven Holl, *Anchoring*, 1989, 109.

21   Here I am benefiting from Adolf Heinrich Borbein's philological investigation which is quoted in Kenneth Frampton, *Studies in Tectonic Culture* (Cambridge, MA: The MIT Press, 1995), 4.

22   Steven Holl, *Anchoring*, 1989, 97.

23   Adolf Loos, "Ornament and Crime," in Ulrich Conrads, ed., *Programs and Manifestoes on 20th-Century Architecture* (Cambridge, MA: The MIT Press, 1970), 20.

24   Steven Holl, *Anchoring*, 1989, 128.

25   Kenneth Frampton, *Steven Holl Architect*, 2003, 14.

26   I visited the building on March 23, 2011, when it was recovered from the flood damage. I want to take this opportunity to thank Eric Dean, Chief Curator of the Office of Visual Resources who walked me through the building and spoke passionately of Steven Holl's design.

27   Kenneth Frampton, *Domus* 896 (October 2006): 42–53.

28   Alberto Perez-Gomez, "Introduction," to Steven Holl, *Intertwining* (New York: Princeton Architectural Press, 1996), 9.

29   Juhani Pallasmaa, "An Architecture of Seven Senses," in S. Holl, J. Pallasmaa, and A. Perez-Gomez, eds, "Question of Perception," *Architecture and Urbanism*, 1994, 35.

30   Kenneth Frampton's introduction in *Steven Holl Architect*, 2003, 13.

31   The association is out of context. However, Otto Wagner's argument that surface embellishment should accentuate construction remains relevant to Steven Holl's project discussed in the main text here. For Wagner see trans. H.F. Mallgrave, *Otto Wagner, Modern Architecture* (Santa Monica, CA: The Getty Center for the History of Art and the Humanities, 1988).

32   On this subject see G. Dodds and R. Tavernor, eds, *Body and Architecture: Essays on the Changing Relation of Body and Architecture* (Cambridge, MA: The MIT Press, 2002).

33   See Kenneth Frampton's introduction in *Steven Holl Architect*, 2003, 21.

34   From Steven Holl's statement in Kenneth Frampton, *Steven Holl Architect*, 2003, 258.

35   Juhani Pallasmaa, *Eyes of the Skin: Architecture of the Senses* (Chichester: Wiley Academy, 2006), 10.

36   Francesco Garofalo, *Steven Holl* (London: Thames & Hudson, 2003), 152.

37   Francesco Garofalo, *Steven Holl*, 2003, 25.

38   Gevork Hartoonian, *Ontology of Construction* (Cambridge: Cambridge University Press, 1994), the final chapter in particular.

39   Walter Benjamin, "The Work of Art in the Age of Mechanical Reproduction," in Hannah Arendt, ed., *Illuminations* (New York: Schocken, 1969), 217–52.

40   Jeffrey Kipnis, "… and then, Something Magical," in Steven Holl, *Stone and Feather: The Nelson-Atkins Museum Expansion* (New York: Prestel-Verlag, 2007), 30.

41   Jeffrey Kipnis, "… and then, Something Magical," 2007, 39.

42   Jeffrey Kipnis, "… and then, Something Magical," 2007, 34.

43   Steven Holl, *Architecture Spoken*, 2007, 30.

9

Surface: The A-tectonic of Roofing and Wrapping

> *The position that an epoch occupies in the historical process can be determined more strikingly from an analysis of its inconspicuous surface-level expressions than from that epoch's judgments about itself ... The surface-level expressions, however, by virtue of their unconscious nature, provide unmediated access to the fundamental substance of the state of things. Conversely, knowledge of this state of things depends on the interpretation of these surface-level expressions. The fundamental substance of an epoch and its unheeded impulses illuminate each other reciprocally.*
>
> Siegfried Kracauer[1]

The following question provides an opening for a discussion of the permeation of roofing and wrapping in architecture today. What is the role of the disciplinary history of architecture when the tendency among architects is to see form as an abstract entity, and to attempt to theorize architecture from an interdisciplinary point of view? That architects should equip themselves with broad available knowledge is obvious and has been part of architectural praxis since Vitruvius's famous text, *De Architectura*. What needs to be added here is that, when built, architecture belongs not so much to the realm of the designer's ideas, let alone concepts developed in other disciplines. It is rather the work's relation to themes, forms, and haptic experiences that are central to differentiating the art of building from other disciplines. The suggested distinction, however, was compromised during the 1970s for reasons that are not the concern of this chapter.[2] Suffice it to say that, in order to move beyond the theoretical premises of post-war architecture, contemporary architects, especially those practicing in America and Europe, seemingly had no choice but to revise their strategies in the light of concepts borrowed from structuralism and post-structuralism. Even if Jacques Derrida's deconstruction theory was once an essential text for theoreticians and some architects, today, architectural form is usually contemplated in reference to Gilles Deleuze's discourse on the fold discussed in the book of that title.[3] The fold has inaugurated a way of seeing and discussing architecture that dispenses with some aspects of classical and anthropocentric assumptions central even to modernist discourse, and it is this that has made the subject so dear to neo-avant-garde architects.

The argument presented in this chapter does not intend to underestimate the role theory plays in architecture. The intention rather is to highlight the fact that theory today operates in an autonomous realm independent of architectural praxis. To map a productive relationship between history, theory, and criticism, this chapter will attempt to turn the focus of analysis to the historicity of architectural discipline. Deploying Gottfried Semper's theory of dressing, the argument presented here gives particular attention to Semper's discourse on the tectonic rapport between the two elements of the roof and the enclosure, and will examine its theoretical implications for contemporary architecture. Semper is important because his idea of theatricality suggests discussing the expressionistic tendencies of computer-generated forms in reference to the aesthetic of commodity fetishism.[4] A different understanding of roofing and wrapping would plot architecture in the domain of landscape. To this end, the final section of this chapter will examine projects designed by diverse architects. The binary underpinning of this comparison is problematized by placing Greg Lynn's views on the tectonics of blob in the fuzzy picture of contemporary architectural practice.

THE RETURN OF SURFACE

Any discussion concerning the tectonic rapport between wrapping and roofing involves examining the historicity of these two architectonic elements. Recent architectural theories discuss "surface" in reference to the visual aesthetics of media technologies with a vague reference to Semper. In "Digital Semper," for example, Bernard Cache dwells on Semper's theory of *Bekleidung*, dressing. However, he fails to notice the difference between "surface" and the idea of dressing, as well as the difference between dressing and the dressed-up.[5] The dressed-up suggests wrapping a constructed form with surfaces that might evoke a particular style or symbolism of the kind in vogue during the 1970s eclecticism. Semper's theory of dressing, in contrast, is primarily concerned with the artistic articulation of the material of the exterior clothing in relation to the load-bearing elements. For Semper, "hanging carpets remained the true walls; they were the visible boundaries of a room. The often solid walls behind them were necessary for reasons that had nothing to do with the creation of space; they were needed for protection, for supporting a load, for their permanence, etc."[6] The difference between surface and dressing should also be discussed in reference to the clothing that corrects or brings forth the shape of the body *vis-à-vis* that used in carnivals. In the latter case the body is dressed-up for theatrical effects with little concern for comfort. Cache uses Semper's theory to justify the present interest in surface, understood as a thin film covering the mass of a building. He also does not discuss the idea of surface with reference to architecture's rapport with landscape. This last point is important for two reasons: firstly, the tectonic evolves primarily in molding the seam connecting the building to its ground. Secondly, any formalistic approach to architecture stops short of historicizing the current visual and tactile experiences in relation to the disciplinary history of architecture. For some, the most significant issue in architecture today is to invent new forms using available digital techniques. To clarify these observations, it is necessary to review Semper's theory of dressing closely.

In the "Preliminary Remarks on Polychromic Architecture," Semper argues that unpretentious lavishness is a natural need for architecture if the whole matter is treated artistically. This conditional endorsement of excess in architecture is fulfilled when, as in the ancient Greek monuments, the architect combines painting, sculpture, and other arts, creating a chorus.[7] Juxtaposing dance and fine art, Semper did underline "necessity" and the architectonic means by which one should handle such a subject artistically. In fact, the theme of necessity was critical for nineteenth-century architecture in more ways than one: a utilitarian understanding of the socio-cultural consequences of the industrial revolution and the emergence of new building materials and institutional needs were both developments instrumental in generating an esteem for realism and "objectivity" which were shared by many architects and artists.[8] Making a distinction between the core-form and the art-form, Semper argued that in early civilization, the interior space was wrapped by carpets hung from a frame that fulfilled the structural and practical needs of sheltering. According to him, the carpets were later conceived as stylistic or tectonic surrogates, dressing the building's physical structure.

Several decades later, in an article titled "The Principle of Cladding," Adolf Loos gave a new twist to Semper's idea of dressing. For Loos the primary task of the architect is to embellish the material of dressing in such a way that its tactile qualities would evoke a particular sentiment. The second task of the architect, he wrote, was to think of a structure that holds the enclosure up, for example, the four carpets implied in Semper's theory of dressing. Obviously there is a rift between Semper's and Loos's interpretations of dressing that sheds some light on the present tendency to wrap the space with surfaces (folds?) that have no tectonic rapport with what holds the enclosure together.

Semper's theory of dressing aimed at two goals: first, to underline the importance of the textile industry for the origin of architecture. For Semper, the idea of the wall evolved through a sequence of spatial enclosures; primitive screen or woven-mall, then metal sheathing, and eventually carpets whose colorful images were applied to the surfaces of masonry building to evoke a sentiment of monumentality.[9] Second, Semper was concerned with the difficulty involved in the artistic use of iron in monumental architecture.[10] His argument was also in response to those who believed that Greek architects shunned the use of color in monuments. Dwelling on necessity, Semper argued for a concept of dressing through which the architect could wrap the structure, the core-form, in an art-form that might even deny the material basis of the former. According to him, "architecture could only attain a pivotal status among the fine arts by elevating the 'poetic idea' of the building's purpose (using types, metaphors, and functional forms) to such a level that the physical material of the building disappeared from the subjective consciousness, leaving only the contemplation of its transcendental meaning."[11] The statement discloses Semper's re-interpretation of the nineteenth-century drive for realism and objectivity with an eye to the disciplinary history of architecture.

There were other interpretations of "necessity" as the nineteenth century came to an end. Otto Wagner, for one, discussed realism in terms of faithfulness to material and practical demands of modern life. In defense of *Nutz-Stil*, Wagner recalls his introduction to *Sketches, Projects and Executed Buildings*, and the French cultural experience where the architect functioned as both artist and building technician. And considering realism in French painting, he observed that, "such Realism in architecture can also bear quite peculiar fruit ... "[12] While challenging Semper's theory of *Bekleidung*, Wagner came short of proposing a clear alternative to the ways in which architecture attains a particular art-form out of a chosen structural system. His early views recall Marc-Antoine Laugier's interest in the rational expression of construction. As Peter Haiko reminds us, Wagner's later practice unfolds a tectonic form in which the actual structure often remains hidden. In the main façade of Postsparkasse, for example, the nails adorning the façade were not used to visualize the structure *per se*, "but [of] that which reminds us of it. ... The task of the bolts is to point out to the viewer the novelty of the encasement, namely the slabs, to make it obvious and eternal."[13] The semantics invested in Wagner's tectonic were mainly motivated by the physical material of construction.

Wagner's understanding of the tectonic could be associated with J. Winckelmann who saw the poetics of Greek temples as driven by a stone construction system. Questioning the rationalist distinction between the structural and the ornamental, Semper's discourse on dressing, instead, equates architecture with dance and music. He referred to architecture as a cosmic art. As discussed in Chapter 2, music and dance differ from the imitative arts in that a distinction between what is essential to them and what is excessive, or ornamental, is almost impossible. The implied idea of theatricality in Semper and his reference to the Greek chorus and dance suggests that excess in architecture should be seen as a conscious attempt by the architect to include architecture within a broader cultural experience. And yet central to the idea of theatricality is the embellishment of the constructed form while mastering the material; the form fakes, according to Semper, if there is nothing behind the mask.[14]

Semper's idea of theatricality is important because, contrary to the accusation that he was a die-hard materialist,[15] he attempted to draw the attention to that aspect of architecture which, like other commodities, has to do with the realm of consumption. In order to be "attractive," like products of fashion, and to be appropriated by the masses, architecture, like every other modern product, should constitute "antiquity anew out of the most recent past." In modernity, "as objects of fetishization, commodities destined for everyday consumption display two closely related features: one is an apparent self-sufficiency or independence from their process of production; the other is the appearance of novelty, required to make them attractive in the face of competing products."[16] The Benjaminian dialectics established between the past and the present demonstrates Semper's inclination to bring architecture together with other cultural products, including motifs produced by the applied arts, such as weaving and ceramics, but also dance and chorus, material experiences that are absent in Wagner's discourse on realism. Obviously Semper was not familiar with the "critical" dimension of Walter Benjamin's discourse. This is one reason why this book wishes to highlight the difference between the tectonic of theatricality and the aesthetic of theatricalization (spectacle) permeating architecture today.

The historicization suggested here perhaps speaks for this author's fascination with Semper. But there is more to it. Besides Semper's belief that fabrication is essential to architecture's interiority, what Semper wrote and built were charged, in a disguised way, with a glimpse of what has become a century later an experience of everyday life:[17] the permeation of the aesthetic of commodity fetishism. The totalization implied in Semper's idea of theatricality, his reference to the Greek chorus, are meaningful today if recoded in the context of a mass culture that is not orchestrated by historical forms, but by animated surfaces, folds, and blob architecture. What the blob, a generic name for computer-generated form, offers is not the new, but a sense of aesthetic appreciation that runs through the entirety of the present culture of spectacle. For further understanding of the difference between "dressing" and "dressed-up," the historicity of blob architecture should be addressed.

THE RETURN OF THE ORGANIC

There is another dimension to the need to historicize current architectural theories. The biomorphic forms permeating digitally produced images might look like the work of modern expressionists, or evoke Wright's organic theory. An argument can be made for suggesting that neither of these tendencies of modernism has any thing in common with the conceptual potentialities vested in the current interest in biomorphic forms. And yet, the "return of the organic" should be understood in conjunction with the recent history of the concept of organic that permeates architectural discourse. Criticizing the totalizing tendency of international architecture, Peter Collins presented the "biological analogy" as one paradigm among four others that frames the horizon of his discourse in a book entitled *Changing Ideals in Modern Architecture, 1750–1950* (1965). Collins traces the origin of the biological analogy back to the mid-seventeenth century when biological studies were used to study laws governing social phenomena.[18] The analogy was further modified during the nineteenth century when vegetation was discussed in reference to a particular environment. Collins's classificatory mode, however, haunts him: in an attempt to contextualize modern architecture, he uses an organic metaphor to show how architecture is "constantly shifting like an evolving, living being."[19] He goes further and recognizes two directions in modern architecture that were influenced by biological studies: the idea that form follows function, and the view that attempts to associate architectural form to a particular environment, i.e., regionalism. Both ideas have a foot in the nineteenth-century discourse on organicism. What is of most interest in organicism, however, is the drive for singularity and individuation without rejecting the totality of history. Caroline van Eck describes the significance of organicism for nineteenth-century architecture:

organicism presented "a strategy of invention, by which stylistic decisions are made and justified, or … a strategy of interpretation, through which the meaning of architecture, and especially the architecture of the past, can be formulated."[20] In any case, Collins's paradigm should be revisited in the light of blob architecture, and the historicity permeating the two concepts of the organic and mechanics.

In a seminal essay Joseph Rykwert locates the etymological roots of the word organic in *organon*, which according to him "came from an archaic term, *ergon*, work." Rykwert suggests that, the Latin use of "*organicus* did not mean anything very different from *mechanicus*: something done by means of instruments indirectly."[21] The Latin use of the term came to an end by the seventeenth century when minerals, plants, and animals were regarded as entities belonging to separate domains. Interestingly enough, the mechanistic philosophy emerging in the seventeenth century supported the idea of using techniques derived from classical aesthetics, thus creating an illusion of life and movement perceivable in nature.[22] The word *organon* and its appeal for the archaic unity between the organic and mechanics, Rykwert reminds us, resurfaced through many nineteenth-century functional theories, especially in the work of those architects and theoreticians who wanted to totalize the rift between structure (mechanics/necessity) and ornament (excess/aesthetic pleasure).[23] Confronted by the orthodox modernist denunciation of ornament, and the postmodernist simulation of historical forms, Rykwert, may have wanted to underline the bad conscience of the 1980s and to draw our attention to the eternity of the classical. His argument is useful if read in conjunction with Walter Benjamin's discourse on the actuality of the present. For Benjamin "the present must be relieved from its identification with the eternal past and be nourished by the now."[24] But the now of the present is pregnant with the most archaic, and for Benjamin the culture of modernity is nothing but the clash between the ever new and the outmoded past.

Benjamin's "doubling," the return of the past in the new, leads us to see the present esteem for biomorphic forms neither as an expression of the *Zeitgeist*, nor as a direct product of electronic technology. In fact an argument can be made to suggest that since antiquity,[25] in addition to plant and animal forms, human figures were utilized for symbolic and structural ends. While Semper's observation concerns the organic idea implied in the tectonic articulation of ornament and structure, the following remarks make a point that is relevant to the present obsession with surface architecture. For Semper, the organic content of the tectonic of Greek order was anticipated in the Assyrian column, though without the "animating spark of Prometheus." Here he presents a perception of shell that permeates *surface*. Following Semper, and to paraphrase him, it might be argued that in blob architecture the function of the structure is transferred to the shell, the "structural scheme and the artistic scheme become one," and that the "organic" haunts the image. Anthony Vidler is correct to characterize the neo-avant-garde architects' interest in fold as part "of conscious literalization, deployed in the service of an architecture that takes its authority from the inherent 'vitalism'— of computer-generated series."[26] What should be added to Vidler's observation is Greg Lynn's discussion of the tectonics of biomorphic forms.

The blob attempts to provide an alternative theory against those architects who invest in contradiction (formal or contextual) and the search for bygone coherencies exemplified in the work of some traditionalists. This third alternative, according to Lynn, wants to do two things: first, to underline the situation where the velocity of computer-generated images has put architects in a defensive position. This is the case with those who are seeking to reassess the importance of architecture's disciplinary history for current practice. Second, dwelling on themes like "anexact geometries" or vague forms, Lynn sees smoothness in the blob having the potentiality to nullify the contradictions so dear to the "reactionary call for unity" and the "avant-garde dismantling of it."[27] Smoothing over contradictions, together with an esteem for pliancy, gives rise to the simultaneous existence of disparate and seemingly distinct elements. Lynn's biomorphic alternative dismisses the possibility of architecture having any rapport with the ideology of late capitalism; the blob indeed represents a totalized space, having the least to do with its context. Also missing in Lynn's theorization is the discussion that concerns the return of the familiar, the organic and its capacity to domesticate both the shock effects and anxieties unleashed by a capitalist system, the culture of which is moving beyond the modernist aesthetic of abstraction. In addition, mention should be made of the alienation induced by the globalization of capital and the information industry. To naturalize, or domesticate the very mechanistic logic of computer technology, the blob wraps "anexact geometries" with surfaces, the very appearance of which might be associated with zoological forms, if not with the tectonic transformations that reshape the landscape.

Any discussion concerning the subject of domestication of the "new" and its implication for architecture needs to be historicized too. Was not "nature" appropriated as a means of domestication when eighteenth-century architecture seemed to depart from classical wisdom? And did not most modernists recode "real" as natural to substantiate their mechanical analogies? One is reminded of the sublime beauty of the so-called French Revolutionary architects and the abstraction envisioned in technological products. Mention should also be made of the silos, the liners, and the machine-objects that were characterized as the second nature. Of interest here is the way neo-avant-garde architects' fascination with digital techniques ends in bringing to the surface once again ideas such as "anthropomorphizing the material world," and the "humanization of nature," which interestingly, had been utilized in ancient sculptures. Speaking of the great collections of natural and human objects, Horst Bredekamp suggests that, "automatons were the most obvious expression of the desire to imitate life by inspiring movement."[28] In any event, there is a difference between blob architecture and the architecture of modern buildings, quite apart from ancient sculptures, that should be addressed. Within the torn-apart landscape of the pre-modern world, the white and abstract forms of early modern buildings stood aloof and looked surreal. On the other hand, the early twentieth century's organic theories of architecture and the work of expressionism were indeed formulated in tandem, if not in opposition, to the emerging metropolis and a straitjacketed understanding of functionalism. This is not the place to discuss these issues; the discussion should rather turn to the postmodernity of blob-form, which does not produce the shock

9.1   Jean Nouvel, Conference Center in Lucerne, 1992–2000. Photograph by Philippe Ruault, courtesy of Ateliers Jean Nouvel

effect that modern architects guarded against. This change in perception and in the appropriation of architecture has to do with the total effects of the commodity-form. What this means is that the phenomenon of blob is the result of the unmediated internalization of technique into the processes of conceptualization and production of architecture. Losing its modernist agenda, architecture today is plunged into the spectacle of the culture industry. One architectonic manifestation of this unique development is the return of surface in architectural discourse. And yet, the blob touches the realm of the uncanny; it neutralizes the animated surfaces of architecture, tossing the Venturisque vanilla ice cream forms to the ashes of history. The disappearance of postmodern historicism from the main scene of today's architecture should be considered the most positive contribution that digital techniques have offered to architecture thus far.

The theoretical position presented in the previous pages gives rise to the following question. Is there another dimension to the notion of organic with positive architectonic implications? Besides the idea of landscape (discussed next), the return of the organic provides an opportunity to recall Steven Holl, an architect who has not joined the club of total digitalization of the architectural form. Even though I suggested earlier that the return of the organic should be considered in conjunction with the dialectics of the organic and mechanics, it is of significance here to highlight the idea of body implied in the word organic. It is not the humanist discourse on the subject of the body and architecture that is of interest,[29] but a phenomenological one that, as discussed in the previous chapter, has been central to the development of Holl's architecture.[30] What makes the return of the organic in this American architect's work singular is his conceptualization of the dialectics involved in art and science where the ontological dimensions of architecture are excessively stressed to balance the aesthetic of theatricalization permeating the age of digital reproduction.

BACK TO ROOFING AND WRAPPING

The theoretical formulation presented thus far provides a lens through which to look at the dialectics of the elements of roof and clothing from a different angle. Consider Jean Nouvel's design for the Conference Centre in Tours, France, and the Culture and Conference Centre in Switzerland (Figure 9.1). In these two projects, the roof is articulated in reference to its ur-form, the idea of sheltering. Thus, the tectonic rapport between the slab and the beam, especially in the Swiss project, recalls Wright's deliberate transgression of the sheltering image of a hip roof, charging the overhanging part of the roof with the modernist esteem for the aesthetic of horizontality. Against, or in spite of the theatricalization of architecture by Frank Gehry and others, Nouvel's tectonic articulation restores the archaic purpose of the roof, rendering it as the foremost architectonic element of monumentality. This aspect of his work not only recalls Mies van der Rohe's National Gallery in Berlin (1968), but also Renzo Piano's design in the Foundation Beyeler, Riehn (1997), a project that is fundamental to presenting a different understanding of the theme of organic (Figure 9.2).

The Beyeler project stresses the essentiality of the roof work and its tectonic dialogue with the wall and the site. Here Piano takes us back to Mies's Barcelona Pavilion where architecture is perceived in dialogue with landscape, water, and sky. Both projects enjoy a lightness of structure experienced in the building's reflection in the pond, and the smooth spatial transition that takes place between interior and exterior spaces. In the Foundation Beyeler, the building's stepping into the water dramatizes the image of ruin in the future: a high-tech glass roof shelters stone-clad columns and walls that are sunken into the water. One is reminded of Carlo Scarpa's fascination with water and landscape, as re-presented in both the Brion Cemetery (Figure 3.10), and the Fondazione Querini-Stampalia, Venice. Roman Hollenstein pushes the envelope of these associations to include Ignazio Gardella's Padiglion d'Arte Contemporary, realized in Milan in 1949–53.

9.2   Renzo Piano Building Workshop Architects in association with Burckhardt + Partner AG, Basel, Beyeler Foundation Museum-Riehen, Basel (Switzerland) 1991–2000. Photograph by Michel Denance, image courtesy of Renzo Piano Building Workshop Architects, Italy

Like Piano's Foundation Beyeler, Gardella's art Pavilion opens via a glazed façade onto the park. … In short: the spiritual kinship between these two buildings—despite technical differences— is so striking that one might be tempted to regard Piano's new building as a contemporary reinterpretation of Gardella's exhibition pavilion.[31]

Piano, however, goes a little further than Scarpa. Looking at the pictures taken from the bird's-eye view of the Foundation Beyeler, one cannot dismiss the tectonic rapport between the surface of the roof and the texture of the adjacent vineyard (Figure 9.3). More important, and perhaps in reference to the de Menil Collection and Cy-Twombly Museum (both in Houston, Texas), Piano treats the surface of the roof almost like an element of clothing in its own right. Similar to the texture of a woven fabric, the roof in the Beyeler building re-presents a hybrid fabric weaving together the grid of structural support (columns and beams) and the in-fill through which light seeps into

9.3   Renzo Piano Building Workshop Architects in association with Burckhardt + Partner AG, Basel, Beyeler Foundation Museum-Riehen, Basel (Switzerland) 1991–2000. Aerial view. Photograph by Niggi Braining, image courtesy of Renzo Piano Building Workshop Architects, Italy

the galleries. Water, sky, and light orchestrate the tectonic of roof and wall evoking the idea of monumentality.

The idea of a building's dialogue with landscape is rather an Oriental phenomenon and its genealogy goes back to Japanese culture. However, the ur-form of a monumental pavilion standing next to a pond can be traced back to the Persian palaces built in the Safavid period, specially the Chihil Suton in Isfahan. The Oriental sense of the tactile and monumental is also discernable in Le Corbusier's design for the High Court of Chandigarh, India (1951–65). I am also reminded of the formativeness of the element of roof in Le Corbusier's later buildings including the Chapel of Notre Dame du Haut, Ronchamp (1951–53), and the Heide Weber Pavilion, Zurich (1961–65). However, in Piano's hands, the modernist notion of monumentality is mediated through landscape. In his words, "a monument evaporates like snow in the sun, that is to say organically, almost like the notion of excellence. Excellence vanishes the moment you proclaim it."[32] In the Foundation Beyeler the "organic" is returned to mediate the building's relation to the landscape. According to Piano, the exterior walls give the impression that "they were part of a terrain, projecting from the ground beneath as static, geological elements. The only additional feature was the transparent glass roof, which had alighted like a butterfly on the wall and spread out its wings."[33] Piano's work recodes the return of the organic in architecture's indispensible coexistence with landscape.

The tectonics of roofing and walling, and the idea of roof as a mediating element between architecture and landscape return in Piano's design for the Tresnick Pavilion, an expansion to the Los Angeles County Museum of Art (2006–10) (Figure 9.4).

9.4   Renzo Piano, County Museum of Art, Los Angeles, California, 2006–10. Photograph by author

Surrounded by a number of existing institutional structures, including a park in the north and Wilshire Boulevard in the south, the design distributes the programmatic needs of the addition into two separated volumes. What brings together the museum's three-story-tall volume, facing the Boulevard, with its large single-story volume, located on the opposite side, is the design's saw-tooth roof. The repetitive and elegantly detailed profile of the truss of this roof, what Piano calls "piece," turns out to be the element that also coordinates the building's structure with the location and dimensions of display rooms. Occasionally, the piece "lends a specific character to the building, which often helps to scale vis-à-vis the site too."[34] The two major volumes of the complex are clad in stone and roofed with metallic trusses, the elegant tectonic language of which sustains the museum's civic image. Whereas the sprouting look of the roof's blades can be associated with the cactus trees planted around the site, its overall detailing demonstrates a deliberate tectonic figuration to integrate ornament with construction. According to Peter Buchanan the "natural evolution" at work in the architect's design of the above mentioned pieces aims to combine "the efficiency of machines and the integrity of the organism."[35] The organic metaphor is further stressed in the surface articulation of the roof of the main gallery, seen from the stairs leading to the taller volume (Figure 9.5). Similar to the Beyeler Foundation, the saw-tooth roof is the major tectonic element that is associable with the idea of landscape,

9.5   Renzo Piano, County Museum of Art, Los Angeles, California, 2006–10. Aerial view. Photograph by author

and it also leaves its mark on the interior spaces of the galleries. It is to Piano's credit to detail the element of the roof as a diaphragm controlling the natural light pouring into the gallery spaces wherever needed (Figure 9.6). His is not a romantic yearning for nature, but the conviction that architecture should mediate between the organic and the mechanics. Of this association mention should also be made of the red painted mechanical machines placed next to the single-story building. Their color and forms recall the Pompidou Center, Paris. In the Tresnick Pavilion, however, Piano makes an attempt to deconstruct the classical notion of monumentality in a tectonic figuration that evolves from architecture's rapport with the landscape.

If Piano's tectonics of roofing and the dialectics of the roof and the wall recall the Semperian tradition, an argument can be made to suggest that Peter Eisenman's later projects attempt to dispense with the essential nature of the tectonic, yet he makes an attempt to place architecture in the fabric of landscape. Consider the Staten Island Institute of Art and Science, where the image of the hurricane-eye is conceptualized in a form that is primarily dictated by a fabric-like layer that wraps the body of the building (Figure 9.7). The reference to the eye of the hurricane is not direct: using morphing techniques, the initial image of an organic phenomenon is transposed into a form whose dressing operates in many ways: at one level, the roof functions as an enclosure, if not a path, but then it becomes the floor for a space beneath. Here the roof-work is reduced to covering spaces that are left between the adjacent and dynamic surfaces, the overall form of which compromises the line separating the element of roof from the wall. Far more interesting is the way this alien-looking object (Eisenman calls it "ghost of the real")[36] sits on the site staring at Manhattan, eye to eye with the destroyed twin towers of the World Trade Center (Figure 9.8). The image recalls mythologies of the metropolis: King Kong conquering the tall buildings, for example. The "soft" alien-looking object of Eisenman's project, with its peculiar gesture towards the metropolis, looks as human as ET in Spielberg's film. The image also discloses Eisenman's misreading, at least at the time of conceiving this project, that postmodernism represents the end of ideology. This limitation has opened a path towards a critical practice, the idiom of which fluctuates between tectonic and topological tectonics.

Eisenman's design strategy aims at transgressing dualities such as inside/outside, figure/ground, real/virtual, and the spectacle/event. Among these it is the second duality that needs to be discussed here, though briefly. Without dwelling on the history of the idea of figure/ground, it is enough to say that the figure necessitates a ground distinct from the object. This compositional principle sustains the classical analogy between the vertical posture of the body and the pavilion-type building, if not the hut discussed by Marc-Antoine Laugier. To weaken the seam connecting the building to the ground (or the earth-work to the frame-work discussed by Semper) entails two developments. First, one that weakens not only the perspectival perception of an object, but also the parallelism that is assumed between the object and the viewer. Second, like Eisenman, we should be keen to rethink the Cartesian perception of space in reference to Deleuzian differentiation between matt and felt.[37] In Eisenman's words:

> The Staten Island project began with a finely gridded Cartesian matt, which was eventually turned into smooth topological strands that retain in their striations a memory of their original gridding. In the twelve diagrams of the process of transgression, the movement from a Cartesian mesh (ground) to figured set of striations is achieved by passing a flow through the matt, analogous to the pedestrian flow through the ferry terminal. The resultant interior space is not formed by function, nor is it centralized, but appears to be a random overlay of layers revealing of spaces which appear and disappear at a glance, not allowing the observer to have a directed route or a fixed gaze.[38]

9.6   Renzo Piano, County Museum of Art, Los Angeles, California, 2006–10. Interior view. Photograph by author

Eisenman's strategy utilizes fabric and separates the interior space from the outside (Figure 9.9). And yet, instead of articulating the tectonic of the enclosure and structure, he seemingly agrees with Loos that the support element is secondary to the idea of wrapping. In doing so he recodes the idea of dressing; his design process Involves laying down a virtual matt, proceeding towards the formation of an object that meets the horizon of the landscape and the verticality of the body midway.

9.7   Eisenman Architects, Staten Island Institute of Arts and Sciences project, New York, 1999. Diagram drawing. Image courtesy of Eisenman Architects, New York City

   This is evident from the City of Culture of Galicia, Santiago de Compostela, Spain (2010), where Eisenman creates a fabricated topography superimposing abstract diagrams drawn in analogy to the plan of the city and the Vieira, a fan-shaped shell, a symbolic icon of Compostela (Figure 3.18). To deconstruct the tectonics of roofing and walling, the building's roof is stretched along the slope of the site. Covered by the stones of Mount Gaias, the roof is morphed in simulation to biological forms and the contours of the earth's surface. The project recalls Rosalind Krauss's discussion of "sculpture in

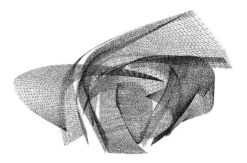

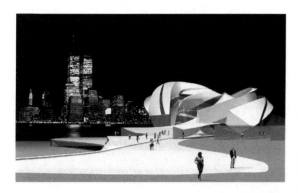

9.8   Eisenman Architects, Staten Island Institute of Arts and Sciences project, New York, 1999. General view. Image courtesy of Eisenman Architects, New York City

9.9   Eisenman Architects, Staten Island Institute of Arts and Sciences project, New York, 1999. Interior space. Image courtesy of Eisenman Architects, New York City

the expanded field," and this in reference to *works* that attempt to mediate between sculpture, landform, and architecture.[39] To sustain an architectonic balance between horizontality (landscape) and verticality (the body), Eisenman had to slice the project's topographic surface, making inroads for light and access to the interior spaces. The cuts are in place to reiterate the architect's lasting struggle to deconstruct architecture's interiority (think of the notion of frontality) creating morphing interior spaces that at times recall the Aronoff Center for Design and Art (1988–96) discussed in Chapter 3.

Of Eisenman's more successful engagements with the tectonics of landform, mention should be made of the Memorial to the Murdered Jew of Europe, Berlin (2005) (Figure 9.10). Designed in collaboration with the American sculptor Richard Serra (1997), the final work juxtaposes landscape with the body, and this in reference to the tomb-shaped concrete volumes of the project. Contrary to conventional memorials and cemeteries, where the spectator stands in front of the status, here, instead, the body walks through a gridded path cut through an artificial topography, consisting of a field of 2,511 concrete slabs. The spacing between these tomb-like masses is narrow enough for one person to pass through. Seemingly Eisenman wanted us to experience one of the most barbaric moments of our very civilized world in solitude, if possible. The experience is intensified by the constant change in the height of each concrete *mass* (bodies?), the totality of which creates an undulating landscape. Eisenman here reverses Loos's famous association of architecture with tomb, suggesting that architecture today can only make sense if it is molded with earth and landscape.

Eisenman's turn to landform is inspired by Georges Bataille's remarks on alteration, another term to associate with Semper's interest in weaving. In discussing surrealist artwork, the idea of alteration meant to Bataille a strategy to recode the classical dualities like high and low and base and figure, and thus the possibility of placing the work somewhere between devolution and evolution.[40] In this process, the "surface" emerges as a symptom of horizontality, if not the "flatbed picture plane" discussed by Leo Steinberg.[41] In Eisenman's architecture, the space is perceived in the interplay established between surfaces needed to wrap the interior space and the play of tectonics. To put it differently, the physicality of Eisenman's architecture is fissured in the diagrammatic representation of topography of the site and the program.

What makes Eisenman's architecture different from Piano's has to do with his formalistic rethinking of the architecture's interiority, discussed in Chapter 3. Taking into

9.10   Eisenman Architects, Memorial to Murdered Jews of
Europe, Berlin, 1998–2005. Photograph by author

consideration the available materials, building techniques, and programmatic needs, Piano's tectonic articulation recollects the modernist's tradition of *Bauen*. We have already noted the Italian architect's attempt to reconcile a craft-oriented practice of tectonic with available high-tech structural systems and landscape. Writing on Piano, Hal Foster sees Le Corbusier a major forerunner in steeping architecture in nature and at the same time making analogies between Greek temples and racing cars.[42] Recalling the Le Corbusier of *L'Art décoratif d'aujourd'hui* (1925), Foster reminds us of the ways in which the French architect would fetishize technology. The conflict between architecture and technology is real; however, Piano is an exemplar among contemporary architects who try to subdue the spectacle of theatricalization in spite of the work's tendency to fetishize technique, noted by Foster. Eisenman, instead, reiterates the ethos of avant-gardism, and yet resists falling into the trap of the *Zeitgeist* entertained by architects who reduce architectural form to the images generated by electronic technologies. In operating in such a contradictory zone, Eisenman wishes to recode the early modernist formalist theories in line with contemporary intellectual life. The Staten Island Institute of Art and Science addresses architecture's relation to a society that is deeply entangled with the spectacle of late capitalism. Eisenman's architecture involves readjusting architecture's interiority, and in doing so, the work highlights the difficulty of retaining some kind of critical distance from that theatricalization of architecture that would submit the art of building to the aesthetic of commodity fetishism.

In discussing Piano in conjunction with Eisenman, the intention is not to pit these two architects against each other. In arguing that wrapping and roofing are formative for any critical engagement with contemporary architecture, the aim was to say something more: we are witnessing a historical situation where Semper's discourse on theatricality might be taken for the present culture of spectacle. Furthermore, if it is still useful to claim that Mies exhausted the tectonic potentialities of steel and glass architecture,[43] then it is necessary to explore the dialogical relationship between the roof-work and clothing differently. It is this last point that makes Semper's idea of theatricality essential for a critique of contemporary architecture.

To begin with, attention should be given to the distinction Semper makes between planar and linear motifs fundamental to any fabric. According to him, "the cover's purpose is the opposite to that of binding … If the basic form of binding is linear, the surface appears as the formative element in everything intended to cover, protect, and close." And he continues, "the most important general factor affecting the style of cover are the attributes of the surface; that is the extension in breadth and length, the absence of the third dimension … "[44] The suggested distinction between linear and planar motifs is critical for understanding Semper's differentiation between the tectonic potentialities of Gothic and Renaissance architecture. It also offers a theoretical paradigm in which to discuss current architecture's turn to surface.

Historically, what is involved in the turn has to do with the ontological rift between construction and representation. Beyond the issue of tectonic, the divide was one reason why most pre-modern architects gave huge attention to the design of the frontal façade. Since the modernist formulation of the free-façade, the representational in architecture has been subdued, and the *look* of the object, instead, has become the prime occupation of most architects. Highlighting the schism between the technical aspects of construction and the representational, David Leatherbarrow and Mohsen Mostafavi explore various strategies that architects have chosen in different periods of history to tackle the subject.[45] And yet, the aforementioned dichotomy should also be addressed in reference to the architecture of blob and fold wherein the modernist grid and the linear dimension of the frame-structure are treated as a surrogate for the representational conventions of the element of wall. Thus the emergence of a different politics of "*faciality*, that are no longer structured on the opposition between front and back, private and public, or roof and wall." Alejandro Zaera Polo writes: "Once cornices, corners, and windows are no longer technically necessary, and the private and public are tangled in an increasingly complex relationship, the hierarchies of the interface become more complex."[46] What this means, as discussed previously in this chapter, is the critical position section drawing occupies in the architecture's twisted and playful surfaces. According to Rafael Moneo, section is central to understanding the best work James Sterling designed, for example. In Leicester, "the section is also the envelope, and the skin. Against the neutral, inert wall of traditional building, the modern architect discovered the lure of manipulating surfaces."[47] From now on, the element of clothing can be seen as a thin membrane, the exterior face of which is embellished in its own right, but is also independent of the frame-structure behind. When the surface is reduced to an all-encompassing unified enclosure, then the seam, "the principle making a virtue out of necessity,"[48] vanishes. In the present rush to digital surface, the latter is treated like a carpet with a major difference: unlike the fabric of a carpet, the digital surface disguises the grid of its fabric on both sides. Thus, the inevitable dismantling of the tectonic rapport between the roof and the structural frame, and the ways which dressing is expected to re-present that relationship.

Greg Lynn's argument in favor of blob tectonics is noteworthy. According to him, in the blob, the element of roof is not made of repetitive and identical elements covering a long span with a singular height. It is rather perceived as "a surface that continuously connects across all heights like a wet-cloth."[49] Here an attempt is made to re-define the tectonic of a trabeated structure in the light of recent advances taking place in the field of structural engineering, and the organic forms in some of the images produced by digital technology. This much is evident from the tectonics of topological roof typologies of the Shoel Yoh's "sport complex," Japan (1992), where, according to Alejandro Zaera-Polo and Moussavi, "construction techniques are developed simultaneously with formal diagram." The return of the organic is given a new twist in the Yokohama International Port Terminal, designed by the Foreign Office. Folding the floor into the roof and back and forth is analogous to "taking a series of sections through the building … virtually like taking sections through an animal." For Kenneth Frampton, the project illustrates "both a topographic sensibility and a display of a parametric method."[50] Hence, the integration of the "organic" implied in digital forms in the architecture's transformative rapport with the urban landscape, including its infrastructure.

Still, recalling the nineteenth-century debate on ornament and structure, Lynn's remark on ornament remains vague, even when he makes a distinction between ornament as applied decoration and that which to him characterizes "a dependency on collaboration that transforms" decoration and structure in "some unforeseen and unprecedented way."[51] When the surface is turned into the structure of ornament, then the organic rapport between the art-form and ornamentation, to recall Semper again, is not bound and influenced by the "principle of surface dressing that [makes it] impossible to consider them separately."[52] Therefore, Lynn's position, like other advocates of "digital tectonics," is primarily informed by the structural-technical, and the aesthetic sensibilities permeating the present culture of spectacle. At a different level, it might be argued that Lynn's alternative is suggestive of a structural organism that is analogous to the global corporate organization where complexity is not achieved through the resolution of contradictions, but through pliancy. Blob is indeed a totalized system, leaving no space outside of its surface. From this point of view, one might argue that the blob maintains a non-critical position against the ideological rapport running between architecture and the visual spectacle created by late capitalism.

In the early decades of the last century there was enough space in the landscape under capitalist reconstruction where architecture could still retain its disciplinary history and yet present itself as the social engine of modernity. That space today has been overtaken by the culture of spectacle. If one agrees with this observation, then it is possible to suggest that Eisenman's architecture attempts to make an opening through the suggested "closure," and thus the possibility of entering into the realm of topology. Lynn, on the other hand, retains the closure as a datum to gauge the contemporaneity of architecture. The comparison raises the following question: In what creative ways can architects today keep a hold of Semper's tectonic of theatricality without dismissing the tactile and visual sensibilities permeating contemporary culture? And, more importantly, and particularly in reference to neo-avant-garde architects, how could architecture deconstruct itself, to go beyond its interiority, and yet retain a level of autonomy that was critical to the modernist departure from the classical language of architecture?

If it is true that architecture cannot touch the realm of landscape (where it belonged in the first place) without overcoming its own limits, what should we make of the association made here between Piano's work and the modernist tradition of the *Neue Bauen*. The association is a useful one: it foreshadows a criticism of the idea of theatricalization that takes advantage of idioms central to modernity even though this project may remain forever incomplete.[53] Lynn's blob, instead, formulates an alternative to Eisenman's intention in dressing-up the void left by the failure of the project of the historical avant-garde. To put it differently, if the culture of building is dispensed with, then the deconstruction of the limits of architecture leads the art of building nowhere but into the whirlpool of the culture of spectacle. As Juan José Lahuerta reminds us, "if architecture had ever desired to become the scenario of human relations—in the heroic period of history—now it had finally achieved this, functioning as an indispensable backdrop for perfumes and automobiles in television advertisements, i.e., becoming raucously visible in the moment of its disappearance."[54] Such a moment, to some architects, alludes to architecture's loss of its own scaffolding, and thus the tendency to legitimize the return of organic forms, the surface of which is scribbled with theories of formal autonomy. The development suggests that the temporality within which architecture was perceived to be the engine of society is gone, and perhaps cannot be regained for a long time to come.

What makes the current situation historically singular is architecture's confrontation with technology. In the age of digital reproduction, technification of architecture entails a production process the final result of which might be called *shape*, to be edited for a particular purpose. If in the dawn of modernism abstraction was a necessary strategy to detach architecture from the technical and aesthetic apparatus of *technė*, digitally produced shapes, instead, facilitate the permeation of the aesthetic of commodity fetishism in all cultural products including architecture. Again if in the early 1920s modern buildings seemed more advanced than most other industrial products, a few of Zaha Hadid's recent projects, for example, have the least affinity with architecture as such. Yes, parametric designs are attractive and look cool, as do most digitally engineered shapes.

Therefore, one possible way to get around the former political agenda of architecture is to exploit the historicity of that loss and to make architecture critical to the present culture of spectacle. To this end, the return of "surface" to the main scene of contemporary architecture should be seen as useful: it sheds a different light on Semper's theory of cladding, and provides an opportunity to underline the essentiality of the tectonics of roofing and wrapping, in spite of architecture's entanglement with a culture that is totally commodified. What this means is that criticism should discuss the work itself; how architecture addresses the culture of building in rapport with the objective and subjective situation of late capitalism. The critique of the theatricalization of architecture presented in this book should be considered a minor attempt to cast a critical light on our understanding of how architecture operates in late capitalism. Interestingly enough, in criticism of the present culture of the visual, Hal Foster underlines the usefulness of what he calls "strategic autonomy" for critical practice.[55] His argument is based on the historicity of the modernism of the 1920s when the situation was sufficiently unclear for the subject to claim autonomy from the fetishism of the past, and thus had no choice but to jump on the machine of progress. Today the situation has changed dramatically: commodification of the life-world is total and the subject is constantly defined and redefined by an everydayness that is saturated by visual images. In the present commodified world, the predicament of architecture centers on the fact that, by definition, architecture is a collective and constructive art, and might never achieve the autonomy of other visual arts. Even modernism's claim for autonomy was nothing but a foil whose ideological delusion needed only a couple of decades to unveil its affiliation with capitalism. In the dialectics of autonomy and semi-autonomy the idea of theatricality, as presented in this book, operates like an antinomy. In an attempt to reach what is architectural, the tectonic of theatricality facilitates architecture's rapport with the constructive structures of capitalism.

NOTES

1   Quoted in Janet Ward, *Weimar Surfaces: Urban Visual Culture in 1920s Germany* (Berkeley, CA: University of California Press, 2001), 32.

2   Elsewhere, I have presented "culture of building" to map themes that are fundamental to the tectonic discourse. See Gevork Hartoonian, *Modernity and Its Other* (College Station, TX: Texas A&M University Press, 1997). Peter Eisenman has introduced the idea of "interiority" to underline an understanding of "form" that is architectural. See Eisenman, *Diagram Diaries* (New York: University Publishing, 1999).

3   Gilles Deleuze, *Fold, Leibniz and the Baroque* (Minneapolis, MN: University of Minnesota Press, 1993). Thus far Anthony Vidler has presented the best criticism of the architects who entertain a literal interpretation of the idea of fold. See Anthony Vidler, *Warped Space: Art, Architecture, and Anxiety in Modern Culture* (Cambridge, MA: The MIT Press, 2000).

4   On this subject see Chapter 2 in this volume.

5   The suggested differentiation was introduced in the final chapter of Gevork Hartoonian *Ontology of Construction* (Cambridge: Cambridge University Press, 1994). For the architectonic implication of the mentioned differentiation see Gevork Hartoonian, "The Tectonic of Camouflage," *Architecture Australia* 92, 2 (March/April 2003): 60–65.

6   H.F. Mallgrave, *Gottfried Semper: Architect of the Nineteenth Century* (New Haven, CT: Yale University Press, 1996), 180.

7   Gottfried Semper, *The Four Elements of Architecture and Other Writings*, trans. H.F. Mallgrave and Wolfgang Herrmann (New York: Cambridge University Press, 1989), 45–73.

8   For a concise summary of the suggested development, see H.F. Mallgrave's Introduction to *Otto Wagner, Modern Architecture* (Santa Monica, CA: The Getty Center for the History of Art and the Humanities, 1988), 1–54.

9   I am benefiting from H.F. Mallgrave, *Gottfried Semper*, 1996, 293.

10   See H.F. Mallgrave, "A Commentary on Semper's November Lecture," *RES: Journal of Anthropology and Aesthetics* 6 (spring 1983): 23–31.

11   Scott C. Wolf, "Karl Friedrich Schinkel: The Tectonic Unconscious and New Science of Subjectivity," 1997, unpublished dissertation submitted to the Faculty of Princeton University, UMI Dissertation Services.

12   Peter Haiko, *Otto Wagner* (New York: Rizzoli, 1987), 18. For the theme of theatricality in French realist painting of the early nineteenth century see Michael Fried, *Courbet's Realism* (Chicago, IL: University of Chicago Press, 1990).

13   Peter Haiko, "Introduction," in *Sketches, Projects and Executed Buildings by Otto Wagner* (New York: Rizzoli, 1987), 10.

14   See Gevork Hartoonian, *Ontology of Construction*, 1994, 89.

15   Many nineteenth-century architects and theoreticians expressed confusing views on Gottfried Semper's discourse. While Otto Wagner pointed at Semper's preference for "symbolic" over material factors, Peter Behrens, among others, followed Alois Riegl's idea of *Kunstwollen* and chastised Semper for his mechanistic views on the essence of art. On these issues see, H.F. Mallgrave, *Gottfried Semper*, 1996, 355–81.

16   Walter Benjamin quoted in Peter Osborne, *The Politics of Time: Modernity and Avant-garde* (New York: Verso, 1995), 184.

17   I am thinking of Henri Lefebvre, but also the host of other thinkers, including Georg Simmel, Siegfried Kracauer, Martin Heidegger, and specially Walter Benjamin's reflections on the everyday life. For a comprehensive discussion of these authors' views on everyday life see Harry Harootunian, *History's Disquiet: Modernity, Cultural Practice, and the Question of Everyday Life* (New York: Columbia University Press, 2000).

18   Peter Collins, *Changing Ideals in Modern Architecture, 1750–1950* (London: Faber and Faber, 1965), 149.

19   Pananyotis Tournikiotis, *The Historiography of Modern Architecture* (Cambridge, MA: The MIT Press, 1999), 191.

20   Caroline van Eck, *Organicism in Nineteenth-Century Architecture* (Amsterdam: A&N Press, 1994), 19.

21   Joseph Rykwert, "Organic and Mechanic," *Res* 22 (autumn 1992): 11–18, 13.

22   Horst Bredekamp, *The Lure of Antiquity and the Cult of the Machine* (Princeton, NJ: Markus Wiener Publishers, 1995), 46.

23   Adolf Behne, for one, suggested that a building becomes organic by compromising its function. He also made a distinction between the utilitarian, the rationalist, and the functionalist approaches to the machine. According to Behne "when functionalist refers to the machine, he sees it as the moving tool, the perfect approximation to organism" (Behne, *The Modern Functional Building*, trans. M. Robinson [Santa Monica, CA: The Getty Center, 1996], 130).

24   See Harry Harootunian, *History's Disquiet*, 2000, 104.

25   Here and in the following, I am benefiting from Gottfried Semper's ideas discussed in *Style in the Technical and Tectonic Arts; or Practical Aesthetics*, trans. H.F. Mallgrave and Michael Robinson (Santa Monica, CA: Texts and Documents, The Getty Research Institute, 2004), 345.

26   Anthony Vidler, *Warped Space*, 2000, 227.

27   Greg Lynn, *Folds, Bodies and Blobs: Collected Essays* (Brussels: La Lettre volee, 1998), 110.

28   Horst Bredekamp, *The Lure of Antiquity*, 1995, 49.

29   On this subject see, G. Dodds and R. Tavernor, eds, *Body and Architecture: Essays on the Changing Relation of Body and Architecture* (Cambridge, MA: The MIT Press, 2002).

30   See "Question of Perception: Phenomenology of Architecture," *A+U*, special issue (July 1994).

31   Roman Hollenstein, "Temple and Pavilion: The Architecture of Foundation Beyeler," in The Foundation Beyeler, ed., *Renzo Piano-Foundation Beyeler* (Boston, MA: Birkhauser, 2000), 73.

32   Renzo Piano in an interview with Lutz Windhofel. See The Foundation Beyeler, ed., *Renzo Piano-Foundation Beyeler*, 2000, 33.

33   Quoted by Markus Brudelin in *Domus* 11 (1997): 60.

34   Hal Foster, *The Art-Architecture Complex* (London: Verso, 2011), 56.

35   Peter Buchanan, *Renzo Piano Building Workshop Vol. IV* (New York: Phaidon, 2005).

36   The full title of Peter Eisenman's presentation is "The Specter of the Spectacle: Ghost of the Real," which alludes in part to the spectacle of Frank Gehry's Bilbao project in Spain. See, Cynthia Davidson, ed., *Anymore* (Cambridge, MA: The MIT Press, 2000), 174–9.

37   I have discussed this difference to associate felt with montage as a technique that encompasses our very contemporary way of seeing and making. See Gevork Hartoonian, *Ontology of Construction*, 1994, 26.

38   Peter Eisenman, "The Specter of the Spectacle: Ghost of the Real," in Cynthia Davidson, ed., *Anymore*, 2000, 179.

39   Rosalind Krauss, "Sculpture in the Expanded Field," *October* 8 (Spring 1979): 30–44.

40   Rosalind Krauss "No More Play," in *Originality of the Avant-garde and Other Modernist Myths* (Cambridge, MA: The MIT Press, 1985), 54. Krauss's idea should be read against the background of Clement Greenberg who saw flatness as a theme working towards a modernist criticism launched from inside the movement. On this subject see the following footnote.

41   Leo Steinberg, "Other Criteria," in *Other Criteria: Confrontations with Twentieth-Century Art* (New York: Oxford University Press, 1972), 55–93. In criticizing Clement Greenberg's formalism, Steinberg used the term "the flatbed picture plane" to discuss the transformation of art's subject from nature to culture, and to avoid perceiving the world from an upright position. Discussing a number of American painters of the 1950s, Steinberg concluded that, "the flatbed picture plane lends itself to any content that does not evoke a prior optical event. As criteria of classification it cuts across the terms 'abstract' and 'representational'" (Steinberg, 1972, 90).

42   Hal Foster "Global Style," *London Review of Books* 29, 18 (September 20, 2007): 10–12.

43   On this subject see Gevork Hartoonian, "Mies van der Rohe: The Genealogy of Column and Wall," in *Ontology of Construction*, 1994, 68–80.

44   Gottfried Semper, *Style*, 2004, 123.

45   David Leatherbarrow and Mohsen Mostafavi, *Surface Architecture* (Cambridge, MA: The MIT Press, 2002).

46   Alejandr Zaera-Polo, "The Politics of the Envelope," *Log* 13/14 (fall 2008): 199.

47   Rafael Moneo, *Theoretical Anxiety and Design Strategies in the Work of Eight Contemporary Architects* (Cambridge, MA: The MIT Press, 2004), 23.

48   Gottfried Semper, *Style*, 2004, 154.

49   Greg Lynn, *Folds, Bodies and Blobs*, 1998, 177.

50   Quoted in "Kenneth Frampton in Conversation with Carlos Brillembourg," *Brooklyn Rail*, December 10–January 11 (2010).

51   Quoted in a conversation with Neil Leach. See "The Structure of Ornament," in N. Leach, David Trunbull, and Chris Williams, eds, *Digital Tectonics* (London: Wiley Academy, 2004), 65.

52   Gottfried Semper, *Style*, 2004, 246.

53   Obviously I am recalling J. Habermas's famous essay "Modernity and Incomplete Project," and Fredric Jameson's observation that modernism flourishing during the 1920s was "abruptly cut short around the same time in the early 1930s." He continues, "On the aesthetic level, this situation certainly justifies Habermas's well-known slogan of modernism as an unfulfilled project" (Jameson, *Singular Modernity* [London: Verso, 2002], 167).

54   Juan Jose Lahuerta, "Spain-For Sale," *Casabella* 697 (February 2002): 4.

55   Hal Foster, *Design and Crime* (London: Verso, 2003), 100–103.

Afterword

In *Vers une architecture* (1924), Le Corbusier wrote:

> You work with stone, with wood, with concrete, you make them into houses and palaces; this is construction. Ingenuity is at work. But suddenly you touch my heart, you do me good, I am happy, I say: "It is beautiful." This is architecture. Art is present.

Since the time these words were penned, many architects have tried to do what might have touched the French architect's heart! Bearing in mind the number of volumes he had read and commented on, it is plausible to say that Le Corbusier was aware of the philosophical discourses dealing with the issue of aesthetics in art and architecture. Likewise, he shared the dominant view of the time that there is something in the prevailing *Zeitgeist* that should be captured if architecture is to be part of the uprooting event later to be termed modernity. Even though the early houses he designed were mostly embellished in the tradition of the arts and crafts movement, the architecture he produced after the invention of the Dom-ino frame took a fresh direction. In theorizing architecture using the famous "five points," and drawing analogies from the precision and beauty of the machine and the ocean liner, Le Corbusier balanced his aspiration for the humanist discourse on the body and its proportions with the ingenuity of construction permeating the work of engineering, the aesthetic of which he praised jealously in the opening statement of the "argument" to the above book.

There is no substantial evidence to show that Le Corbusier had read Gottfried Semper's theory of architecture. What we do know is that, in thinking architecture simultaneously into the two realms of construction and art, he endorsed the separation of the column from the wall, to mention one architectonic consequence of the French Enlightenment advocated by Perrault. All these might be considered *history* today, except for one thing that Le Corbusier did not explain, that is, how aesthetics works in architecture. The question is still important if we agree with the proposition that architecture is construction plus something else; and that, visual excess is what makes architecture today part of the culture of spectacle produced and sustained by late capitalism operating on a global scale.

In the introduction to this book, the same question was raised albeit implicitly: should the inquiry into aesthetics be reapproached along the romanticist understanding of the artist as a God-given genius, or pursued in the line of the contemporary phenomenological attitude to perception and the body? In addition to these two possibilities, we are reminded of recent attention given to neuroscience,[1] and the theoretical drive to uphold the mechanism of the brain (its capacity to reason?) as an explanatory reference to the survival of the humanist discourse on architecture. Following the Lacanian discourse on *desire*, another tendency attempts to historicize contemporary neo-avant-garde architecture beyond the historicist's take on the subject[2] If, during the high point of phenomenology, "intention" was the word promoted in his interpretation of the state of post-war architecture,[3] the titles of the last abovementioned two books speak for themselves, and go further. Highlighting "architect" and "architecture," these books allude to the autonomy of the body and architecture in spite, or because, of the humanist conviction that the body of building is inseparable, metaphorically, from the body as such. Two things are significant in this brief reiteration of recent theoretical developments: first, that the four suggested positions and their variants emerged in the context of either socio-political upheavals, or technological transformations; and second, that the aesthetic consciousness in architecture is an old issue, and can be related to the split between thinking and making, a phenomenon relevant to the design of the dome of Florence Cathedral where, in addition to conceiving the idea, Brunelleschi had to design its construction system.[4] His was an historical event wherein the work neither perfectly coincided with nor adjusted itself to the demands of the time.

There is no need here to further highlight the criticality of the technification of architecture in the context of the present technological turn to digital reproductivity. The subject and its consequences for architecture are discussed in most significant volumes published during the first decade of this new millennium. What this book wished to accomplish, among other things, is the idea that in capitalism, the operative domain of technology is *collective* with unpredictable economic, political, and cultural repercussions. To compensate for the conditions when the nihilism of technology is shaking the foundations of both humanism and modernism, it is essential to re-think architectural praxis along with those aspects of the art of building that have the closest ties with capitalism. In the age of digital reproduction, architecture is in a privileged position in the sense that its technically induced aesthetics are overwhelmingly present in the cultural realm beyond the modernist moment, and definitely beyond the white abstraction with which Le Corbusier glossed over the free-façades of his early buildings. To show the extent to which the present image-laden spectacle is absorbed by architecture, it seems reasonable to recode the nineteenth-century discourse on the tectonic, highlighting the seeds of the aesthetic of animation present in Semper's theorization of how the art-form relates to the core-form. The idea of the tectonic of theatricality was indeed Semper's response to the crisis of an object unfolding at the dawn of modernization. The concept of theatricality discussed throughout this volume offered a strategy for criticism wherein the artistic articulation of the constructed form does two things simultaneously. On the one hand, it draws attention to the thematic of the culture of building (autonomy) and its potential for representing architecture as a constructed form. On the other, it offers a critical understanding of architecture's relationship with the larger picture of spectacle fostered by the present age of digital reproduction.

NOTES

1   Harry Francis Mallgrave, *The Architect's Brain: Neuroscience, Creativity, and Architecture* (London: Wiley-Blackwell, 2010).

2   K. Michael Hays, *Architecture's Desire: Reading the Late Avant-Garde* (Cambridge, MA: The MIT Press, 2010). For this author's review of Hays's book see Gevork Hartoonian, *Architectural Science Review*, 53:2, 2010, pp. 276–7.

3   See for example, Christian Norberg-Schulz, *Intentions in Architecture* (Cambridge, MA: The MIT Press, 1963).

4   Here, I am following Giulio Carlo Argan, *The Renaissance City* (New York: G. Braziller, 1970). For a recent account of the subject see Mario Carpo, *The Alphabet and the Algorithm* (Cambridge, MA: The MIT Press, 2011).

Index